OFF THE BEATEN PATH® SERIES

Florida

SIXTH EDITION

by Diana and
Bill Gleasner

Guilford, Connecticut

Cover and text design by Laura Augustine
Cover photo by © Chip Henderson/Index Stock Imagery
Maps created by Equator Graphics © The Globe Pequot Press
Illustrations by Carole Drong

Library of Congress Cataloging-in-Publication Data
Gleasner, Diana C.
    Florida : off the beaten path / Diana and Bill Gleasner. —6th ed.
    p. cm. —(Off the beaten path series)
Includes index.
ISBN 0-7627-0794-1
1. Florida—Guidebooks. I. Gleasner, Bill. II. Title. III. Series.
F309.3.G55 2000
917.5904'64—dc21   00-032148

Manufactured in the United States of America
Sixth Edition/Second Printing

To Ed and Susan Cottle—
Intrepid Florida Explorers

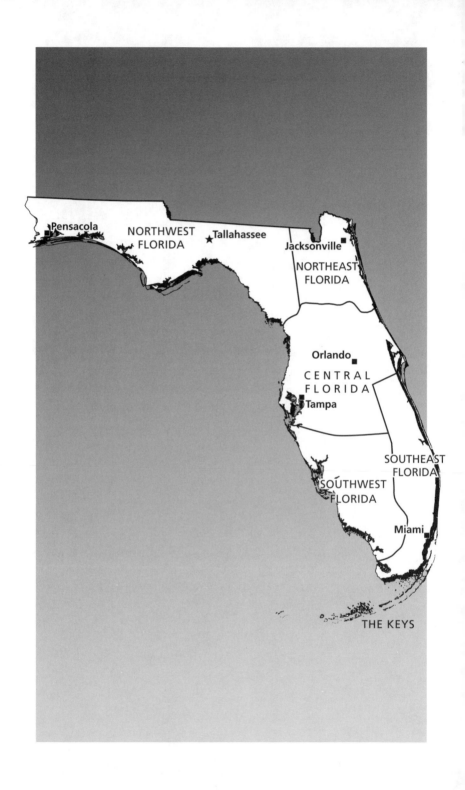

Pensacola

NORTHWEST
FLORIDA

Tallahassee

Jacksonville

NORTHEAST
FLORIDA

Orlando

CENTRAL
FLORIDA

Tampa

SOUTHEAST
FLORIDA

SOUTHWEST
FLORIDA

Miami

THE KEYS

Contents

Acknowledgments

To our able assistants, Lesa Ritter and Patsy Kiszely, a round of grateful applause.

Introduction

Warning! Straying from the beaten interstate can be addictive. But is it ever fun!

By poking and prowling around this incredible state, we discovered a high-rise for bats, the world's smallest police station, a McDonald's complete with salt licks and hitching posts, a museum dedicated to the inventor of air-conditioning, and an Arctic blizzard (Eglin Air Force Base Climatic Laboratory).

Florida seems to have cornered the "world's largest" market. We saw the largest concentration of saw grass; the largest bald cypress tree; and the largest collections of Frank Lloyd Wright buildings, Art Deco buildings, Salvador Dali artworks, and Tiffany glass in the world. We even strolled the world's longest continuous sidewalk.

We traveled by inner tube, pontoon boat, car, motor home, houseboat, sailboat, seaplane, canoe, motorized gondola, and airboat. Our meanderings took us through Little Havana, the Greek community of Tarpon Springs, and a Miccosukee Indian Village.

We heard a dolphin take a deep breath in the Everglades, toured a thoroughbred farm, and chatted with a cow hunter rounding up one of the few remaining herds of scrub cattle in existence. We saw manatees, wood storks, a herd of buffalo, and alligators romping in the surf!

We slept in a lighthouse, cheered ourselves hoarse at a rodeo, hunted for fossil shark teeth, lunched in an indoor swimming pool (luckily for us, it was dry), nibbled on alligator tail (lucky for us, it was not connected to anyone), and pitched a tent on more than a few of the Ten Thousand Islands.

In short, we have enjoyed an abundance of serendipitous experiences. But there are many more discoveries waiting to be made in Florida. Write us (c/o The Globe Pequot Press, P.O. Box 480, Guilford, CT 06437) and tell us your special finds.

Travel safely and have a terrific time!

Florida Fact Block

Name: Discoverer Ponce de Leon named it "Florida," the Land of Flowers, for its abundant flora.

Official Nickname: The Sunshine State

Location: Southeastern United States. Florida's southern tip is 1,700 miles (2,737 kilometers) north of the equator.

History: Florida has belonged to five different nations—Spain, England, France, the Confederacy, and the United States.

State Capital: Tallahassee was selected as the capital in 1824; a compromise between Pensacola in west Florida and St. Augustine on the east coast.

Population: It has 14.4 million people, the fourth most populous state in the United States after California, Texas, and New York. The largest concentration of Finns (17,000) outside of Finland lives in the Lake Worth/Lantana area. When asked where they would most like to live other than their current residence, Americans made Florida their first choice.

Time: Most of Florida is in the Eastern Time Zone. The area west of the Apalachicola River is in the Central Time Zone.

Weather: Abundant sunshine, pleasant coastal breezes during summer months, and 53 inches of annual rainfall.

Average Annual Temperatures: Summer: 80.5 degrees in north Florida and 82.7 in south Florida. Winter: 53 degrees in north Florida and 68.5 in south Florida.

Geography: Total area is 58,560 square miles. From Pensacola to the southernmost point of Key West is 832 miles (1,339 kilometers).

Lakes: Florida is sprinkled with more than 7,800 lakes ranging in size from an acre to the 448,000-acre Lake Okeechobee, the second largest freshwater lake in the United States.

Rivers: Florida has thirty-four major rivers. Certainly one of the best-known rivers (thanks to Stephen Foster's song "Old Folks at Home") is the Suwannee, in the northern part of the state.

Springs: There are 320 known springs in the state and 27 are classified as "first magnitude." First magnitude springs produce at least 100 cubic feet of fresh water per second. One of the longest underwater cave systems in the continental United States (over 28,000 feet), Peacock

Springs State Recreation Area *is* a popular place for cave diving.

Beaches: A beach is no more *than 60* miles (96.6 kilometers) away no matter where you are in Florida. *Sand* beaches account for 1,200 miles (1,932 kilometers) of the state's 1,800 *miles* (2,898 kilometers) of coastline. Florida's beaches are rated among *the finest* in the country by University of Maryland coastal geologist *Stephen* Leatherman, who researches and rates the nation's beaches on *forty different* criteria.

Shoreline: Florida has more tidal shoreline than any *other* state except Alaska.

Islands: Florida has 4,510 islands of ten acres or more in *size*, more than any state except Alaska.

Elevations: Florida's highest points are 325 feet at the summit of Iron Mountain near Lake Wales and 345 feet at Lakewood near DeFuniak Springs in the northwest.

Tourism: Tourism is the state's number-one industry, followed by agriculture. In 1997 a record 46.95 million tourists visited Florida. Approximately six million people camp in Florida each year, choosing from more than 100,000 campsites.

National Parks: Florida has two national parks, Biscayne National Park has over 180,000 acres of water and is the largest marine park under the protection of the National Park Service. Everglades National Park, with more than 1.4 million acres, is the largest subtropical wilderness in the United States.

National Forests: Florida's four national forests—Apalachicola, Choctawhatchee, Osceola and Ocala—cover more than one million acres. Nearly half the state is covered with uninhabited forests.

National Sanctuary: Florida Keys Marine Sanctuary, the largest U.S. marine sanctuary, covering 2,600 nautical square miles, extends from Biscayne National Park south to Fort Jefferson National Monument and northward to Everglades National Park on the tip of the Florida Peninsula.

State Parks: Florida's park system, consisting of more than 100 recreational areas, is one of the finest in the nation. All state parks open at 8:00 A.M. and close at sunset year-round.

Seaports: The Port of Miami is the busiest cruise port in the world, serving over three million passengers, which is two-thirds of the world's cruise-ship passengers.

Professional Sports: Professional sports franchises in the state include:

National Football League: Miami Dolphins, Tampa Bay Buccaneers, and Jacksonville Jaguars.

Arena Football: Orlando Predators, Florida Bobcats, and Tampa Bay Storm.

National Basketball Association: Miami Heat and Orlando Magic.

Major League Baseball: Florida Marlins and Tampa Bay Devil Rays.

National Hockey League: Tampa Bay Lightning and Florida Panthers.

Daily Newspapers:

More than 250,000 circulation: *Fort Lauderdale Sun-Sentinel,* 200 East Las Olas Boulevard, Fort Lauderdale 33301; *Orlando Sentinel,* 633 North Orange Avenue, Orlando 32801; *Tampa Tribune,* 202 South Parker Street, Tampa 33606; *Miami Herald,* One Herald Plaza, Miami 33132; *St. Petersburg Times,* 490 First Avenue South, St. Petersburg 33701.

100,000–250,000 circulation: *Daytona Beach News-Journal,* 901 Sixth Street, Daytona Beach 32017; *Florida Today,* One Gannett Plaza, Melbourne 32940; *Sarasota Herald Tribune,* 801 South Tamiami Trail, Sarasota 34236; *Florida Times-Union,* One Riverside Avenue, Jacksonville 32202; *Fort Myers News-Press,* 2442 Martin Luther King Boulevard, Fort Myers 33901; *Palm Beach Post,* 2751 South Dixie Highway, West Palm Beach 33405.

Transportation:

Car: Florida has spent far more money on highways than on mass transportation, so it should come as no surprise that roads are excellent while public transportation opportunities are limited. The best way to travel in Florida is by car, and major airports have extensive fleets of rental cars with economical rates. Recreation Vehicles (RVs) are also available for rent. Often the most economical way to vacation in Florida is a package deal that includes car rental and/or lodging with the cost of the flight.

Train: Amtrak serves Florida from both the east and west coasts. There are Amtrak stations in the following cities: Pensacola, Tallahassee, Jacksonville, Ocala, Sanford, Orlando, Tampa, West Palm Beach, Fort Lauderdale, and Miami. A rail pass providing unlimited travel during a certain period of time must be purchased from an Amtrak agent before arrival. Amtrak buses, known as "Thruway" buses, run from Winter

x

Haven, near Orlando, to Fort Myers via St. Petersburg and Sarasota to connect with Amtrak rail services.

Amtrak's Auto Train, for visitors who want to travel by train and then have use of their own car when they arrive, runs daily from Virginia to Sanford. For information on all rail service to Florida, call Amtrak's toll-free number: (800) USA–RAIL.

Tri-Rail, linking fifteen stations between Miami and West Palm Beach, runs frequently during the week, less often on weekends. (800) TRI–RAIL.

Bus: Greyhound buses usually offer the best value in public transportation, and passes purchased in advance provide unlimited travel for set periods of time; (800) 231–2222.

Famous People of Florida (people who were born, died, or lived a significant portion of their lives in Florida):

> Marjorie Kinnan Rawlings, Author
>
> John and Charles Ringling, Circus Owners
>
> John Gorrie, Inventor of Refrigeration
>
> Thomas E. Dewey, Politician
>
> Faye Dunaway, Actress
>
> William Deering, Manufacturer (Deering, Harvester Company)
>
> Frank Doubleday, Publisher
>
> Jose Ferrer, Actor
>
> Jackie Gleason, Actor/Comedian
>
> Pat Boone, Singer
>
> Lillian Smith, Author
>
> Red Grange, Football Player
>
> Sidney Poitier, Actor
>
> Janet Reno, U.S. Attorney General
>
> Nelson Eddy, Singer/Actor
>
> Melville Grosvenor, Publisher and president of the National Geographic Society

Philip Wylie, Author

Al Capone, Criminal

Harvey Firestone, Manufacturer (Firestone Tire and Rubber Company)

Thomas Alva Edison, Inventor

John D. Rockefeller, Oilman and founder of Standard Oil Company of Ohio

Meyer Guggenheim, Industrialist/Philanthropist

Addison Mizner, Architect

Jack Kerouac, Author/Poet

Douglas Edwards, Broadcast Journalist

Mackinlay Kantor, Author/Journalist

Vaughn Monroe, Singer/Bandleader

Red Barber, Sportscaster

Lois Lensky, Children's Author/Illustrator

Henry Morrison Flagler, Cofounder of Standard Oil Company/Builder of railways in Florida

Jacob Javits, Politician

John Pillsbury, Manufacturer (Pillsbury Mills, Inc.)

For more information:

State Parks: Department of Environmental Protection, Office of Recreation and Parks, Mail Station 536, 3900 Commonwealth Boulevard, Tallahassee, FL 32399–3000; (850) 488–9872.
Web site: www.dep.state.fl.us/parks.

State Forests: Department of Agriculture and Consumer Services, Division of Forestry, 3125 Conner Boulevard, Tallahassee, FL 32399–1650; (850) 488–6611.

Historical Sites: Division of Historical Resources, Florida Department of State, R.A. Gray Building, 500 South Bronough Street, Tallahassee, FL 32399–0250; (850) 488–1480. Web site: www.flheritage.com.

Attractions: Florida Attractions Association, P.O. Box 10295, Tallahassee, FL 32302; (850) 222–2885. Web site: www.floridaattractions.org.

Sports: Florida Sports Foundation, 2964 Wellington Circle, N. Tallahassee, FL 32308; (850) 488–8347; e-mail: fsf@tdo.infi.net.

Accommodations: Florida Hotel & Motel Association, P.O. Box 1529, Tallahassee, FL 32302; (850) 224–2888.

Inn Route, Association of smaller and historic lodging properties of Florida, P.O. Box 6187, Palm Harbor, FL 34684–0787; (407) 648–5750. Web site: www.florida-inns.com.

Statewide information about Florida:

General Information:
Florida Chamber of Commerce, P.O. Box 11309, Tallahassee, FL 32302; (850) 425–1200; www.flchamber.com.

Florida Division of Tourism, Visitor Inquiry, 107 West Gaines Street, Tallahassee, FL 32399; (888) 735–2872.

Vacationers planning a trip to Florida may receive a free official Florida Vacation Guide by contacting VISIT FLORIDA, 661 East Jefferson Street, Tallahassee FL 32301; toll-free at (888) 7FLAUSA or visiting Florida's Web site at www.flausa.com.

The prices and rates listed in this guidebook were confirmed at press time. We recommend, however, that you call establishments before traveling to obtain the most current information.

Northeast Florida

or leisurely exploration, it's hard to beat an old, ocean-hugging route like SR A1A. Amelia Island, at the northern border of Florida, was the state's first resort destination. The southernmost in a chain of large barrier islands known as the Golden Isles, Amelia's beauty includes both expansive beaches with rolling dunes and lush interior forests.

Continue south on A1A, via the Mayport ferry (a ten-minute ride across the St. Johns River) to Jacksonville and St. Augustine. After Bulow Plantation ruins (south of Palm Coast), turn inland via SR 100 to Palatka. Follow SR 20 to the Gainesville area, then I–75 northward to O'Leno State Park and Ichetucknee Springs.

Amelia Island

melia Island, with its 13 miles of uncrowded sandy beaches, has already been discovered. In fact, it is the only United States location to have been under eight different flags: French, Spanish, British, American Patriots (1812), Green Cross of Florida (1817), Mexican, Confederate, and American.

The Timucuan Indians' simple life was disrupted first by the French in the sixteenth century and then by the Spanish. The Union Jack was raised in 1763, but the Tories who converged on the island during the Revolutionary War left when Florida was ceded to Spain. A military adventurer, General Sir Gregor MacGregor, captured the island and claimed it as his for a brief time but was ousted by a pirate who took over ostensibly for Mexico. After the United States government took formal possession, the claim was disputed by the Confederacy, which raised its flag here during the Civil War.

> ### Amelia Island
>
> Amelia Island: "It is a place wonderfull fertill, and of strong scituation, the ground fat so that it is lekely that it would bring fourthe wheate and all other corn twise a yeare . . . yt is a country full of havens, rivers and islands of suche frutefullnes as cannot with tonge be expressed . . . the fairest, frute-fullest and pleasantest of all the worlde . . ."
>
> —Jan Ribaut, French colonizer, 1563

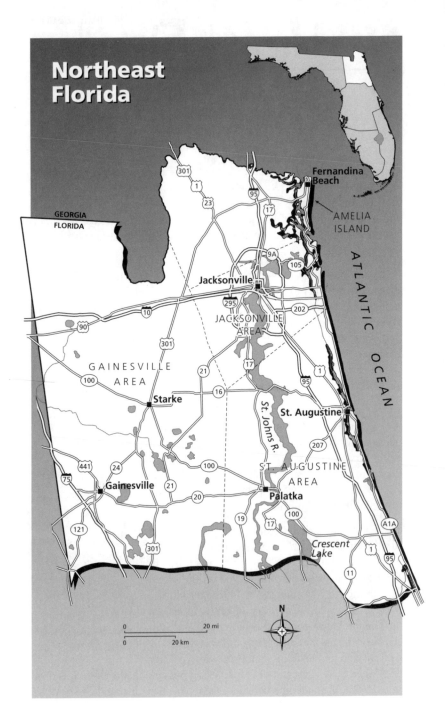

Northeast Florida

GEORGIA
FLORIDA

Fernandina
Beach

AMELIA
ISLAND

ATLANTIC OCEAN

Jacksonville

JACKSONVILLE
AREA

GAINESVILLE
AREA

Starke

St. Augustine

St. Johns R.

ST. AUGUSTINE
AREA

Gainesville

Palatka

Crescent
Lake

0   20 mi
0   20 km

N

NORTHEAST FLORIDA

Top Events in Northeast Florida

Hoggtown Medieval Faire,
Gainesville, February,
(352) 334–2197

**Gatornationals
(drag racing spectacle),**
Gainesville, March,
(800) 884–6472

Shrimp Festival,
Fernandina Beach, May,
(800) 2–AMELIA

Days in Spain,
St. Augustine, September,
(904) 829–1711

Jacksonville Jazz Festival,
Jacksonville, November,
(904) 353–7770

**British Night Watch and
Grand Illumination,**
St. Augustine, December,
(904) 825–1010

Federal occupation during the Civil War triggered a tourist boom. This, with an impressive flow of money created by the shipping business, made Fernandina Beach a prosperous community. Before long, handsome Victorian homes lined the residential streets. These architectural gems, dating from 1857 and ranging in style from old steamboat Gothic to Queen Anne, earned the 30-block Old Town district, also known as *Centre Street Fernandina,* a listing on the National Register of Historic Places. Be sure to stop at the chamber of commerce near the city docks for walking or driving tour directions to this gingerbread seaport.

It was from these docks that the country's first offshore shrimp trawlers sailed early in this century. For a look at the multicolored shrimp nets being made, go through the back door of *Standard Marine Supply Corporation* on Alachua Street. This father-and-son operation does not offer a formal tour, but keep in mind that Fernandina Beach is the only town in the country that has a shrimp net manufacturer on site to accommodate the fleet. Be sure to be at the docks at sunset to watch the shrimping fleet return with the day's catch.

Stroll past the old *Palace Saloon,* or better yet, stop in to inspect its splendid carved mahogany bar, which a reliable source has called "the best bar east of Boise." Be sure to sample a miniplatter of fresh boiled shrimp while enjoying local color in the oldest saloon in Florida. The Palace Saloon is on the corner of Second and Centre; (904) 261–6320.

Historic Centre Street bristles with fascinating shops and boutiques. *The Ships Lantern* (210 Centre Street, Fernandina Beach 32034) offers a fine selection of paintings, prints, woodcarvings, scrimshaw, and jewelry made from shark teeth found in the area.

Even if you don't stay in the *Bailey House,* be sure to take a good look at this 1895 Victorian bed-and-breakfast inn in the heart of the historic district. Its turrets, gables, bays, fish-scale decoration, and stained-glass windows make it a showcase. No wonder it cost $10,000—an outrageous amount in 1895! The rooms are filled with carved furniture, brass beds, pump organs, fringed lamps, and footed bathtubs, and

Palace Saloon

guests are served a continental breakfast in the elegant dining room. No children, pets, or smoking in the building. The Bailey House address is 28 South Seventh Street, Fernandina Beach, FL 32034; (904) 261–5390 or (800) 251–5390; Web site: www.bailey-house.com.

Fort Clinch State Park on Atlantic Avenue in Fernandina Beach welcomes visitors to the most northeasterly point in Florida. Its European-style brick masonry is unique in this country, and you'll get a splendid view of the Atlantic Ocean and Georgia's Cumberland Island from the fort's ramparts. On the first full weekend of every month, rangers and volunteers reenact the 1864 occupation in full period costume. The park's recreation facilities include saltwater fishing (1,500-foot lighted pier), swimming, camping, picnicking, and hiking. The park, which is on Atlantic Avenue in Fernandina Beach (off SR A1A), opens at 8:00 A.M. and closes at sunset year-round. Fort Clinch State Park, 2601 Atlantic Avenue, Fernandina Beach, FL 32034; (904) 277–7274.

If you've always wanted to stay in a *lighthouse* right on the beach, this is your chance. Four floors include two bedrooms (sleeps up to four), two baths, a kitchen and dining area, and an observation deck for expansive viewing of the great Atlantic Ocean. Wallpapered in nautical charts, this is the place for faraway dreams. Breakfast and the morning paper are delivered to your door. The lighthouse is on the ocean side of SR A1A on the northern end of Amelia Island. Write to Amelia Island Lodging Systems, 584 South Fletcher, Amelia Island, FL 32034; (904) 261–4148 or (800) 872–8531; Web site: www.amelialodging.com.

Amelia Island Plantation is a low-key, four-star resort offering a wide range of accommodations and amenities ranging from a beautiful beach and complete health club to a well-supervised children's program. Tennis enthusiasts have the run of twenty-five courts at *Plantation Racket Club,* and golfers play on forty-five challenging holes, which architect Pete Dye claims are the only true links on the East Coast. The fishing is fine whether it's deep-sea tarpon and kingfish charter, freshwater lagoon angling, or crabbing.

Nature lovers should follow the *Plantation's Sunken Forest Trail.* The dense semitropical growth includes palms, magnolias, and live oaks festooned with Spanish moss. About a quarter of this resort community has been set aside as a nature preserve enjoyed by raccoons, opossums, armadillos, and alligators. There are 7 miles of bike and nature trails, and a full-time naturalist offers tours daily.

Amelia Island Plantation's Pool Villas provide the last word on romantic getaways. Imagine rolling out of bed and into your own private indoor swimming pool in a villa hidden deep in a moss-draped forest. Add a nearby beach and candlelight dinners overlooking the ocean, and you have the ingredients of a perfect lovers' retreat. The Plantation is on the southern end of Amelia Island off SR A1A, 29 miles northeast of Jacksonville International Airport. Amelia Island Plantation, Amelia Island, FL 32034; (800) 874–6878; Web site: www.aipfl.com.

Bailey House

Kayak Amelia offers visitors an opportunity to discover the tranquil backwaters of Amelia Island by kayak. Experienced guides teach visitors the how-tos of kayaking and will take them on guided tours of the island's many creeks, marshes, and rivers. Nature discovery tours are also available for the entire family. For more information, call Kayak Amelia at (904) 321–0697.

The **Voyager,** an authentic 105-foot replica of a nineteenth-century gaff-rigged packet schooner, is docked at the Fernandina Beach Marina. The experienced crew will take visitors into the Amelia River/Intracoastal Waterway or into the Atlantic Ocean. For information on regularly scheduled sails, call Voyager Ventures at (904) 321–1244.

Jacksonville Area

ittle Talbot Island State Park embraces a quiet curving beach hidden beyond the dunes and framed by graceful sea oats. This is a delightful spot to camp, swim, and picnic on an unspoiled beach. Open 8:00 A.M. to sunset year-round, Little Talbot Island is 17 miles northeast of Jacksonville, off SR A1A; (904) 251–2320.

The house at *Kingsley Plantation,* believed to be the oldest plantation house in Florida, has been restored in pre–Civil War style. Long rows of crumbling quarters are a mute reminder of the days of slavery. Open 9:00 A.M.–5:00 P.M. daily. This national park is on Fort George Island, off SR A1A; (904) 251–3537; Web site: www.nps.gov.

The *Marine Science Education Center* welcomes visitors to a marine museum, wet lab (with more than a dozen different aquaria), and a collection of marine specimens including everything from giant clam shells to huge whale vertebrae. The center, in the historic village of Mayport, is 1 block south of the ferry slip on SR A1A (1347 Palmer Street, Mayport 32233). The reason the center looks like a school is because it is one. Although this resource is primarily for students, visitors are welcome

Time Warp

*W*e camped at Fort Clinch State Park, which commands a splendid view of Georgia's Cumberland Island and the Atlantic Ocean. The park, the most northerly point in Florida, takes full advantage of its Atlantic beach, Cumberland Sound, and salt marsh. Besides, it's the only place for RVs on the island. Certainly it boasts one of the most impressive fishing piers (1,500 feet long with night lighting) we have ever seen. If the strings of fish coming off that pier are any indication, Amelia Island is an extremely fertile fishing ground.

The fort is a fascinating reminder of a less complicated time. We roamed the ramparts and inspected exhibits in the small museum. Quite by accident, we

happened to be there the first weekend of the month, when costumed rangers reenact the 1884 occupation of the fort. These folks really take this time-warp business seriously. They feigned total ignorance when we mentioned computers or men on the Moon.

As we were leaving, a soldier stepped in front of us and ordered us to halt. Did we have permission to leave? Well, not exactly. We had to return to the office where a young man laboriously filled out the necessary form with a quill pen. Still not satisfied, the guard at the gate quizzed us as to the president's name. We stammered for a moment, finally came up with "Abraham Lincoln," and only then were granted permission to leave.

AUTHORS' FAVORITE ATTRACTIONS IN NORTHEAST FLORIDA

8:00 A.M.–2:00 P.M. Monday through Friday except school holidays; (904) 247–5973; Web site: www. educationcentral.org\msec.

Fort Caroline National Memorial commemorates the only French attempt to establish a colony in Florida (1564). The 138-acre park features exhibits, guided tours, and an interpretive model of the original fort. The story told is a tragic one, ending in the massacre of most of the French settlers by the Spanish from St. Augustine. Located about 5 miles from the mouth of the St. Johns River. Open daily 9:00 A.M.–5:00 P.M. Free. Fort Caroline National Memorial, 12713 Fort Caroline Road, Jacksonville, FL 32225; (904) 641–7155. Web site: www.nps.gov.

Jacksonville is Florida's largest and most populous city as well as its leading financial, industrial, transportation, and commercial center. Situated on a bend in the St. Johns River, this bustling and prosperous port is a skyscrapered showcase of sophisticated urban amenities. The St. Johns, the only major river in the United States to flow from south to north, has been the focus of the city's development since Jacksonville was founded in 1822. An ambitious riverfront beautification program has spiffed up the south bank with its attractive **Riverwalk.** Be sure to stroll the boardwalk and enjoy a fine view of this bustling city.

Centre Street Fernandina, Fernandina Beach

Fort Clinch State Park, Fernandina Beach

Fort Caroline National Memorial, Jacksonville

Castillo de San Marcos, St. Augustine

St. George Street, St. Augustine

Spanish Quarter, St. Augustine

Palatka Ravine State Gardens, 1 mile southeast of Palatka

Marjorie Kinnan Rawlings State Historic Site, Hawthorne

Florida Museum of Natural History, Gainesville

Ichetucknee Springs State Park, north of Gainesville

Adjacent to the Riverwalk are several fine restaurants, an excellent museum, and one of the world's tallest fountains, which erupts after dark into a spirited rainbow of beautiful colors. The **Museum of Science and History** is a treasure house of exploration for the whole family. Attractions include a 28-foot dinosaur skeleton, an exhibit of Florida Indian culture, and the **Alexander Brest Planetarium** with its daily multimedia productions. The museum is at 1025 Museum Circle in Jacksonville. Open Monday through Friday 10:00 A.M.–5:00 P.M., Saturday 10:00 A.M.–6:00 P.M., and Sunday 1:00–6:00 P.M.; (904) 396–7061.

How grand to be able to promenade the Riverwalk, explore the museum, and then satisfy your appetite in style. **Crawdaddy's** looks like a disaster from the outside, but that's part of its charm. The front yard of this ramshackle fish-camp shanty features rusting skeletons of old cars, a rooster, and chickens. Beneath the corrugated tin roof you'll find a fine restaurant. Try an appetizer of Florida alligator chased by beer cheese soup, Cajun chicken, and upside-down apple walnut pie. Crawdaddy's is at 1643 Prudential Drive, Jacksonville 32207. Most dinner entrees range from moderate to expensive; (904) 396–3546.

The *Cummer Museum of Art and Gardens* features a permanent collection particularly rich in Baroque and American art, traveling exhibitions, an award-winning interactive education center known as Art Connections, and two and one-half acres of formal gardens on the west bank of the St. Johns River. Open Tuesday and Thursday 10:00 A.M.–9:00 P.M., Wednesday, Friday, Saturday 10:00 A.M.–5:00 P.M., Sunday, noon–5:00 P.M.; closed Monday; (904) 356–6857. Admission fee.

The brew master's art is on display at the *Anheuser-Busch Brewery.* After your tour enjoy a free taste of the product or soft drinks in the hospitality room. Take I–95 north to the Busch Drive exit. The brewery is at 111 Busch Drive, Jacksonville 32218. Self-guiding and conducted tours are available 9:00 A.M.–4:00 P.M. Monday through Saturday; (904) 751–8118. Free.

Ever dream of chocolate? *Peterbrooke Chocolatier* has the answer to your dreams. The store overflows with chocolate tennis rackets, golf balls, and teddy bears. The candy is made from a secret recipe (known only to three people), and you may view the hand dipping on the premises.

The specialty here is fresh creme truffles, but you may also indulge yourself in chocolate-smothered Oreos, chocolate-covered popcorn, fresh strawberries dipped in chocolate, or ice cream appropriately named Total Decadence (loaded with milk chocolate, semisweet chocolate, and macadamia nuts).

The chocolatier ships products all over the world but maintains a keen interest in the local community. Peterbrooke was the inspiration for much of the impressive restoration of the San Marco area, and you will want to visit other shops and restaurants in the area. Peterbrooke is at 2024 San Marco Boulevard, Jacksonville, FL 32207; (904) 398–2488; Web site: www.peterbrooke.com.

St. Augustine Area

S t. Augustine, 40 miles south of Jacksonville, is an important repository of history, not only for the community and the state but for the entire nation. In a cheerful if sometimes unsettling mix, the city's carefully preserved past rubs shoulders with the most blatant commercialism, but it is impossible not to be impressed by the city's antiquity. A history that spans four centuries covers a lot of territory.

Ponce de Leon, landing in this general vicinity, claimed the region for Spain, but it was Pedro Menendez de Aviles, sent by the king of Spain to get rid of the French, who established the first settlement. Continuously occupied since 1565, St. Augustine was founded forty-two years before the colony at Jamestown and fifty-five years before the ocean-weary Pilgrims set foot on Plymouth Rock! A highly recommended movie, *Dream of Empire*, brings this dramatic story to life. The film is shown at the Visitors Center, 10 Castillo Drive 32084, 9:00 A.M.–4:00 P.M. on the hour daily; (904) 824–0339 or (904) 825–1000.

Imposing **Castillo de San Marcos** is well worth a visit. The king of Spain spent $30 million on this fort, which took nearly a quarter century to build. Overlooking Matanzas Bay, this national monument withstood many a siege but was never captured. Reenactors in Spanish uniforms provide plenty of smoke as well as action with their demonstrations of old-time firearms. Castillo de San Marcos National Monument, 1 South Castillo Drive, St. Augustine 32084. Open 8:45 A.M.–4:45 P.M. every day except Christmas; (904) 829–6506.

A faithful reconstruction of the 1750–1845 period centers on **St. George Street.** To absorb the Old World atmosphere, take a leisurely stroll by

St. Augustine

*I*n April 1513 Ponce de Leon landed in Florida. He may have been seeking the legendary fountain of youth as the myth says. After all, he was over fifty and no doubt could have used an elixir guaranteed to roll back the years. More likely, he was hoping to increase his net worth. Other Spanish explorers had returned from adventurous forays into Central and South America laden with gold. Ponce de Leon had every reason to think this new land might be similarly endowed. The king of Spain promised treasures beyond imagining. All Ponce de Leon had to do was find them.

The intrepid explorer claimed the region for Spain, but it was Pedro Menendez de Aviles, sent by the king of Spain to get rid of the French, who first sighted land during the Feast of St. Augustine and named the settlement in honor of the saint.

Although sacked by pirates, burned by the British, attacked, counterattacked, and ravaged by a raging yellow fever epidemic, St. Augustine managed to serve as the capital of colonial East Florida for 259 years. Control shifted from the Spanish to the English, then back to the Spanish, who finally turned it over to the Americans in 1821.

coquina-stone houses with overhanging balconies and walled garden patios that line the narrow streets. Be sure to visit the exquisite **St. Photios National Greek Orthodox Shrine** at 41 St. George Street, St. Augustine 32084. (Open 9:00 A.M.–5:00 P.M.) Attractive shops and restaurants lure visitors. You'll want to browse the **Ancient Mariner** gift shop and follow your nose to the **Spanish Bakery.** Ask for Spanish meat turnovers, better known as empanadas, to eat in the picnic area. (The bakery is open 9:00 A.M.–3:00 P.M.) The historic area is immediately south of the Old City gate.

Don't miss the **Spanish Quarter** in the restoration area. Here the daily lives of soldiers and settlers are re-created by costumed guides and craftspeople who welcome your questions. Look for the red-and-white Spanish flag and enter at 29 St. George Street. Operated by the city, this quality attraction is open 9:00 A.M.–5:00 P.M. daily. Information and ticket window at 29 St. George Street, St. Augustine; (904) 825–6830; e-mail: sqmuse@aug.com.

St. Augustine experienced its first tourism boom at the turn of the century, thanks to Henry Flagler. Impressed with the city's possibilities, he linked St. Augustine and Jacksonville by railroad. While he was at it, Flagler turned the town into a fashionable resort by building two grand hotels, the **Ponce de Leon** and the **Alcazar.** Visitors should not leave the city without at least a look at these two lavish hotels, their gardens, and fountains. The Ponce de Leon serves as **Flagler College** (no charge to roam the campus), and the restored Alcazar houses the

Truly Weird

*R*ipley's Believe It or Not! Museum, Ripley's oldest and original museum, in St. Augustine has some displays that will make your skin crawl. This collection features bizarre and unusual oddities from around the world. So if it's a two-headed lamb you want to see, a bunch of shrunken heads, the "Oldest Mother," or the man with the largest nose, this is the place.

If these items don't entice you, perhaps the 2,000-year-old Egyptian mummi-

fied cat, a sculpture of the Last Supper made entirely of pecans, or a collection of paintings done on potato chips will. Not yet convinced? Wax figure heads of the Double-Eyed Man, the Human Unicorn, or a 17-inch dwarf named Alypius should do it.

Still have an appetite? The museum makes some of the best fudge in town in its very own fudge factory. I dare you to bypass it without sampling at least one little piece.

Ghost Town

Lightner Museum with its three floors of fascinating collections. Open 9:00 A.M.–5:00 P.M. daily; (904) 824–2874. Both are at Cordova and King Streets, St. Augustine.

What better spot to lunch than in the indoor swimming pool (fortunately it was drained some time ago) of the fantastic Alcazar Hotel (now the Lightner Museum). *Cafe Alcazar* is located in the rear of the museum right in the center of the *Lightner Antique Mall.* You may investigate the antiques shops while waiting for a sandwich, salad, or freshly baked quiche. Appropriately, considering the grand setting, the dozen tables are set with real flowers, linen tablecloths, and china. Open 11:00 A.M.–3:00 P.M. every day except Sunday and Monday; (904) 824–7813.

Imagine having dinner in your own private thatched hut overlooking the water at sunset. The *Conch House Restaurant* is known for succulent seafood as well as an enchanting tropical atmosphere. This unusual restaurant is the brainchild of the Ponces, who are descended from the Solanas, believed to be the oldest documented family in the United States. Family records on file in the Catholic Cathedral in St. Augustine date back to 1594.

The owners' interest in local history is evidenced in the extensive collection of nautical antiques used throughout the restaurant. The thatched roof, made of more than 8,000 palm fronds, is the work of the Ponce brothers and a Seminole Indian and his son.

The Conch House Restaurant steams its seafood entrees in special spices and sauces and offers, as well, grilled, broiled, and fried dishes. Specialties of the house include conch chowder, conch fritters, and Caribbean cuisine. Try the steamed seafood for two. Sensational!

You have your choice of dining on the outdoor deck, in a private dining pod, or inside the restaurant. Come by sea (free dockage while dining) or by land. After crossing the Bridge of Lions from the historic area of St. Augustine, take SR A1A South for 6 blocks, turn left at sign, go 2$^1/_2$ blocks to 57 Comares Avenue, St. Augustine 32084. Open Sunday through Thursday 8:00 A.M.–9:00 P.M. and Friday and Saturday 8:00 A.M.–10:00 P.M. Most dinner entrees range from moderate to expensive; (904) 824–2046.

Are there ghosts in St. Augustine? Are you kidding? Of course there are. This is, remember, the oldest continuously occupied European settlement in the continental United States.

If you care to meet them, take a colorful **"Ghost Tour"** *hosted by knowledgeable tour guides in period costume. As you wind through the narrow byways of the oldest city and feel the hairs on your neck stand on end, you'll understand why this is one of the city's most memorable tours. For more information, call (800) OLD–CITY (653–2489).*

The Conch House Restaurant

Those seeking a spot to spend the night that is as charming as it is convenient should make reservations at **The Kenwood Inn.** This bed-and-breakfast hostelry (built between 1865 and 1886) is located within the Historic District between the Oldest House and the famous Castillo de San Marcos. Most of St. Augustine's historic sights and fine restaurants are within walking distance.

The fourteen rooms range in size from small and cozy to spacious; each has its own unique personality (choose Shaker, Colonial, or Victorian), and all have private baths. A small outdoor swimming pool is an appreciated extra, and innkeepers Mark and Kerrianne Constant make everyone (except small children and pets) feel warmly welcome. The Kenwood Inn, 38 Marine Street, St. Augustine 32084; (904) 824–2116.

South of St. Augustine are sights in Bunnell and Palatka not to be missed. The **Bulow Plantation Ruins Historic Site** features an old sugar mill and the crumbling foundation of an ancient mansion destroyed during the Seminole Indian Wars. Guided tours are available on request. The ruins are southeast of Bunnell on Old Kings Road. Open 9:00 A.M.–5:00 P.M.; (904) 517–2084.

A Medieval Moment

*R*olling into St. Augustine just about dusk, we spotted combatants in medieval garb hacking away at one another to the tune of flailing swords and clanking armor. All this on the library grounds, no less, and not a movie director in sight—our first clue that St. Augustine is not your everyday, run-of-the-mill city.

Since whacking one another with broadswords is not what folks in our hometown generally do in their spare time, we stopped to watch. These earnest warriors, we learned, belonged to a group dedicated to reenacting medieval battles as authentically as possible and were in dress rehearsal for a major contest in another state.

Strange as it seemed at first, this was oddly appropriate. After all, St. Augustine is old.

OTHER ATTRACTIONS WORTH SEEING
IN NORTHEAST FLORIDA

Amelia Island Museum of History, Fernandina Beach

Jacksonville Zoo, Jacksonville

St. Augustine Beach, St. Augustine

Fountain of Youth Park, St. Augustine

Kanapaha Botanical Gardens, Gainesville

Marineland Ocean Resort, St. Augustine

If your thoughts turn to **Palatka Ravine State Ornamental Garden,** it's probably spring. During February and March, the azaleas and camellias are at their peak. You may drive the road that loops around the edges of three steep ravines, jog the popular exercise course, or just stroll the paths thinking end-of-winter thoughts. One hundred thousand azaleas can't be wrong. A mile southeast of Palatka on Twigg Street (off Moseley Avenue); (904) 329–3721. Open daily 8:00 A.M. to sunset.

Gainesville Area

Marjorie Kinnan Rawlings found inspiration in the backwater community of Cross Creek. This semitropical low country was the setting for her Pulitzer Prize–winning novel, *The Yearling.* The author's rambling farmhouse, complete with old-fashioned canned goods on the kitchen shelves and her antique typewriter on the screened porch, looks as though she had just stepped out for a moment.

Rawlings quickly grew to love this place and its people, which she immortalized in her autobiographical book, *Cross Creek.* Her neighbors were "crackers," rural folk native to the region who were used to "making do." They made what living there was from the land, put on no airs, and wore their Southern heritage with pride. The author also compiled a book of regional recipes titled *Cross Creek Cookery.*

The **Marjorie Kinnan Rawlings State Historic Site** is in Cross Creek, off CR 325. Open Thursday through Sunday 10:00–11:00 A.M. and 1:00–4:00 P.M. Tours are given every hour from 10:00 A.M.–4:00 P.M. (except noon). House closed August and September. Marjorie Kinnan Rawlings State Historic Site, Route 3, Box 92, Hawthorne, FL 32640; (352) 466–3672.

Florida's home where the buffalo roam is **Payne's Prairie State Preserve** just south of Gainesville. Indian artifacts dating back to 7000 B.C. have been unearthed here. The visitor center contains interesting exhibits on the natural and cultural history of the preserve. (It was once a large Spanish cattle ranch.) A nearby observation tower provides a scenic overlook of this vast, marshy sea of grass.

The park offers boating (no gasoline-powered boats allowed) and fishing in Lake Wauberg, as well as camping, bird-watching, and horseback riding. (Bring your own horse.) The entrance is on U.S. 441, 10 miles south of Gainesville. Open 8:00 A.M. to sunset year-round. Payne's Prairie

Castle Warden

Castle Warden, the building housing Ripley's Believe It Or Not! Museum, was built in 1887 by William G. Warden, once a partner of John D. Rockefeller and Henry Morrison in the early development of the Standard Oil Company. Henry Morrison Flagler was convinced Florida would become the "Riviera of the Americas." He asked Warden to invest in the construction of a great railroad to connect St. Augustine with New York.

Warden went to Florida, studied the railroad project, and declared (the story goes) he would not put a cent into the railroad. However, he liked the climate and decided to build a large home here. He wanted to be in Florida, he said, to watch Flagler go broke.

The Warden family and its heirs lived here for many years until Marjorie Kinnan Rawlings, the well-known Florida author of The Yearling, *bought the home in 1941. In 1950 Castle Warden became the original Ripley's Believe It or Not! Museum.*

State Preserve, Route 2, Box 41, Micanopy, FL 32667; (352) 466–3397.

The *Wine and Cheese Gallery* in Gainesville, with umbrellaed tables in a shady courtyard, is a fine spot for lunching. Go right on through the front of the Gallery—which is a gourmet food and wine shop—and hang a left to reach the courtyard. In inclement weather, take a right to the inside dining room. As you might imagine, they offer a super selection of wines, or you may choose from more than a hundred kinds of imported beer. The sandwiches are a treat, as are the salads. Try the Big Cheese, a fat sandwich consisting of Cream Havarti, Jarlsberg, and Gouda, or a lettuce salad loaded with rare roast beef, fresh mushrooms, and Jarlsberg. The Wine and Cheese Gallery is at 113 North Main Street in Gainesville 32601. Restaurant open 11:00 A.M.–2:15 P.M. Monday through Saturday. Retail store open 10:00 A.M.–6:00 P.M.; (352) 372–8446. Inexpensive to moderate.

Gainesville's outstanding *Florida Museum of Natural History* offers fascination for all ages with its replica of a Mayan palace and reconstructed Florida cave. (The cave comes complete with cave critters, but don't worry, they don't fly.) What a find! The museum has one of the largest natural history collections in the United States. The museum is on the University of Florida campus at the corner of Newell Drive and Museum Road. Open Monday through Saturday 10:00 A.M.–5:00 P.M. and Sunday and holidays 1:00–5:00 P.M. Admission and parking are free; call (352) 846–2000. The museum's Collectors Shop, open during museum hours, carries a fine selection of items relating to the natural and social sciences.

Just down the road from the museum is the lush *Lake Alice Wildlife Preserve,* home base for alligators that fit easily into the whopper category. Don't mess with them, but do enjoy this lovely spot. The preserve is on Museum Road, a mile west of Southwest Thirteenth Street.

Some fossils that have shed light on Florida's ancient history were found 2 miles northwest of Gainesville at the **Devil's Millhopper State Geological Site.** This huge five-acre sinkhole has yielded shark teeth and other evidence of the prehistoric sea that once covered the state. Some of the plants and animals in the 120-foot-deep collapsed caverns are more typical of the Appalachian Mountains than of Florida. Off SR 232 (Millhopper Road). Devil's Millhopper State Geological Site, 4732 Northwest Fifty-third Avenue, Gainesville, FL 32606. Open 9:00 A.M.– 5:00 P.M. October to the end of April, April to September 9:00 A.M. to sunset; (352) 955–2008.

At **O'Leno State Park,** the scenic Sante Fe River performs a real disappearing act as it flows underground for more than 3 miles before coming to the surface. Other natural features of O'Leno are sinkholes, hardwood hammocks, river swamp, and sandhill communities. You'll find a good view of the river from the suspension bridge built by the Civilian Conservation Corps in the late 1930s. A fine place to camp, canoe, fish, swim, or walk the nature trails. The park is off U.S. 41, 35 miles northwest of Gainesville. Open 8:00 A.M. to sunset year-round. O'Leno State Park, Route 2, Box 1010, High Springs, FL 32643; (904) 454– 1853; Web site: www.dep.state.fl.us/parks.

Ichetucknee Springs State Park features a pristine crystal-clear river, but it is not exactly undiscovered. Floating down the scenic Ichetucknee in an inner tube has become so popular that the park limits the number of tubers to protect vegetation. Spending a day (or a few hours) on this river is a perfectly splendid thing to do. The current moves you effortlessly along so that you can enjoy the surrounding beauty. No wonder this is such a popular pastime.

The river's source is a group of springs that boil out of limestone sinks and trickle out from under cypress tree roots to the tune of 233 million gallons a day. Ichetucknee is the state's third largest spring, an impressive statistic in a state that claims more springs than any other.

The day was warm, the water cool (72 degrees). We parked all our cares on the river's banks, plopped into our inner tubes, and dedicated the day to drifting. We bobbed along beneath an emerald canopy on crystal-clear water. Sunlight flickering through Spanish moss created moving light patterns on the river floor. We could see each fish. A great blue heron fanned us with massive wings as it passed just overhead. Early tubers reported seeing beavers and otters.

We moved along at a good clip with only an occasional steering stroke. Every turn offered a new view of this dense wilderness area studded with cypress knees and limestone outcrops. No motor noise spoiled the tranquility.

We did our tubing one gorgeous October Saturday, a day we'll remember always. This has to be one of Florida's most enjoyable (and economical) off-the-beaten-path adventures.

At the park entrance you will receive a map of tubing options. No food, drink, tobacco, disposable items, or pets are allowed on the river. The peak season is May through September, when the park is apt to be most crowded. At other times, you can occasionally have the river to yourself. The water is 72 degrees year-round. Local vendors rent tubes and canoes. The park, which is north of Gainesville, off I–75 and 4 miles northwest of Fort White, off SR 27 and CR 238, is open 8:00 A.M. to sunset. For maps and details contact the north entrance of Ichetucknee State Park on CR 238, or call (904) 497–2511. For recorded information call (904) 497–4690.

STATE PARKS IN
NORTHEAST FLORIDA

**Amelia Island State
Recreation Area**
(904) 251–2320

**Anastasia State
Recreation Area**
(904) 461–2000

**Big Talbot Island
State Park**
(904) 251– 2323

Bulow Creek State Park
(904) 676–4040

**Devil's Millhopper
State Geological Site**
(352) 955–2008

Faver-Dykes State Park
(904) 794–0997

Fort Clinch State Park
(904) 277–7274

**Fort George Island State
Cultural Site**
(904) 251–2320

**Gainesville-Hawthorn
State Trail**
(352) 466–3397

**Gamble Rogers Memorial
State Recreation Area at
Flagler Beach**
(904) 517–2086

Guana River State Park
(904) 825–5071

**Ichetucknee Springs
State Park**
(904) 497–2511

**Little Talbot Island State
Park** *(904) 251–2320*

**Marjorie Kinnan
Rawlings State
Historic Site**
(352) 466–3672

**Mike Roess Gold Head
Branch State Park**
(352) 473–4701

O'Leno State Park
(904) 454–1853

**Olustee Battlefield State
Historic Site**
(904) 758–0400

**Paynes Prairie State
Preserve** *(352) 466–3397*

Ravine State Gardens
(904) 329–3721

**San Felasco Hammock
State Preserve**
(352) 462–7905

**Washington Oaks State
Gardens** *(904) 446–6780*

PLACES TO STAY IN
NORTHEAST FLORIDA

AMELIA ISLAND
Florida House,
22 South Third Street;
(904) 261–3300

Williams House,
103 South Ninth Street,
Fernandina Beach;
(904) 277–2328

The Ritz-Carlton,
Amelia Island, 4750 Amelia
Island Parkway;
(904) 277–1100

GAINESVILLE
Magnolia Plantation,
309 Southeast Seventh
Street; (352) 375–6653

JACKSONVILLE
Courtyard by Marriott,
4600 San Pablo Road;
(800) 321–2211

Holiday Inn–Airport
North, P.O. Drawer 18409,
12 miles north on
Airport Road;
(904) 741–4404

Visitor Information for Northeast Florida

Alachua County Visitors and Convention Bureau,
30 East University Avenue, Gainesville 32601;
(352) 374–5231;
Web site: www.co.alachua.fl.us/~acvacb

Amelia Island Tourist Development Council,
102 Centre Street, Amelia Island 32034;
(800) 2–AMELIA;
Web site: www.ameliaisland.org

Beaches Chamber & Visitor Center,
1101 Beach Boulevard, Jacksonville Beach 32250;
(904) 249–3868

Flagler County Chamber of Commerce,
Star Route Box 18–N, Bunnell 32110; (800) 881–1022

Jacksonville and the Beaches
Convention & Visitors Bureau,
3 Independent Drive, Jacksonville 32202;
(800) 733–2668

Putnam County Chamber of Commerce,
1100 Reid Street, Palatka 32177; (904) 328–1503;
Web site: www.putnam.special.net/chamber

St. Johns County Visitors and Convention Bureau,
88 Riberia Street, Suite 400, St. Augustine 32084;
(800) OLD–CITY; Web site: www.visitoldcity.com

Starke–Bradfod County,
202 South Walnut Street, Starke 32071; (904) 964–5278

Omni, 245 Water Street;
(904) 355–6664

JACKSONVILLE BEACH
The Lodge and Beach Club
at Ponte Vedra Beach,
607 Ponte Vedra Boulevard,
Ponte Vedra Beach;
(904) 273–9500

Marriott At Sawgrass,
1000 TPC Boulevard,
Ponte Vedra Beach;
(904) 285–7777

Ponte Vedra Inn & Club,
200 Ponte Vedra Boulevard,
Ponte Vedra Beach;
(904) 285–1111

ST. AUGUSTINE
Monterey Inn,
16 Avenida Menendez;
(904) 824–4482

Casa de La Paz,
22 Avenida Menendez;
(904) 829–2915

Old City House,
115 Cordova Street;
(904) 826–0113

Old Powder House,
38 Cordova Street;
(904) 824–4149

PALATKA
Holiday Inn Riverside,
201 North First Street;
(904) 328–3481

**PLACES TO EAT IN
NORTHEAST FLORIDA**

AMELIA ISLAND
Beech Street Grill,
801 Beech Street,
Fernandina Beach;
(904) 277–3662

The Grill,
The Ritz–Carlton,
Amelia Island Resort,
4750 Amelia Island
Parkway; (904) 277–1100

JACKSONVILLE
Cafe Carmon,
1986 San Marco Boulevard;
(904) 399–4488

David's (Italian/American),
834 Kingsley Avenue,
Orange Park;
(904) 264–7431

The Wine Cellar,
1314 Prudential Drive;
(904) 398–8989

JACKSONVILLE BEACH
Aw Shucks,
950 Sawgrass Village Drive,
Ponte Vedra;
(904) 285–3017

Dolphin Depot,
704 North First Street;
(904) 270–1424

ST. AUGUSTINE
Creekside Dinery,
160 Nix Boatyard Road;
(904) 829–6113

Le Pavillon,
45 San Marco Avenue;
(904) 824–6202

Raintree,
102 San Marco Avenue;
(904) 824–7211

Salt Water Cowboy's,
299 Dondanville Road;
(904) 471–2332

Santa Maria,
135 Avenida Menedez;
(904) 829–6578

GAINESVILLE
The Chuck Wagon,
3483 Williston Road;
(352) 336–5677

Sovereign,
12 Southeast Second
Avenue; (352) 378–6307

From the Lake City area, the most direct route to Cedar Key is south on I–75 and west on Florida 24. From Cedar Key travel north on U.S. 19/98 to Perry, then follow U.S. 98 west as it passes one sugar-white beach after another clinging to the Gulf of Mexico all the way to Pensacola. Side roads reveal all sorts of surprises, from dead lakes sprouting tree skeletons to verdant offshore islands.

If you take the northern route (I–10) from Pensacola to Tallahassee, you'll discover a Florida few folks are familiar with. Sometimes the scenery resembles Maine, Canada, or the foothills of Virginia. Byways off this main road lead to fall color, one of only two perfectly round lakes in the world, stalactites and stalagmites, and the state's only waterfalls.

Lake City Area

The **Stephen Foster State Folk Culture Center** pays tribute to the man who made the Suwannee River famous, wrote "Old Folks at Home" (Florida's official state song), and gave us such long-standing favorites as "Oh Susannah" and "Camptown Races." One of America's best-loved composers, Stephen Foster was born in Pennsylvania in 1842 and died at the age of thirty-seven in New York City with 38 cents in his pocket. He never did get to see the Suwannee, but you should. It's the second-largest river in the state, and you may camp, boat, fish, and explore nature trails.

The **Foster Museum** is housed in an antebellum-style mansion that conjures up all sorts of romantic images of the Old South. The Carillon Tower chimes forth hourly concerts of Foster favorites. Inside you may take a trip through yesteryear as you inspect Foster memorabilia, antique musical

Way Down Upon the Suwannee River

In the late 1700s the Suwannee River was called the little San Juan, possibly because a Spanish mission, San Juan de Guacara, was located on its banks. Some historians suspect local dialect changed the name to San Juanee and hence Suwannee. Others believe the river's name was derived from the Creek Indian word Suwani, which means "echo."

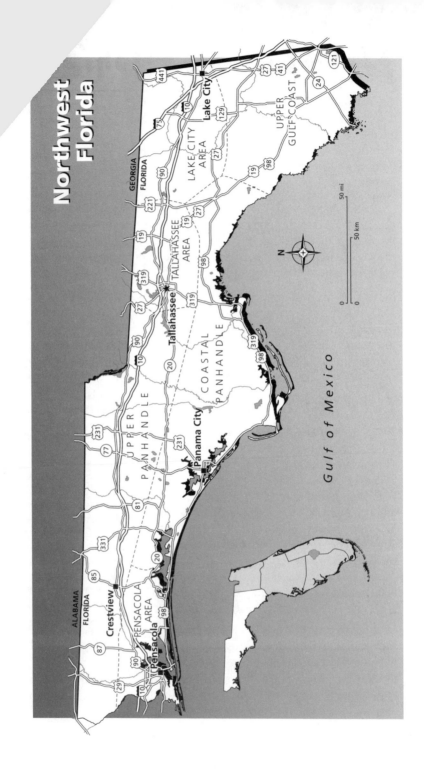

instruments, original manuscripts, and animated dioramas.

The *Florida Folk Festival,* an annual gathering of folk musicians and craftspeople in May, is a well-attended event. The Jeanie Ball (named for "Jeanie with the Light Brown Hair") is the highlight of October, and December features popular Christmas Concerts. For a complete schedule of events, write Stephen Foster Center, P.O. Drawer G, White Springs, FL 32096; (904) 397-2733. The Stephen Foster Center is open every day 9:00 A.M.–5:00 P.M. White Springs is 3 miles east of I–75 and 10 miles northwest of Lake City at the junction of U.S. 41 and SR 136.

For another look at this well-known river, head west for *Suwannee River State Park.* The overlook above the confluence of the Suwannee and the Withlacoochee provides a commanding view of both rivers as well as a fine place for a picnic. Notice the remains of Confederate earthworks built to protect the railroad bridge across the Suwannee. Oaks bearded with moss and cypress trees canopy the tranquil river creating a scenic setting for those who enjoy camping, boating, fishing, and hiking. Open 8:00 A.M. to sunset. The park is 13 miles west of Live Oak off U.S. 90; (904) 362-2746.

Upper Gulf Coast

The *Forest Capital State Museum,* just south of Perry ("Tree Capital of the South"), pays tribute to forestry, the state's third-largest industry. This cypress geodesic dome features an old turpentine still as well as exhibits on such things as modern day turpentine production and the sex life of the pine tree. After learning about Florida's 314 known species of trees and the 5,000 products manufactured from the longleaf pine tree, take time to wander through the turn-of-the-century *Cracker Homestead*

TOP EVENTS IN NORTHWEST FLORIDA

The Chautauqua Assembly, DeFuniak Springs, February, (850) 892-4300

Suwannee River Country Jam, Live Oak, October, (904) 364-1683

Springtime Tallahassee, Tallahassee, April, (850) 224-5012

Fort Walton Beach Seafood Festival, Fort Walton Beach, April, (850) 651-7131

Gulf Coast Triathlon, Panama City Beach, May, (850) 235-0720

Destin Mayfest, Destin/Fort Walton Beach, May, (850) 837-6241

Billy Bowlegs Festival, Destin/Fort Walton Beach, June, (850) 651-7131

Fiesta of Five Flags, Pensacola, June, (850) 433-6512

Pensacola Seafood Festival, Pensacola, September, (850) 433-6512

Boggy Bayou Mullet Festival, Niceville, October, (850) 678-1615

Destin Fishing Rodeo, Destin/Fort Walton, October, (850) 837-6734

Indian Summer Seafood Festival, Panama City Beach, October, (850) 785-8591

Old Tyme Farm Days, Live Oak, November, (904) 364-1683

Winter Festival, Tallahassee, December, (850) 891-3866

Jail Time

Longing for the good old days? Perhaps a visit to the **Old Jail** *in Jasper will cure that longing. Inspect the hangman's noose—thirteen knots swinging freely in the hanging tower constructed over the front entrance— and the dungeon where the most dangerous criminals were kept. Photos of what is believed to be the last legal hanging in Florida are on display. The Old Jail is at 501 Northeast First Avenue in Jasper, Florida. The museum is open most weekdays and every Sunday afternoon. Call the Hamilton County Chamber of Commerce at (904) 792–1300 for a private tour or the weekly schedule.*

behind the visitor center. This log cabin home has a "dogtrot" (a breezeway), mosquito netting on the beds, and a kitchen that is separated from the house in case of fire. Near the well, tubs for washing clothes stand ready for action. (Keep in mind, these are the "good old days.") A grape arbor, outhouse, pantry house, chicken pen, barn, corncrib, cane grinder, and smokehouse round out the self-sufficient scene of yesteryear.

The Visitor Center Museum and Cracker Homestead are off U.S. 98-27A just south of Perry. The center is open 9:00 A.M.–5:00 P.M. (except noon–1:00 P.M.) every day except Tuesday and Wednesday and Thanksgiving, Christmas, and New Year's days. Forest Capital State Museum, 204 Forest Park Drive, Perry, FL 32347; (850) 584–3227.

In October the **Florida Forest Festival** celebrates by crowning a Forestry Queen and holding chain saw championships and arts and crafts shows. For festival information call the Taylor County Chamber of Commerce; (850) 584–5366.

Halfway between Tallahassee and Tampa but a world apart from both, **Cedar Key** is far enough off the beaten interstate to have preserved the flavor of old Florida. (Take SR 24 off I–19 and 98.) This tiny fishing village is on the largest of more than a hundred islands clustered in the Gulf of Mexico. Three miles from the mainland, Cedar Key is officially on Way Key, which is connected to the mainland by causeway. Local restaurants, the beneficiaries of fishing, crabbing, scalloping, and oystering, are known for their sumptuous repasts.

Settled in the early 1840s, Cedar Key began to blossom in 1861 with the completion of Florida's first major railroad, which ran from Fernandina in the northeast corner of the state to Cedar Key. This led to a boom in the lumber business and brought trainloads of tourists. It seems incredible today, but Cedar Key was once the second-largest city in Florida.

After the Civil War, Cedar Key developed a reputation as a center for shipbuilding and manufacturing of wooden pencils. When the cedar forests had all been leveled, residents turned to the sea for their living. For a brief time the manufacture of brushes and brooms from palmetto fiber created a flurry of business activity, but the discovery of plastics decisively ended that enterprise. As if it needed a final "blow," this bustling port was devastated by the hurricane of 1896, from which never fully recovered.

All these ups and downs are carefully documented at two pleasant little museums, **Cedar Key State Museum** and the **Cedar Key Historical Society Museum.** The State Museum, on Museum Drive, is open 9:00 A.M.–5:00 P.M. except for Tuesday and Wednesday; (352) 543–5350. The Cedar Key Historical Society Museum, on the corner of Second and D (SR 24) Streets, is open Monday through Saturday 11:00 A.M.–5:00 P.M., Sunday 2:00–5:00 P.M., during winter and Sunday through Thursday 2:00–5:00 P.M., Friday and Saturday 11:00 A.M.–5:00 P.M., during summer (May through October); (352) 543–5549.

Cedar Key's **National Wildlife Refuge,** covering three islands, gives rattlesnakes the same preferential treatment as birds. Sea views are embellished by the pink flash of a rare roseate spoonbill, freewheeling frigates, and pelicans crashing into the Gulf in search of supper. The refuge is strictly an environmental study area and not open for visitor use. But bird-watchers who rent a boat and cruise near the islands will be well rewarded.

Festival followers flock to the Cedar Key **Sidewalk Arts Festival** in

Ghost Ship

*I*f you haven't done any underwater sight-seeing lately, perhaps the time has come. For almost a hundred years, from 1834 to the 1920s, more than fifty steamboats plied the Suwannee River. Today, the remains of a dozen steamboats can be found along the riverbed, including the especially well-preserved **City of Hawkinsville,** the largest and last steamboat to be stationed on the Suwannee. Looking like a storybook ghost ship, the wreckage can be viewed by swimmers and divers.

The site, accessible only by boat, is located in shallow water on the river's west bank south of the railroad trestle at Old Town. The City of Hawkinsville is marked by a series of buoys on her starboard side and by mooring buoys approximately 50 feet downstream from her stern. Visitors are asked to tie up to the mooring buoys to prevent anchor damage to the boat. This underwater archaeological site is a well-preserved but fragile piece of Florida history. Please take care to leave it as you found it. For more information, contact Florida Department of State, Division of Historical Resources, Bureau of Archaeological Research, R.A. Grey Building, 500 South Bronough Street, Tallahassee, FL 32399; (904) 487–2333.

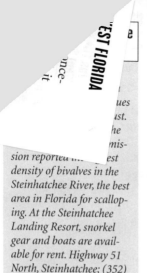

sion reported ... est density of bivalves in the Steinhatchee River, the best area in Florida for scalloping. At the Steinhatchee Landing Resort, snorkel gear and boats are available for rent. Highway 51 North, Steinhatchee; (352) 498–3513.

April and the **Seafood Festival** in mid-October. For information contact the Cedar Key Area Chamber of Commerce at Second Street and SR 24, or call (352) 543–5600.

Coastal Panhandle

t. Marks National Wildlife Refuge, 25 miles south of Tallahassee, comprises nearly 70,000 acres of forests, water areas, and the coast on the Gulf of Mexico. Stop in the Visitor Center for a look at the interpretive displays, to pick up leaflets and maps, and to browse in the gift shop. Then take the 7-mile wildlife drive to the **St. Marks Lighthouse,** one of the oldest in the Southeast. Constructed in 1831 from stones removed from old Fort San Marcos de Apalache, this lighthouse guides modern vessels with the same lens it used during the Civil War.

If you are a bird-watcher or an alligator watcher, you will be in your glory. (You'll feel even more glorious if you remembered the bug repellent.) Hike miles of primitive walking trails, including a 42-mile section of the Florida National Scenic Trail, and enjoy a picnic lunch overlooking the water near the lighthouse. The Visitor Center, 3 miles south of U.S. 98 on Lighthouse Road, is open 8:15 A.M.–4:00 P.M. Monday through Friday and Saturday and Sunday 10:00 A.M.–5:00 P.M. You are welcome in the refuge anytime during daylight hours to picnic, launch a boat, crab, or fish. Call (850) 925–6121.

San Marcos de Apalache State Museum is also the site of a fort first built in 1679 by the Spaniards. The fort was held at various times by the British, Spanish, and Confederate forces. Its capture by General Andrew Jackson in 1818 was an important factor in the United States' acquisition of Florida the next year. The museum contains artifacts spanning the area's history from the Spanish occupation to the Civil War. A lovely trail winds through Confederate earthworks, climbs to the top of a powder magazine, follows crumbling fort walls along the banks of the Wakulla River, and ends at the original site of early Spanish fortifications where the Wakulla and St. Marks Rivers merge. The museum is 24 miles south of Tallahassee on SR 363 in St. Marks. Open Thursday through Monday 9:00 A.M.–5:00 P.M. San Marcos de Apalache, Box 27, St. Marks, FL 32355; (850) 925–6216.

Right around the corner from the museum is **Posey's,** "The Home of the Topless Oyster." Try the topless oyster, smoked mullet, baked oysters with bacon and cheese, or boiled shrimp. A live band entertains Friday, Saturday, and Sunday nights. Posey's, on the road to the museum in St. Marks, is open year-round. Inexpensive; (850) 925–6172.

Posey's "Home of the Topless Oyster"

Folks from Tallahassee head to the coast for fresh seafood, and one of their favorite destinations is **Spring Creek Restaurant.** This family operation hides out under live oaks festooned with Spanish moss where, according to the menu, "fresh spring water merges with the Gulf, creating the finest seafood in the world." Spring Creek serves up generous portions of mullet, crab fingers, oysters, lobster, deviled crab, and grouper, to name just a few. If you are partial to truly fresh seafood, the owners raise their own softshell crabs. The salad bar comes to the table so you can build your own. Specialties are cheese grits and homemade desserts such as chocolate peanut butter pie and coconut cream pie. Take U.S. 363 (South Monroe Street) south from Tallahassee and go west on U.S. 98 and south on CR 365 to the tiny community of Spring Creek. Open at 5:00 P.M. daily (dinner), noon on weekends (lunch and dinner). Prices are mostly in the moderate range; (850) 926–3751.

Once you've started, there's no stopping. Fresh seafood is a fun addiction. **Angelo's Seafood Restaurant's** roomy wraparound deck is just the place to relax in a rocking chair and have a cocktail while the sun sets over the river. Try the charbroiled grouper and, for sure, their Greek salad. Each table is served a corked wine bottle full of dressing. Angelo's "over the water" restaurant is right by the bridge in Panacea. The owners take a lot of pride in their handsome restaurant, which is open Friday and Saturday 4:30–11:00 P.M., Sunday noon–10:00 P.M., and 4:30–10:00 P.M. every other day but Tuesday. Prices are mostly moderate; (850) 984–5168.

You really shouldn't drive through Carrabelle without tipping your hat to the **world's smallest police station.** You can't miss it. It's a public phone

St. Marks Lighthouse

The original St. Marks Lighthouse was built in 1829 by Winslow Lewis of Boston for $11,765, but the structure was judged unacceptable because the tower walls were found to be hollow rather than solid. Calvin Knowlton reconstructed the 80-foot tower using limestone blocks taken from the ruins of old Fort San Marcos de Apalache. The reflector lens, from Paris, was installed in 1829. On a clear evening the light, now triggered by an electric eye, can be seen 15 miles away.

booth right on the main drag with an American flag painted on it. Often the patrol car is parked beside it waiting for the next call. If it is, why not wave? Carrabelle doesn't even remotely resemble the Naked City.

A British fort once stood at the **Fort Gadsden State Historic Site.** Held for a time by Indians and runaway slaves, it was destroyed by American forces in 1816. In 1818 Andrew Jackson ordered the fort to be rebuilt, but today only a bare outline is visible. A miniature replica of Fort Gadsden, some British muskets, and Indian artifacts are on display in an open-sided interpretive center. You may picnic, fish, and explore the nature trails. A short walk will take you to the remains of the renegade cemetery where grave robbers left nothing but shallow depressions. Fort Gadsden is 24 miles north of U.S. 98 just off SR 65 (21 miles of good road, the last 3 miles are rough) or 6 miles south of Sumatra off SR 65. Open daily 8:00 A.M. to sunset; (850) 643–2282. Free.

If you love the beach—the sand, the sea, and the sky—uncluttered by honky-tonk attractions, head for **St. George Island State Park** at the end of Apalachicola Bay. The miles of undeveloped beaches, sand dunes, and marshland are not totally wild. You'll find nature trails, boardwalks, observation platforms, picnic and camping areas, and bathhouses. Take the turnoff from U.S. 98 that leads across the bridge to St. George Island. Open daily 8:00 A.M. to sunset; (850) 927–2111.

Apalachicola's **Trinity Church,** one of the oldest (1830s) in the state, was cut in sections in New York and floated by schooner down the Atlantic Coast and around the Florida Keys. The original church bell was melted down to make Confederate cannon. Trinity, sometimes called the nation's first prefabricated church, is on Sixth Street, a block off U.S. 98, across from the Gorrie Museum in Apalachicola; (850) 653–9550. Free.

Whether you know it or not, you owe a lot to John Gorrie. He's the physician whose inventions make it possible for you to enjoy air-conditioning, refrigeration, and ice cubes in your drink. Back in the days when ice had to be shipped all the way from the Great Lakes, it was a precious commodity in Florida. Dr. John Gorrie wanted a way to cool the rooms of patients suffering from malaria. The only problem was that the pipes in his experimental machine kept clogging with ice. When he realized the importance of this accidental discovery, he immediately built a small ice-making machine. You may inspect a replica of the machine (patented in 1851) that paved the way for modern refrigeration and air-conditioning in the *John Gorrie Museum.* (The original machine is in the Smithsonian Institution.) This one-room museum also has displays on cotton, lumbering, fishing, and other aspects of early Apalachicola history. The museum is at Avenue D and Sixth Street, 1 block off U.S. 319-98 in Apalachicola. Open 9:00 A.M.–5:00 P.M. daily except Tuesday and Wednesday; (850) 653-9347.

St. Vincent National Wildlife Refuge on St. Vincent Island is a bridgeless gem given over to some interesting animals and birds. White-tailed deer, wild hogs, raccoons, and opossums share the triangular-shaped refuge with sambar deer, which were imported from India by early owners. Red-tailed hawks, peregrine falcons, bald eagles, and a host of songbirds and waterfowl come and go. The deserted beaches are a favorite nesting ground for sea turtles. Most alligators hang around the freshwater ponds and marshes, while a few individualists choose to sun on the beach and enjoy the surf. Something to remember when taking a swim! This splendid place, with mile after mile of unspoiled beach, can be reached only by water. Contact the refuge manager for information on freshwater fishing, island exploration, and the cost of managed hunts for deer and wild hog. No charge for using the island, but you'll have to make your own

Abandon Hope

*I*f you're into snakes—really dangerous, poisonous snakes—have I got a place for you. **Tate's Hell Swamp** *(shown on some maps as Tates Hell State Forest) is not a tourist attraction where a friendly herpetologist demonstrates how to milk snakes. It's a real, live swamp located just north of Apalachicola. Well named, it is infested with deadly water moccasins. Abandon hope, all ye who enter.*

Get lost in this 70,000-acre swamp, and you're apt to be lost a long time. Fossils found in the tangled interior indicate it may have been a bog for more than a hundred centuries. According to the lumber company that owns the land, some of the trees deep in the swamp are more than 600 years old.

No one's quite sure if Old Man Tate, who gave his name to this watery wilderness, is still in there or not. Legend has it he was mad as hell because a panther had been killing his cattle. Following the panther's tracks, Tate disappeared into the morass. Some claim he was bitten by a snake and died somewhere deep in the quagmire. A folk song says he lived just long enough to tell of the hell he'd been through. In any case, he was not a pretty sight. Don't say you weren't warned.

arrangements to get there. Refuge Manager, St. Vincent National Wildlife Refuge, P.O. Box 447, Apalachicola, FL 32329; (850) 653–8808.

If you would like to see where the first of Florida's five constitutions was written, stop in at the *Constitution Convention State Museum.* Here you'll view an impressive replica of the Convention Hall's west wing, see eighteenth-century artifacts, and learn the story of the town of St. Joseph, which vanished forever after the 1844 hurricane. The museum is a quarter mile east of U.S. 98, just south of Port St. Joe. Open Thursday through Monday 9:00 A.M.–noon and 1:00–5:00 P.M.; (850) 229–8029.

Strange as it might seem, the Dead Lakes are alive with fish. Named for thousands of cypress, oak, and pine trees that drowned in the natural overflow of the Chipola River, *Dead Lakes State Recreation Area* enjoys a reputation as one of the best freshwater fishing spots in the Florida Panhandle. A longleaf pine forest shelters a tranquil picnic and camping area, and large stands of bare trees create a place of haunting beauty. One mile north of Wewahitchka on SR 71. Open 8:00 A.M. to sunset year-round. Dead Lakes State Recreation Area, P.O. Box 989, Wewahitchka, FL 32465; (850) 639–2702.

Another state recreation area that takes advantage of the Panhandle's gloriously white beaches is *St. Andrews* near Panama City. The water is unusually clear, the dunes are picturesque, and the pine woods shade fine campsites. Be sure to take a look at the restored old-time "cracker" turpentine still. St. Andrews is 3 miles east of Panama City Beach on SR 392, 4607 State Park Lane, Panama City, FL 32408. Open 8:00 A.M. to sunset; (850) 233–5140.

One of the most popular boat trips along the Panhandle Gulf Coast is to *Shell Island.* This undeveloped treasure of long, white beaches and windswept dunes is perfect for barefoot beachcombers and those who enjoy long, uninterrupted views of the Gulf between swims. Seven and a half miles long and more than a mile wide, this pristine island boasts a freshwater lake and teems with wildlife. From St. Andrews State Park, boats leave four times daily for the western end of the island. Shell Island trips leave for the eastern end of the island from Captain Anderson's Marina on Thomas Drive at Grand Lagoon in Panama City. Boats make the trip twice daily from mid-March to mid-September at 9:00 A.M. and 1:00 P.M. Inquire about sight-seeing and dinner cruises. Call (850) 234–3435. From *Treasure Island Marina* at Grand Lagoon on Panama City Beach, a glass-bottom boat departs daily during the summer for a three-hour adventure called "Sea School." You will see dolphins, examine the contents of a shrimp net, and feed birds. Glass-bottom boat cruises:

Authors' Favorite Attr/
Northwest Florida

(850) 234–8944. Treasure Island Marina: (850) 234–6533.

The Beaches of South Walton span 26 miles along the clear blue-green waters of the Gulf of Mexico in Northwest Florida. Between Destin to the west and Panama City Beach on the east, these eighteen small beach neighborhoods specialize in dazzling white sand hugging the Gulf's gentle waters.

These beaches have always been favorites for summer vacations, but they are quickly becoming a year-round destination. Along with mild temperatures, fall, spring, and winter bring quiet, peaceful beaches and low season prices. Winter, with an average temperature of 68 degrees, means sweater weather for Florida residents but feels like Indian summer to most people. The average high fall and spring temperatures are 79 and 80 degrees, respectively. October and November are the least humid months of the year.

These communities take a great deal of pride in being one of the most pristine destinations in Florida. Of 53,000 acres, an astonishing 23,000 is undeveloped state-owned property. With nary an amusement park, chain motel, T-shirt shop, or honky-tonk bar in sight, these relaxed beach communities still offer plenty of fascinating things to see and do. For more information: Beaches of South Walton, P.O. Box 1248, Santa Rosa Beach, FL 32459; (800) 822–6877; Web site: www.beachesofsouthwalton.com.

For a sample of the natural splendor of the area, head straight for ***Grayton Beach State Park***. This beach was recently retired as the "Nation's Best Beach." (Dr. Stephen Leatherman ["Dr. Beach"], director of the University of Maryland's Laboratory for Coastal Research, names certain U.S. beaches "best beach." After a beach is given this honor, it becomes ineligible for the designation for ten years.) In fact, each year the University of Maryland Geological Survey, an independent study, ranks the beaches of South Walton among the best in the nation.

Chosen from 650 other U.S. beaches for its quality of sand, accessibility, natural beauty, water temperature, pristine nature trails, and safe, uncrowded environment, Grayton Beach State Park is the beach of your fantasies. Here sugar-white sand dunes crested by dense stands of sea oats and wind-sculpted trees lure artists to capture stunning seascapes.

Stephen Foster State Folk Culture Center, White Springs

Cedar Key, Cedar Key

Gulf Islands National Seashore, Gulf Breeze

Seville Square, Pensacola

National Museum of Naval Aviation, Pensacola

Falling Waters State Recreation Area, Chipley

Florida Caverns State Park, Marianna

Maclay Ornamental Gardens, Tallahassee

Tallahassee Museum of Natural History and Science, Tallahassee

Wakulla Springs, Wakulla Springs

Grayton Beach State Recreation Area offers an extensive, self-guided trail system that provides an up-close look at the diverse ecosystems that comprise Northwest Florida's coastal areas. Dramatic examples of dune migration and dune building are seen along the trail. Hours are from 8:00 A.M. to sundown daily. (Park closes at 5:00 P.M. during the winter months.) Grayton Beach State Park Recreation Area is located on CR 30–A, 1 mile east of Grayton Beach, about 25 miles east of Fort Walton Beach by way of U.S. 98 and SR 30–A. Grayton State Recreation Area, 357 Main Park Road, Santa Rosa Beach, FL 32459; (850) 231–4210.

Cassine Garden Nature Trail and boardwalk meanders through 3 scenic miles of marshlands, forests, and pure white sand beaches and includes a 1-mile fitness trail. Visitors are welcome to use the trail at any time, but it is not lighted at night. Located behind Cassine Garden family resort 1 mile east of CR 395 on CR 30–A. For more information call (850) 231–5721.

Grayton Beach is a hundred-year-old community with sand streets, lots of trees, and homes made of weathered cypress. Ask a friendly local to point out the "Washaway" house built in the early 1900s by a veteran of the Civil War. If you want handcrafted furniture, hand-painted clothes, or would just like to meet some personable pigs and goats, *Patrone's* is the place. This working artist colony comes complete with a cluster of small art studios and a lively barnyard zoo. A great place for the kids! The community of Grayton Beach is located off CR 30–A at CR 283.

Topsail Hill State Park, just off Highway 98, is a $2\frac{1}{2}$-mile stretch of beach held in trust by the state as a nature conservatory. High dunes, a longleaf pine forest and two freshwater lakes create a safe haven for wildflowers, plants, and native wildlife. This 3-mile undeveloped beachfront has been identified as the most pristine and environmentally protected piece of coastal property in Florida. When you've had it with the clang, clatter, and fax warbles of modern living, Topsail is an ideal antidote.

For a serene glimpse of the area's past, you'll want to tour the landscaped grounds and mansion of *Eden State Gardens,* overlooking Choctawhatchee Bay. Once the hub of a large sawmill complex, the lumber baron's antebellum residence now stands alone, framed by gnarled oaks dripping with Spanish moss. Camellias and azaleas add color to the enchanting scene, especially during the peak bloom season around mid-March.

The stately white-columned mansion with a fireplace in every room preserves a fragment of the 1800s, the Old South that has mostly gone with the wind. You may picnic, fish, and take a guided tour of this splendid old home. A picnic area with adjacent parking is available at the old mill site on Tucker Bayou. Five miles north of Grayton Beach, Eden State Gardens in on CR 395, 1 mile north of U.S. 98 in Point Washington. Tours of the house are offered Thursday through Monday on the hour, 9:00 A.M.–4:00 P.M., and the park is open daily 8:00 A.M. to sunset. Admission to the park is free. Cost for the mansion tour is $3.00 for adults and $1.00 for children under twelve. Eden State Gardens, P.O. Box 26, Point Washington, FL 32454; (850) 231–4214.

The *Gourd Garden and Curiosity Shop* features decorative gourds, art, and herbs and flowers from the Deep South and around the world. You won't believe the many uses for gourds on display, ranging from birdhouses to gourd jewelry. Pick up a hand dipper from Mali, Africa, or a tiny nativity scene from El Salvador. Be sure to chat with Randy Harelson, garden designer, native plant expert, graphic artist, and owner of The Gourd Garden. Located in an old Florida cottage and garden at 4808 East CR 30–A in Seagrove, FL 32459, 2 miles east of Seaside; (850) 231–2007.

Bayou Arts & Antiques is a woodsy little complex overlooking tranquil Hogtown Bayou. Besides an antiques store bristling with oddities, there is garden statuary, an art studio, a display of old fishing boats, a children's pet cemetery, and the hand-painted St. Francis Wildlife Chapel. Once a year kids bring their pets here to be blessed. Imagine all those cats, dogs, and turtles lining up together! Located at Cessna Park and Highway 393 in the abandoned town of "Old Santa Rosa" just north of CR 30–A at 105 Hogtown Bayou Lane, Santa Rosa Beach, FL 32459. Open Tuesday through Saturday 10:00 A.M.–4:30 P.M.; (850) 267–1404.

The beaches of South Walton offer an impressive array of dining choices. The primary focus is on fresh seafood from the Gulf. And why not? It comes straight from the harbor docks of the largest charter boat fleet in the state. But just about everything else, from Cajun and Caribbean cuisine to down-home Southern cooking, is also on tap.

Donut Hole, a popular local watering hole, is especially good for hearty breakfasts. Try the pastries and European artisan breads made right on the premises. When was the last time you took three days to make a loaf of bread using wild yeast? Better take home a loaf or two of Tuscan bread. Open every day from 6:00 A.M. until 10:00 P.M. On Highway 98 West, 2½ miles east of Sandestin/Santa Rosa Beach; (850) 837–8824.

If you just can't stand to leave the beach long enough for lunch, *Pompano Joe's* is the place for you. This open-air, right-on-the-beach neighborhood favorite specializes in seafood with a Caribbean flair. You can't

OFF THE BEATEN PATH

go wrong with fried blue crab claws and a char-grilled amberjack sandwich. Open every day 11:00 A.M.–10:00 P.M. On the beach, Pompano Joe's is at 2237 Old Highway 98 East South Walton, FL 32541; (850) 837–2224.

For the sophisticated palate, South Walton offers a selection of award-winning five-star restaurants. *Criolla's* offers imaginative cuisine ranging from rabbit and chanterelle soup to seared grouper and apple brown Betty served with their own caramel pecan ice cream. On Scenic CR 30–A in Grayton Beach; (850) 267–1267.

You have to get off the beaten path to find **Elephant Walk** nestled in the dunes overlooking the Gulf of Mexico. Elephant Walk, Sandestin Resort's signature restaurant, has won many awards in addition to its five-star rating. Choose from Tamarind Tango Tuna, Tahitianese duck or shrimp, and lobster ragout. Open every day, Sunday to Thursday 5:00–9:00 P.M., Friday and Saturday 5:00–10:00 P.M. Located on the Gulf at Sandestin Beach and Golf Resort, 9300 Highway 98 West, Destin, FL 32541; (850) 267–4800.

If you aren't an artist already, **Seaside** will make you long to be one. Perhaps the most widely painted and photographed community in Northwest Florida, this pretty pastel town fronts a wide, sugar-white beach. Wood-frame cottages with front porches, tin roofs, gazebos, and picket fences evoke a feeling of nostalgia. Brick streets designed for leisurely strolling lead to lovely pavilions opening onto the beach. Town Center, with a village green, colorful shops, and restaurants, is but a short stroll away. Internationally acclaimed for its distinctive architecture and vision of what beach living should be, Seaside is a stunning success as well as a visual treat. Seaside Visitors Center, P.O. Box 4730, Seaside, FL 32459; (800) 277–TOWN.

Perspicasity, a Mediterranean-type, open-air bazaar, has an intriguing selection of clothes and wickerware. On the beach side of CR 30–A in Seaside. **Modica Market**, surely one of north Florida's most unusual grocery stores, is the place to go when you're fresh out of Scottish smoked salmon or just have a taste for a New Orleans–style muffaletta or just-made tiramisu. Be sure to sample their fresh-squeezed lemonade. Modica Market is located near the center of Seaside.

Bud & Alley's restaurant in Seaside combines Mediterranean cuisine with Deep South and Old Florida influences in a relaxed beach atmosphere. So if you're hankering for some fried green tomatoes, wood-grilled Cobia Crostini, Southern-fried soft-shell crabs, or apple-and-walnut–stuffed quail, you're in the right place. Open every day in summer. Sunday through Thursday, 6:00–9:30 P.M., Friday and Saturday, 6:00–10:00 P.M. Closed January and Tuesdays in winter. Other days open 6:00–9:00 P.M., Friday and Saturday 6:00–9:30 P.M. Scenic CR 30–A in Seaside; (850) 231–5900.

Rocky Bayou State Recreation Area provides an opportunity to see what the real Florida looks like. Located within Eglin Air Force Base, this park sits on the arm of Choctawhatchee Bay known as Rocky Bayou. A freshwater lake by the unlikely name of Puddin Head is home to largemouth bass, alligators, and a colony of beavers; nature trails wind through a pine forest shading reindeer moss and scrub oaks. The area is good for camping, swimming, boating, and fishing. Open 8:00 A.M.–sunset; located 3 miles east of Niceville off Highway 20. Fred Gannon Rocky Bayou State Recreation Area, 4281 Highway 20, Niceville, FL 32578; (850) 833–9144.

How do you like your mullet—smoked, baked, broiled, fried, or in gumbo? The great thing about the *Boggy Bayou Mullet Festival* is that you don't have to decide—you can try it every which way. In the early 1900s mullet was a very important food source as well as the primary livelihood for most of the settlers who lived in this area. Mullet were caught, salted, and shipped by boat first to Pensacola, then to other communities in the South.

Of course the festival offers plenty of other tempting things to eat, including specialties from many foreign lands, and you can feast your eyes on the Queen of the Mullet Festival Pageant. The Boggy Bayou Mullet Festival is held the third weekend in October at College Boulevard and Highway 85 north of Niceville. The festival address is P.O. Box 231, Niceville, FL 32588; (850) 678–1615.

Local history takes on new meaning at the *Heritage Museum* in Valparaiso. Besides an extensive library of old documents and maps (including *The Complete and Official Records of the Union and Confederate Armies*), the museum houses a collection of artifacts that provide insight into the challenges faced by prehistoric Indians and early pioneers. You'll want to inspect the steam-powered cotton gin as well as tools used in farming, lumbering, and producing turpentine. Classes are offered in weaving, quilt-making, needlepoint, tatting, and basket-weaving, and handcrafted items are for sale. The Heritage Museum is at 115 Westview Avenue in downtown Valparaiso. Open Tuesday through Saturday 11:00 A.M.–4:00 P.M.; (850) 678–2615. Free.

The *Air Force Armament Museum* is outside the west gate of Eglin Air Force Base, the largest air force base in the world. The awesome SR–71 Blackbird spy plane and other military aircraft outside compete with interior displays and ongoing movies. The Desert Storm section brings you up to the minute weaponwise. Eglin Air Force Base is 7 miles northeast of Fort Walton Beach on SR 85; 100 Museum Drive, Eglin Air Force Base, FL 32542–1497. For information call (850) 882–4062.

The historic fishing village of Destin was founded in the 1830s when Captain Leonard A. Destin sailed into Choctawhatchee Bay and decided it was a fine place to raise his family. The two-room *Old Destin Post Office Museum* is full of artifacts and photos that tell of the early days of this community. The staff may be able to help with genealogical research on early Destin families. The museum is on Stahlman Avenue, across from the Destin Library in Destin. Open Wednesdays 1:30–4:30 P.M. Old Destin Post Office Museum, P.O. Box 691, Destin, FL 32540–0691. No admission fee and no charge for guided tour; (850) 837–8572.

In 1933 the isolated fishing village of Destin underwent a dramatic change. A wooden bridge was built connecting it to the outside world. Before long, folks began to notice Destin was not only the "luckiest fishing village" but also had some of the finest beaches anywhere. From red snapper to yellowfin tuna, an abundance of incredibly fresh and delectable seafood lands in area restaurants. Emerald Coast favorites include *Marina Cafe,* whose gifted young chef dresses grilled grouper with Louisiana crawfish tails and sauce meunière. For lunch savor a seafood combo at *Fudpuckers;* a juicy burger at *Harry T's Boathouse,* where circus memorabilia includes Stretch, Harry's beloved (stuffed!) giraffe; or the superb chargrilled amberjack sandwich, served with a side-order view of parasailers and other assorted beach action, at the *Back-Porch* on Old Highway 98.

Indians were dining on fresh seafood long before the Europeans "discovered" Florida. Some of them were mound builders, and they left a fine example of their work on the main drag in *Fort Walton Beach.* Imagine 500,000 basketloads of dirt hauled one at a time to create this impressive landmark. To learn more about the seven pre-Columbian cultures who inhabited this area for more than 10,000 years, drop in at the *Indian Temple Mound Museum* on the east flank of the mound. Here you'll see the re-creation of an ancient temple, a four-legged bowl that has been called the most unique ceramic artifact in the Southeast, and various artifacts from recent archaeological excavations.

The museum and mound (which is a National Historic Landmark), at 139 Miracle Strip Parkway on U.S. 98, are owned and operated by the City of Fort Walton Beach, FL 32548. The mound may be viewed during daylight hours. The museum is open 11:00 A.M.–4:00 P.M. Monday through Friday and 9:00 A.M.–4:00 P.M. Saturday, September to May; (850) 833-9595.

Once upon a time a buccaneer known as Billy Bowlegs decided being a run-of-the-mill pirate wasn't classy enough, so he assembled a group of followers—Indians, deserters, bandits, and the like—and proclaimed himself King of Florida. He did all the things pirates were supposed to do—scared folks out of their wits, took their money and buried it, and, in general, made a nuisance of himself. For more than forty years Fort Walton Beach has been annually reviving his swashbuckling spirit in the rollicking **Billy Bowlegs Festival.** The first week in June erupts in mock pirate attacks, parades, concerts, boat races, crafts exhibits, and, of course, treasure hunts. For information write Greater Fort Walton Beach Chamber of Commerce, P.O. Box 640, Fort Walton Beach, FL 32549; (850) 244–8191.

Don your darkest shades and prepare to be bedazzled. The brilliant white beaches of Northwest Florida glitter and gleam their way through 343 sunny days each year.

How is this sand different? For starters, it's not beige, nor is it made of pulverized seashells. It's 99 percent pure quartz crystal formed in the Appalachian Mountains and refined by a millennium of grinding, polishing, and bleaching during its long river journey to the Gulf of Mexico. It's soft, squeaks underfoot, and is as clean and white as fresh snow.

Pensacola Area

each lovers can rest easy. **Gulf Islands National Seashore** protects shimmering white sand and swaying sea oats along a 150-mile stretch of islands and keys between Destin, Florida, and Gulfport, Mississippi. The Florida section of the national seashore includes **Naval Live Oaks Area** (where you may hike through groves once prized for shipbuilding), part of **Perdido Key,** the forts on the **Pensacola Naval Air Station,** and part of **Santa Rosa Island.**

At the western end of Santa Rosa is stabilized, historic **Fort Pickens,** which saw action during the Civil War and where Apache chief Geronimo was held prisoner for two ignominious years. Today the beach gets better use as a bird sanctuary and camping and recreation site. Ask the park rangers or local dive shops to recommend the best scuba diving locations. Besides the usual beach activities, you'll want to explore this massive five-sided fort and visit the small museum. Take U.S. 98 and SR

Union Stronghold

After Florida left the Union in 1861, nearly all federal property in the state was seized by Secessionists, but a notable exception occurred at Pensacola. Rebel troops were never able to take Fort Pickens, but they did take control of all other installations in the area. In a November 1861 battle, Fort Barrancas had its flagstaff shot away and its walls slightly scarred, but casualties were light due to the strong walls. That combat turned out to be the last for the fort. In May 1862, the Confederates pulled out of Pensacola, and Union forces reoccupied all the harbor installations.

399 south to Pensacola Beach, then follow signs west to Fort Pickens. Museum open 9:30 A.M.–5:00 P.M. daily April through October and 8:30 A.M.–4:00 P.M. November through March. For information: Superintendent, Gulf Islands National Seashore, 1801 Gulf Breeze Parkway, Gulf Breeze, FL 32561; (850) 934–2600.

Fisherfolk should not miss the opportunity to drop a line from the *"world's longest fishing pier,"* as the old Pensacola Bay Bridge is now known. Judging from the number of fishing poles sprouting from the bridge, this is one hot spot. And no through traffic interferes with your concentration. Easy to find, this bridge parallels the new Pensacola Bay Bridge.

The heart of Pensacola is in **Seville Square,** a historic district between East Government and South Alcaniz Streets where shops, restaurants, museums, and art galleries inhabit a hodgepodge of restored eighteenth- and nineteenth-century cottages and mansions. Pick up a free map and brochures at the Visitor Information Center, 1401 East Gregory Street (at the foot of the bridge), Pensacola, FL 32501; (800) 874–1234 or (850) 434–1234.

Stop in at the **Pensacola Historical Museum** for local history including everything from displays on ancient Indian culture and Mardi Gras costumes to a fully equipped 1915 kitchen. Located at 115 East Zaragoza Street, Pensacola, FL 32501; (850) 433–1559. Open Monday through Saturday 10:00 A.M.–4:30 P.M.

For a delightful glimpse into Pensacola's past, browse the **Museums of Industry and Commerce,** chat with costumed interpreters in five different house museums, and shop a wide variety of attractive boutiques in **Historic Pensacola Village.** Don't miss the truly weird collection (including both shrunken heads and a petrified cat) in the newly renovated **T. T. Wentworth, Jr., Florida State Museum.** Kids love **Discovery!,** the lively hands-on children's museum upstairs.

Hungry? Try **McGuires,** one of Pensacola's favorite watering holes. The fare is top-notch, the portions generous, and the atmosphere, well, loaded. Thirty thousand one-dollar bills adorn the walls from which stuffed hippos, moose, and Cape buffalo stare. Prices are reasonable,

unless (lottery winners take note!) you're hankering f
famous $100 burger. You might want to try **Skopelǐ**
Seafood and Steak Restaurant or **Jamie's French R**
nineteenth-century cottage in historic Seville Square.
eatery is **Jubilee Restaurant and Oyster Bar** with qu
on the lower level and elegant Florida cuisine upstairs.

Not to be missed is **Seville Quarter** with **Rosie O'Grady's Good Time
Emporium** and seven other saloons and restaurants. Even if you're not
hungry, thirsty, or in need of entertainment, you really should stop in
for a look. Besides an impressive collection of local antiques, the
gaslights are from Liverpool, the parliament benches are from London,
the disco booth was once an English pulpit, the ships' wheels in Copper-
smith's Gallery are from schooners that made tea and spice runs to
China, and Rosie's main door at one time graced a mansion in Mobile.

Seville Quarter overflows with choices. Should you down a Flaming
Hurricane drink at Rosie's, catch the show on big-screen TV in **Lili
Marlene's World War I Aviators Pub,** or tap your feet to **Apple Annie's**
wonderful bluegrass music? While you're deciding, you might want to
order red beans and rice, jambalaya, or beignet doughnuts in the
Palace Oyster Bar. For an inexpensive lunch, choose oysters on the half
shell or a Cajun sausage sandwich. Those great pub mirrors on the walls
were imported from Edinburgh, Scotland. The Seville Quarter is at 130
East Government Street in Pensacola, FL 32501, and the prices range
from inexpensive to expensive; (850) 434–6211.

Take a ride, or better yet a walk, through **North Hill Preservation District.** This 50-block area, bounded by LaRua, Palafox, Blount, and Reus
Streets, is a treasure trove of fancy turn-of-the-century houses. You'll be
able to appreciate the details—the wide verandas, turrets, and elaborate
gingerbread trim—better on foot. Maps and touring information are free
from the Visitor Information Center (open 8:30 A.M.–5:00 P.M.), 1401 East
Gregory Street, Pensacola 32501, at the foot of Pensacola Bay Bridge.

All your roaming through the North Hill Preservation District is sure to
give you a stupendous appetite. You'll need it if you try to do justice to
the good Southern cooking at **Hopkins' Boarding House.** This bustling
establishment is the real thing, an authentic boardinghouse where you
join other diners at big round tables and get to try out your boardinghouse reach. The place is usually pretty packed, and you may have to
wait a few moments to be seated. If so, just grab a chair on the wraparound porch and think ravenous thoughts.

Most first-timers are overwhelmed by the great steaming bowls of food are replaced before they are emptied. A recent offering included fried chicken, rice, gravy, coleslaw, potato salad, corn muffins, black-eyed peas, cucumber salad, greens, succotash, macaroni and cheese, cake, Jell-O, and lots of iced tea. Before you get so stuffed you can hardly see, take a look around at the religious pictures, collections of plates, and family photographs that adorn the walls.

You are expected to clear your own plate and to pay cash. Hopkins' Boarding House is at 900 North Spring Street in the North Hill Preservation District of Pensacola, FL 32501. Opens at 11:00 A.M. Tuesday through Saturday for lunch and 5:00–7:30 P.M. for dinner. Closed Mondays. Inexpensive; (850) 438–3979.

The expansive *National Museum of Naval Aviation* is a real prize—a beautifully designed, fascinating tribute to aviation history on the grounds of the world's largest naval air station. You'll follow the growth and development of our country's naval aviation from the first aircraft the Navy purchased in 1911 (replica) to the Skylab command module. Especially fascinating is the movie of the inspiring *Great Flight,* the first successful crossing of the Atlantic Ocean by air in 1919. The only museum in the world devoted exclusively to naval aviation, this one has something for everyone. You can try out the controls of a jet trainer, wander among full-size aircraft, or browse the bookstore and gift shop. An impressive wing features a dramatic seven-story atrium with four full-size Blue Angel Sky Hawks soaring in permanent diamond formation. Use the main entrance of the Naval Air Station. In Pensacola take Palafox Street south to Garden Street, which becomes Navy Boulevard (SR 295). Follow the signs to the Naval Air Station; (850) 452–3604. Open 9:00 A.M.–5:00 P.M. Closed Thanksgiving, Christmas, and New Year's days. A real bargain, it's free.

The *Naval Air Station* features a number of other attractions visitors sometimes miss because they simply don't realize they are so close by. The *Spanish Fort San Carlos de Barrancas* (part of the Gulf Islands National Seashore) is practically across the road from the museum. First, stop in the visitor center to get some background information, then explore the fort and enjoy its commanding view. Be careful in the dark, steep, and sometimes slippery tunnel to the water battery.

You can't enter the *Old Pensacola Lighthouse,* but as you drive by it's nice to know it has been operating since 1825. You will also want to take a look at *Sherman Field,* home of the famous precision flying team known as the Blue Angels. The Pensacola Naval Air Station main entrance is on Navy Boulevard, SR 295. Free.

While you're in the area, take advantage of the fine facilities at **Big Lagoon State Recreation Area** where you may picnic, camp, boat, fish, and swim. An elaborate boardwalk network and observation tower at East Beach provide bird-watchers with an excellent view overlooking the marsh. This is definitely the place to watch the great blue heron stalking his dinner! Also, you may soak up panoramic vistas of Big Lagoon, the park, and Gulf Islands National Seashore across the Intracoastal Waterway. The park is about 10 miles southwest of Pensacola off SR 292A. Big Lagoon State Recreation Area, 12301 Gulf Beach Highway, Pensacola, FL 32507; (850) 492–1595.

Upper Panhandle

Canoeists and campers will appreciate **Blackwater River State Park** on the shores of one of the cleanest rivers in the country. Dark water contrasts with dazzling white sandbars at bends in the river. Especially good for novice paddlers and inner tubers, the river winds its way from Alabama to Blackwater Bay at the leisurely rate of 3 to 4 mph. The park is 15 miles northeast of Milton, 3 miles off U.S. 90. Blackwater River State Park, 7720 Deaton Bridge Road, Holt, FL 32564; (850) 983–5363. Open 8:00 A.M. until sunset.

Put on your hiking shoes and heed the call of the **Jackson Red Ground Hiking Trail.** Located in Blackwater River State Forest, this old 21-mile Indian trading trail was used by General Andrew Jackson on his historic 1818 journey to the Florida Territory. Follow the red paint marks on trees from Karick Lake to the Red Rock Picnic Area over a combination of footpaths and forest roadways.

The Jackson Trail, which is part of the National Recreation Trail System and designated as a section of the Florida Trail System, has a camping shelter. For information weekdays 7:00 A.M.–4:00 P.M., contact Blackwater Forestry Center, 11650 Munson Highway, Milton, FL 32570; (850) 957–6140. At other times park rangers are available at the Krul Recreation Area and the Coldwater Recreation Area.

What if you are overcome by a craving for pizza and you happen to be in Crestview, Florida? Consider yourself lucky and head on down to the **Hideaway** on Main Street. The dough is made from scratch twice daily, the sausage is cut, ground, and seasoned on the premises, and the sauce, according to a special recipe, is made fresh every morning. The Hideaway takes pride in not using any artificial emulsifiers or preservatives; its salad bar is crispy fresh, and a glass partition gives you a view of its immaculate kitchen. The Hideaway is at 326 North Main Street in Crestview, FL 32536. Open Monday through Thursday 11:00 A.M.–9:00 P.M., Friday and Saturday 11:00 A.M.–10:00 P.M., closed Sunday. To order ahead or place a take-out order, call (850) 682–3225. Inexpensive.

Lake DeFuniak, halfway between Pensacola and Tallahassee, is well worth a visit. For one thing, this claims to be one of only two perfectly round lakes in the world; for another, the area has a rich and fascinating heritage. During the 1880s a railroad executive envisioned a splendid winter resort here. Later, the Chautauqua Committee decided this would make a fine winter site for its program of concerts and lectures given each summer at Lake Chautauqua, New York. Take some time to admire the late nineteenth-century *Chautauqua Assembly Building* and the grand old homes that surround the lake. The U.S. Department of the Interior and the National Parks Service recently placed the *Town of DeFuniak Springs* on the National Register of Historic Districts, citing some 285 structures of significant historic value. The Great Depression ended this glorious era, but an annual festival helps preserve memories of the past. The lake is in DeFuniak Springs near U.S. 90 and SR 83. For information on the festival held each year in April, call the Walton County Chamber of Commerce; (850) 892–3191.

Don't miss seeing one of the town's most historically significant structures, the *Walton-DeFuniak Public Library.* Opened on December 20, 1887, this is believed to be the state's oldest public library continuously operating in its original building. Its one room measured 24 by 17 feet and cost just under $580 when built. This charming library holds 20,000 volumes, including some rare books as old as the library itself.

You really wouldn't expect to find a fine European armor collection in such a modest little library, but that is one of the bonuses of getting off the beaten path. When Wallace Bruce was ambassador to Scotland and living in Edinburgh in the 1880s, his son Kenneth began collecting armor. The family came to DeFuniak Springs about 1890 when Mr. Bruce became president of the Chautauqua winter program. Some of the pieces of this unusual collection date back as far as the Crusades (A.D. 1100–1300). Besides European pieces there are Kentucky rifles from the Daniel Boone era.

The entire collection was willed to Palmer College, but when the college closed in the 1930s, it was given to the city in partial payment of its debts. The city had no suitable place for it, so it eventually wound up in the library for you to enjoy. You won't have any trouble finding the library. Just drive around Lake DeFuniak and look for a tiny building. Closed Sunday. The library's phone number is (850) 892–3624.

Waterfalls in Florida? Strange as it may seem, they do exist in *Falling Waters State Recreation Area.* Though they don't exactly create a neck-craning Niagara, these waters do, just the same, fall. You see, some of the most notable geological features in Florida are its sinkholes. A small stream meanders into a 100-foot sinkhole, and *voilà,* a "waterfall!" A few

Walton-DeFuniak Public Library

caveats—you will be looking down, not up, and during the dry season there may not be any water to fall.

Not to worry. This forested area, the site of the first attempt (1919) to find oil in Florida, is lovely to stroll through. Limestone sinkholes honeycombing the hilly terrain may be viewed from a series of boardwalks. Take the self-guiding nature trails, picnic, camp, and swim. Located 3 miles south of Chipley, off SR 77A, the area is open 8:00 A.M. to sunset year-round. Falling Waters State Recreation Area, 1130 State Park Road, Chipley, FL 32428; (850) 638–6130.

Florida's caverns are another feature to come under the heading of strange quirks of geology. Over the millennium, mineral-rich drops of water have created the enchanting formations in *Florida Caverns State Park.* Among other sights, you'll see the *Waterfall Room,* the *Cathedral Room,* and the *Wedding Room*—all decked out in natural splendor. The caverns are as impressive, if not as large, as some of the country's most famous underground attractions. An enlightening audiovisual show in the visitor center explains how the caverns were formed, and exhibits on natural and cultural history shed some light on the early Indians who found shelter here.

The park also has a disappearing river, a natural bridge, and a natural beach rimming Blue Hole Springs. You may camp, swim, fish, canoe, and picnic. The park, off SR 167, is 3 miles north of Marianna. Open 8:00 A.M. to sundown daily. Tours 9:00 A.M.–4:00 P.M. Florida Caverns

A Sinking Feeling

Falling Waters Sink, a cylindrical, smooth-walled chimney 100 feet deep with a diameter of 15 feet, is in Fallings Waters State Recreation Area near Chipley. Here a small stream creates a waterfall and then flows into an underground cavern at the bottom of the sink, where hand-hewn timbers of an early gristmill can still be seen. This is a classic example of one of Florida's notable geological features, the limestone sinkhole.

State Park, Marianna, FL 32446. Recorded message: (850) 482–9598.

If New England and Canada seem a trifle far to go for fall color, try **Torreya State Park.** Here rugged bluffs and ravines forested by flowers and hardwoods common to the North Georgia Appalachians provide the state's prettiest autumn display. The park, a botanist's paradise, protects the Torreya tree, which is native only to the 20-mile surrounding area. Be sure to tour the restored **Gregory Mansion** (1849), once home of an affluent cotton planter, and hike the trails to the Apalachicola River. The park, on CR 1641 (which is off SR 12) between Bristol and Greensboro, is open 8:00 A.M. to sunset year-round. Guided tours of the house are given during the week at 10:00 A.M. and on weekends and holidays at 10:00 A.M., 2:00 P.M., and 4:00 P.M. Torreya State Park, HC 2, Box 70, Bristol, FL 32321; (850) 643–2674.

The fishing is fine at **Three Rivers State Recreation Area.** Named for the Chattahoochee and Flint Rivers, which merge to form the Apalachicola, this scenic area includes 4 miles of shoreline on Lake Seminole at the Florida-Georgia border. Home to a slew of alligators and huge alligator snapping turtles as well as fish, Three Rivers is the place to wet a line, boat, picnic, or camp. Located a mile north of Sneads off SR 271, it's open 8:00 A.M. to sunset year-round. Three Rivers State Recreation Area, 7908 Three Rivers State Park Road, Sneads, FL 32460; (850) 482–9006.

Tallahassee Area

*A*t the **Maclay Ornamental Gardens** near Tallahassee, the peak blooming season begins in December and continues through April, when dogwood, redbud, and more than a hundred varieties of camellias and azaleas create a fairyland of flowers. The gardens are an oasis of beauty all year, but spring is spectacular! This 307-acre park was once the home of Alfred B. Maclay, a New York financier who made his winter home here starting in 1923.

He developed the grounds as a hobby, using exotic plants to complement the native varieties and adding reflecting pools and avenues of stately palms. Stroll the brick walkways to the tiny walled garden where a graceful fountain provides the only sound except for the distant coo of the doves. If it's serenity you're after, you've come to the right place. Picnic grounds overlook Lake Hall, which is fine for swimming and boating (only electric motors allowed).

The park is open daily 8:00 A.M. to sundown year-round. The gardens and the *Maclay House Museum* are open daily 9:00 A.M.–5:00 P.M. January through April. The Maclay Gardens are north of Tallahassee, half a mile from exit 30 on I–10. Alfred B. Maclay State Gardens, 3540 Thomasville Road, Tallahassee, FL 32308; (850) 487–4556 or (904) 487–4115.

The tradition of wintering in Florida was apparently started by Hernando de Soto in 1539. He and his men celebrated Christmas mass in the vicinity of *Lake Jackson Mounds State Archaeological Site* in what is believed to have been the first Christmas in the New World. That doesn't seem like such a long time ago when you consider that, on the basis of recent excavations, archaeologists now speculate the area was inhabited as early as 1,300 years before the birth of Christ.

The dominant features of this state park are impressive pyramid-shaped mounds that are the remains of the largest known Indian ceremonial center in north Florida. A way of life flourished here from A.D. 1300 to 1600 that revolved around a village, six temple mounds, and a burial mound. The Indians who lived here were farmers who traded their surplus crops with nearby villages. After you climb to the top of the highest mound, you will more fully appreciate the fact that these mounds were created by Indians carrying sand and clay, one basketful at a time! This is a lovely spot for a picnic and a walk through the woods. The Butler Mill Trail through a hardwood ravine and upland pine woods leads to an early 1880s gristmill site. The mounds are located 6 miles north of Tallahassee off U.S. 27. Call Lake Jackson Park Service at (850) 922–6007.

For more information about ancient Florida—its ice age, huge mastodons, resourceful Indians, and Spanish explorers—stop in at the *Museum of Florida History* in downtown Tallahassee. This is the place to learn abut Florida's role on the high seas, to inspect a pre–Civil War dugout boat, and to view precious gold doubloons. Florida's wild booms and busts, complete with a colorful cast of characters from pirates to lumber tycoons, are all part of the story. Fascinating for all ages, the museum is housed in the R. A. Grey Building (500 South Bronough) across from the state Supreme Court in Tallahassee, FL 32399. Open every day but Christmas and Thanksgiving, 9:00 A.M.–4:30 P.M. Monday through Friday, 10:00 A.M.–4:30 P.M. Saturday, and noon–4:30 P.M. Sunday. No admission fee; (850) 488–1484.

The *LeMoyne Art Center and Sculpture Garden* is an oasis of peaceful beauty tucked into the middle of Tallahassee. The area's leading artists are represented in this compact gallery. A few metal sculptures adorn a small but lovingly cared for garden behind the gallery. For information write to LeMoyne Art Foundation, Inc., 125 North Gadsden Street, Tallahassee, FL 32301. Open Tuesday through Saturday 10:00 A.M.–5:00 P.M., Sunday 1:00–5:00 P.M.; closed holidays; (850) 222–8800 or (850) 681–0576.

The *Florida State Flying High Circus* serves up excitement the first two weekends in April. Students perform under the Big Top at Florida State University at West Pensacola Street and Chieftain Way. Performances are Friday and Saturday at 7:00 P.M. with a matinee at 2:00 on Saturday afternoon. For details call (850) 644–4874. Campus tours and maps are available at the Visitor Information Center in Tallahassee; (850) 644–3246.

The *Tallahassee Museum of History and Natural Science* is a favorite haunt for adults as well as children who are curious about the way things were. At this authentic 1890 pioneer farm and community, you'll see demonstrations of blacksmithing, syrup making, sheep shearing, spinning, and weaving during the month of November. There are nature trails, exhibits of wild animals native to the area, a one-room schoolhouse, a gristmill, and the Bellevue Plantation, once the home of Prince and Princess Murat. The museum is at 3945 Museum Drive, Tallahassee 32310, on Lake Bradford bordering Apalachicola National Forest. Open Monday through Saturday 9:00 A.M.–5:00 P.M. and Sunday 12:30–5:00 P.M.; (850) 575–8684. Recorded information: (850) 576–1636.

If you'd like to peer into the world's deepest spring, head south of Tallahassee to *Wakulla Springs,* where limestone-filtered water gushes forth at more than 600,000 gallons per minute. Wakulla has been a sanctuary for wildlife and people ever since Indians fished its 185-foot depths and Spanish explorers refreshed themselves in its clean, clear waters. Tourists after the Civil War thought the springs well worth the trip, as did underwater filmmakers, who came as early as the mid-1940s.

The resort still has an old-fashioned flavor due to its emphasis on conservation rather than razzle-dazzle tourism. This 2,888-acre wildlife sanctuary provides a glorious glimpse into precondominium Florida. Jungle cruises and glass-bottom boat tours reveal an enchanting blend of scenery and wildlife. You'll see lots of alligators and elegant birds including snowy egrets, herons, and ibis.

One common meaning given for the Indian word *wakulla* is "mysteries of strange waters." The spring has its share of mysteries, including complete mastodon skeletons, which have been found in the bottom of the spring. It seems appropriate that this was the location for the filming of *Creature from the Black Lagoon.*

After exploring the nature trails or taking a swim, enjoy historic **Wakulla Springs Lodge.** This Spanish-style inn, built in the 1930s of Tennessee marble, has unusual wood ceiling beams decorated with Florida scenes and flowers. The lodge dining room serves up Southern cooking at a reasonable cost. Wakulla Springs is 15 miles south of Tallahassee on SR 267. The lodge is open twenty-four hours; the park closes at dusk. Edward Ball Wakulla Springs State Park and Lodge, Wakulla Springs, FL 32305; (850) 224–5950. The park number is (850) 922–3632.

Civil War buffs will not want to miss the **Natural Bridge Battlefield State Historic Site.** Young cadets from West Florida Seminary (now Florida State University) and old men (Gadsden County Grays) joined Confederate forces to inflict heavy casualties on Union soldiers here on March 6, 1865. Thanks to their efforts, Tallahassee was the only Southern capital east of the Mississippi that did not fall into Union hands. Each year, in early March, the battle is reenacted.

This is a fine place to do a little fishing in the St. Marks River or to have a picnic, but don't go looking for an impressive arch like Virginia's Natural

The Pole-vaulting Fish

*A*t **Wakulla Springs** *we took both boat trips offered, the jungle cruise and the glass-bottom boat tour, and saw all manner of birds and fish. The endangered limpkin thrives here, primarily because its food, the applesnail, is abundant in the area. Often called the "crying bird," the limpkin's distinctive call has been described as sounding like "a woman lost forever in the swamps." This is one bird that has perfected extracting escargots down to a science, judging from the empty shells piled along the banks of the Wakulla.*

We saw an alligator carrying several small progeny on its head, mullet jumping all over the place, and, yes, a pole-vaulting fish. Now Henry, the fish, doesn't pole-vault just for the fun of it. Our guide worked awfully hard to pull off this particular feat.

"Henry," he called out loudly, "I want you to meet us at the pole." Well, that didn't do it. After calling again and again in a special singsong that apparently is supposed to provoke action, our guide was reduced to pleading. He tried in a more threatening tone: "Henry! Henry Junior! Henrietta!"— all to no avail. Then suddenly a fish appeared, grinned, and vaulted over the pole. Everyone cheered.

Bridge. This was originally a place where the river flowed underground for a ways, but the county has modified the "bridge" for drainage purposes. The battlefield site is 10 miles southeast of Tallahassee. Take U.S. 363 to Woodville, then go east on Natural Bridge Road; (850) 922–6007. Free.

STATE PARKS IN
NORTHWEST FLORIDA

**Alfred B. Maclay
State Gardens**
(850) 487–4556

**Big Lagoon State
Recreation Area**
(850) 492–1595

**Blackwater River
State Park**
(850) 983–5363

**Blackwater Heritage
State Trail**
(850) 623–2363

Cedar Key State Museum
(352) 543–5350

**Cedar Key Scrub
State Reserve**
(352) 543–5567

**Constitution Convention
State Museum**
(850) 229–8029

**Dead Lakes State
Recreation Area**
(850) 639–2702

Econfina River State Park
(850) 922–6007

Eden State Gardens
(850) 231–4214

**Falling Waters State
Recreation Area**
(850) 638–6130

**Florida Caverns
State Park**
(850) 482–9598

**Forest Capital
State Museum**
(850) 584–3227

**Grayton Beach State
Recreation Area**
(850) 231–4210

**Henderson Beach State
Recreation Area**
(850) 837–7550

**John Gorrie
State Museum**
(850) 653–9347

**Lake Jackson Mounds
State Archaeological Site**
(850) 922–6007

**Lake Talquin/River Bluff
Picnic Site**
(850) 922–6007

**Manatee Springs
State Park**
(352) 493–6072

**Natural Bridge Battlefield
State Historic Site**
(850) 922–6007

**Ochlockonee River
State Park**
(850) 962–2771

**Peacock Springs State
Recreation Area**
(904) 776–2194

**Perdido Key State
Recreation Area**
(850) 492–1595

**Ponce de Leon Springs
State Recreation Area**
(850) 836–4281

**San Marcos de Apalache
State Historic Site**
(850) 922–6007

**St. Andrews State
Recreation Area**
(850) 233–5140

**St. George Island
State Park**
(850) 927–2111

**St. Joseph Peninsula
State Park**
(850) 227–1327

**Stephen Foster State
Folk Culture Center**
(904) 397–2733

**Suwannee River
State Park**
(904) 397–2733

**Tallahassee–St. Marks
Historic R.R. State Trail**
(850) 922–6007

**Three Rivers State
Recreation Area**
(850) 482–9006

Torreya State Park
(850) 643–2674

**Waccasassa Bay
State Preserve**
(352) 543–5567

**Wakulla Springs State
Park & Lodge**
(850) 922–3632

PLACES TO STAY IN
NORTHWEST FLORIDA

LAKE CITY
Holiday Inn,
Drawer 1239, Junction of
I–75 and U.S. 90;
(904) 752–3901

CEDAR KEY
Island Place,
Box 687, First and C Streets;
(352) 543–5307

Island Hotel,
Second and B Streets;
(352) 543–5111

TALLAHASSEE
Cabot Lodge,
2735 North Monroe Street;
(850) 386–8880

Shoney's Inn,
2801 North Monroe Street;
(850) 386–8286

Radisson,
415 North Monroe Street;
(850) 224–6000

Governors Inn,
209 South Adams Street;
(850) 681–6855

WAKULLA SPRINGS
Wakulla Springs Lodge,
550 Wakulla Park Drive;
(850) 224–5950

APALACHICOLA
Gibson Inn, 51 Avenue C;
(850) 653–2191

PANAMA CITY
Comfort Inn,
1013 East Twenty-
third Street;
(850) 769–6969

Holiday Inn Select,
2001 North Cove
Boulevard;
(850) 769–0000

PANAMA CITY BEACH
Inn at St. Thomas Square,
8730 Thomas Drive;
(850) 234–0349

Edgewater Beach Resort,
11212 Front Beach Road;
(850) 235–4044

Holiday Inn
Sunspree Resort,
11127 Front Beach Road;
(850) 234–1111

Visitor Information for Northwest Florida

Apalachicola Bay Chamber of Commerce,
99 Market Street, Suite 100, Apalachicola 32320;
(850) 653–9419;
Web site: www.homtown.com/apalachicola

Destin Area Chamber of Commerce,
P.O. Box 8, Destin 32540;
(850) 837–6241;
Web site: www.destin.com/chamber.htm

Emerald Coast Convention & Visitor Bureau,
1540 Highway 98 East, Ft. Walton Beach 32549;
(800) 322–3319; Web site: www.destin-fwb.com

Greater Fort Walton Beach Chamber of Commerce,
34 S.E. Miracle Strip Parkway, Fort Walton Beach 32548;
(850) 244–8191;
Web site: www.hometown.com

Gulf County Chamber of Commerce,
301 Fifth Street, Port St. Joe 32457; (850) 227–1223,
(800) 239–9553 (U.S. only);
Web site: www.homtown.com/gulfco

Hamilton County Tourist Development Council,
207 Northeast First Street, Room 106, Jasper 32052;
(904) 792–1300

Columbia County Tourist Development Council,
P.O. Box 1847, Lake City 32056–1847; (904) 758–1312

Levy County Development Authority,
P.O. Box 1112, Bronson 32621; (352) 486–5470;
Web site: www.levycounty.org

Navarre Beach Tourist Information Center,
P.O. Box 5337, Navarre 32566; (850) 939–2691,
(800) 480–SAND (U.S. only);
Web site: www.navarrebeachfl.com

Marriott's Bay Point,
4200 Marriott Drive;
(850) 234–3307

FORT WALTON BEACH
Four Points by Sheraton,
1325 Miracle Strip Parkway;
(904) 243–8116

Holiday Inn,
1110 Santa Rosa Boulevard;
(850) 243–9181

Ramada Plaza Beach
Resort, 1500 Miracle Strip
Parkway Southeast;
(850) 243–9161

PENSACOLA
Holiday Inn–
University Mall,
7200 Plantation Road;
(850) 474–0100

Hampton Inn,
7330 Plantation Road;
(850) 477–3333

Best Western Village Inn,
8240 North Davis Highway;
(850) 479–1099

New World,
600 South Palafox;
(850) 432–4111

DE FUNIAK SPRINGS
Best Western
Crossroads Inn,
Junction I–10 and U.S. 331;
(850) 892–5111

MARIANNA
Comfort Inn,
Junction I–10 and FL 71N;
(850) 526–5600

**PLACES TO EAT IN
NORTHWEST FLORIDA**

LAKE CITY
Chasteen's
On U.S. 90 East;
(904) 752–7504

CEDAR KEY
Blue Desert Cafe,
12518 Highway 24;
(352) 543–9111

Island Hotel,
Second and B Streets;
(352) 543–5111

Visitor Information for Northwest Florida

Panama City Beach Convention & Visitors Bureau,
P.O. Box 9473, Panama City Beach 32417–9473;
(800) 553–1330;
Web site: pcbeach.com

Pensacola Convention & Visitor Center,
1401 East Gregory Street, Pensacola 32501;
(850) 434–1234, (800) 874–1234 (U.S. only);
Web site: www.visitpensacola.com

Perry-Taylor Chamber of Commerce,
428 North Jefferson Street, Perry 32348–0892;
(850) 584–5366, (800) 257–8881 (U.S. only);
Web site: www.asksam.com/chamber

South Walton Tourist Development Council,
P.O. Box 1248, Santa Rosa Beach 32459;
(800) 822–6877 (worldwide);
Web site: www.beachesofsouthwalton.com

Suwannee County Tourist Development Council,
P.O. Drawer C, Live Oak 32060;
(904) 362–3071
Web site: www.suwanneechamber.com

Tallahassee Area Convention & Visitors Bureau,
106 East Jefferson Street, Tallahassee 32301;
(800) 628–2866;
Web site: www.co.leon.fl.us/cvb.homepage.htm

Wakulla County Chamber of Commerce,
P.O. Box 598, Crawfordville 32327;
(850) 926–1848, (888) WAKULLA (U.S. only);
Web site: www.freenet.tlh.fl.us/~wakullac/

TALLAHASSEE
Andrew's 2nd Act,
228 South Adams Street;
(850) 222-3444

Chez Pierre (French),
1215 Thomasville Road;
(850) 222-0936

Cafe Di Lorenzo (Italian),
1002 North Monroe Street;
(850) 681-3622

APALACHICOLA
Seafood Grill
& Steakhouse,
100 Market Street;
(850) 653-9510

PANAMA CITY
Uncle Ernie's Bayfront Grill
and Brewhouse,
1151 Bayview Avenue;
(850) 763-8427

PANAMA CITY BEACH
Boar's Head,
17290 Front Beach Road;
(850) 234-6628

Capt. Anderson's,
5551 Lagoon Drive;
(850) 234-2225

Fiddler's Green,
Marriott's Bay Point Resort,
4200 Marriott Drive;
(850) 234-3307

Hamilton's,
5711 North Lagoon Drive;
(850) 234-1255

FORT WALTON BEACH
Harpoon Hanna's,
1450 Miracle Strip Parkway;
(850) 243-5550

Los Rancheros (Mexican),
300 Eglin Parkway NE;
(850) 862-2007

Staff's Seafood Restaurant,
24 Miracle Strip Parkway;
(850) 243-3526

PENSACOLA
The Angus (Greek),
1101 Scenic Highway
(U.S. 90); (850) 432-0539

Cock of the Walk,
550 Scenic Highway
(U.S. 90); (850) 432-6766

Jamie's,
424 East Zaragoza Street;
(850) 434-2911

McGuire's Irish Pub
& Brewery,
600 East Gregory Street;
(850) 433-6789

Skopelos Seafood & Steak,
670 Scenic Highway
(U.S. 90E); (850) 432-6565

MARIANNA
Tony's,
4133 West Lafayette;
(850) 482-2232

Central Florida

Starting in Daytona, you can travel a roughly circular route to see Central Florida, but be sure to allow plenty of time for exploration off the beaten path. Whenever you can use A1A (which parallels the great Atlantic) rather than U.S. 1, try to do so, but on occasion the ocean intercedes and pushes you inland.

The Orlando area is so congested, it's probably best to take major routes to your destination. The benefits of getting there outweigh the pleasures of wandering. As soon as you drop south of Orlando, you'll begin to enjoy less hectic travel by taking Alternate 27 instead of 27 through the orange grove country surrounding peaceful Bok Tower.

The St. Petersburg/Tampa area is another driving challenge, but look at it this way: There isn't any snow or ice to contend with. Traveling north from Tampa on U.S. 19 is a pleasant way to reach attractions on or near the Gulf. Take your choice of little roads to get from U.S. 19 to the Ocala area. To complete the circle, drive east through the sand pine woods of Ocala National Forest on SR 40 and south on U.S. 19 toward Blue Springs and Hontoon Island State Parks.

Central Atlantic Coast

Ormond Beach and Daytona Beach owe their starts to the irrepressible Henry Flagler, who extended his railroad south and built the ornate Hotel Ormond in the late 1880s. The monied set was not far behind. When the Vanderbilts, Astors, and Goulds started wintering in Ormond Beach, it became known as the "millionaires' colony."

Rich men shipped their automobiles to Florida because the 500-foot-wide beach with its hard-packed sand was perfect for running flat out. By the turn of the century, Henry Ford, Louis Chevrolet, and R. E. Olds were comparing times on the beach's measured mile. Things moved quickly. In 1903 Alexander Winton set a world record of 68 mph on the sands of Daytona. A Stanley Steamer was clocked at 127.66 mph in 1906. The next year Ralph Owens made the first car trip from New York

Central
Florida

EASTERN
INTERIOR

ATLANTIC
OCEAN

Ocala

OCALA
AREA

CENTRAL
ATLANTIC
COAST

GULF
COAST

FLORIDA'S TPK

Orlando

Titusville

Weeki
Wachee

ORLANDO
AREA

Kissimmee

CENTRAL
HEARTLAND

FLORIDA'S TPK

Tampa

TAMPA-
ST. PETERSBURG
AREA

St. Petersburg

Sebring

N

| 0 | 30 mi |
| 0 | 30 km |

Top Events in Central Florida

Indian River Native American Festival, New Smyrna Beach, January, (904) 424–0860

Epiphany Celebration, Tarpon Springs, January, (727) 937–3540

Annual Florida Citrus Festival and Polk County Fair, Winter Haven, January, (863) 292–9810

Daytona 500 NASCAR Stock Car Race, Daytona Beach, February, (904) 253–RACE

Cracker Country, Tampa, February, (813) 621–7821, ext. 276

Fiesta Day, Ybor City, February, (813) 247–4951

Florida State Fair, Tampa, February, (813) 621–7821

Gasparilla Pirate Fest Weekend, Tampa, February, (813) 353–8070

Florida Strawberry Festival, Tampa, March, (813) 752–9194

Central Florida Balloon Rally, Deland, March, (904) 736–1010

Deland Outdoor Art Festival, Deland, March, (904) 734–8333

Spring Daytona Beach Car Show and Swap Meet, Daytona Beach, March, (904) 253–RACE

Kissimmee Bluegrass Festival, Kissimmee, March, (407) 856–0245

Spring Flower Festival, Cypress Gardens, Winter Haven, March, (863) 324–2111

Annual Chasco Fiesta, New Port Richey, March, (727) 842–7651

Arts in April, Orlando, April, (407) 425–0277

Sun 'N Fun EAA Fly-in, Lakeland, April, (863) 644–2431

Fun 'N Sun Festival, Clearwater, April/May, (727) 462–6531

Zellwood Sweet Corn Festival, Zellwood, May, (407) 886–0014

Annual Space Week Celebration, May, (407) 452–2121, ext. 235

Annual Harvest Festival, Clermont, June, (800) 768–WINE

Flagler County's Fabulous Fourth Festivities, July, (904) 439–0995

Pepsi 400 Stock Car Race, Daytona Beach, July 4, (904) 253–RACE

Taste of Clearwater, Clearwater, September, (727) 461–0011

Great Florida Triathlon, Clermont, October, (352) 394–1320

Clearwater Jazz Holiday, Clearwater, October, (727) 461–JAZZ

Biketoberfest, Daytona Beach, October, (800) 854–1234

Seminole Indian & Florida Pioneer Festival, Cocoa Beach, October, (407) 632–1111

Guavaween, Ybor City, Tampa, October, (813) 248–3712

St. Petersburg Fall Boat Show, St. Petersburg, November, (727) 892–5767

Chrysanthemum Festival, Winter Haven, November, (863) 324–2111

Christmas in the Park, Winter Park, December, (407) 645–5311

Poinsettia Festival and Garden of Lights, Cypress Gardens, Winter Haven, December, (941) 324–2111

to Daytona in an amazing seventeen days. Thirteen auto speed records were set here between 1902 and 1935, earning the area the reputation as the "birthplace of speed."

Faster cars and larger crowds gradually outgrew the oval raceway that had been dug into the Daytona dunes. A 2$^1/_2$-mile asphalt track, opened in 1959, offered new challenges to the growing sport. World attention is riveted on the famous *Daytona International Speedway* during the Fourth of July 400-mile stock car race and its Daytona 500 in February. No tours of the Speedway are offered during races and special tests, but at other times a half-hour tram tour will fill you in on all the details. Open 9:30 A.M.–5:00 P.M. daily. The Speedway is at 1801 Speedway Boulevard. For tickets to special events, write Daytona International Speedway, 1801 West International Speedway Boulevard, Daytona, FL 32114; (904) 947–6800.

Medium Well

*I*f you are hungering for spiritual growth or would like to communicate with a deceased loved one, perhaps you should seek out the **Cassadaga Spiritualist Camp.** *Designated a Historic District on the National Register of Historic Places, the Southern Cassadaga Spiritualist Camp Meeting Association is the oldest active religious community in the Southeastern United States. The association celebrated its 100th birthday in 1994.*

While residents may own the homes they live in within the camp grounds, the church retains ownership of the land and offers lifetime leases to the homeowners. Incidentally, there are no camping facilities in Cassadaga. "Camp Meeting" is an old term referring to the annual gathering of a religious group.

Cassadaga, complete with an education center devoted to the science, philosophy, and religion of Spiritualism, is a sanctuary where Spiritualists live and work together. Spiritualists believe that life continues after "the change called death" and that those who have passed through this transition can communicate with the living through mediumship.

About twenty-five of the camp's residents are mediums who offer counseling from their homes. A medium, a spiritual counselor with proven capabilities of communicating with Spirit through various forms of phenomena, acts as a channel for information between the Spirit and Earth Planes.

The camp welcomes the curious and skeptical as well as believers to its Sunday services, Wednesday night services, and candlelight healing services on the second Friday of each month.

Contact the Camp Bookstore for a listing of all certified mediums in the Camp and call the medium of your choice for a private appointment. Or you may wish to attend a workshop, seminar, or educational program listed on the camp's fascinating schedule. Cassadaga Spiritualist Camp (P.O. Box 319, Cassadaga, Florida) is midway between Daytona and Orlando and easily accessed from I–4, exit 54; (904) 228–2880.

CENTRAL FLORIDA

AUTHORS' FAVORITE ATTRACTIONS IN
CENTRAL FLORIDA

Merritt Island National Wildlife Refuge,
near Titusville

Bok Tower Gardens,
north of Lake Wales

Salvador Dali Museum,
St. Petersburg

Homosassa Springs Wildlife Park,
Homosassa Springs

Weeki Wachee Springs,
Weeki Wachee

Ocala National Forest,
east of Ocala

Silver Springs,
east of Ocala

Daytona Beach's *Museum of Arts and Sciences* has a fine collection of Cuban paintings, a skeleton of a giant ground sloth, interesting fossils, and a planetarium. Open Tuesday through Friday 9:00 A.M.–4:00 P.M. and Saturday and Sunday noon–5:00 P.M. At 1040 Museum Boulevard (Daytona Beach, FL 32114) in Tuscawilla Park; (904) 255-0285.

You don't have to be an RVer to stay at *Great Outdoor RV/Nature & Golf Resort,* but most are. If you love the natural beauty of the outdoor world and enjoy golf, fishing, and the camaraderie of other like-minded folks, this is definitely the place for you.

No wonder this is considered one of the finest RV destinations in the South. Miles of scenic nature trails through forests and around lakes and wetlands reveal the beauty of these 3,000 acres. Woodlands shelter Sabal palms, holly, pines, wax myrtles, palmettos, and huge live oaks dripping with Spanish moss.

Besides fishing and golf, the Great Outdoors has two swimming pools, lighted tennis and shuffleboard courts, a health club with a well-equipped exercise room, sauna and steam rooms, a recreation hall with dance floor, a restaurant, a lounge, bathhouses with laundry facilities, a beauty salon, a hobby shop, croquet lawn, a library, a fire station, and a country store complete with deli.

The Great Outdoors Resort, 135 Plantation Drive, Titusville, FL 32780 is on Highway 50 just west of I–95, 6½ miles from Kennedy Space Center. (800) 621-2267 or (407) 269-5004; Web site: www.tgoresort.com

The *Kennedy Space Center Visitor Complex,* just south of Titusville, will test the limits of your imagination. At the Visitor Complex the past, present, and future of our country's inspiring probe into the mysteries of outer space are packed into one memorable visitor attraction. Admission and parking are free, as are the *Gallery of Spaceflight, NASA Art Exhibit,* the outdoor *Rocket Garden,* and live shows on a variety of current space-related topics presented in *Spaceport Theater.* A *Spaceman,* who loves to pose for photographs, appears for several hours daily.

You'll want to purchase tickets for a bus tour of Kennedy Space Center's *Launch Complex 39,* where NASA prepares and launches the Space

Shuttle. Also available are tours of the historic **Cape Canaveral Air Force Station,** where the U.S. space program began in the early 1960s.

Don't miss the three impressive IMAX movies shown on a five-and-one-half-story screen in **IMAX Theater.** *The Dream Is Alive* (thirty-seven minutes) shows NASA astronauts working and living in space; *Mission to Mir* (forty minutes) shows Russia's space station, home to scientists since 1986; and *L5: First City in Space,* a 3-D adventure, which depicts a future space city based on data from NASA and leading scientists. The **Astronauts Memorial,** honoring U.S. astronauts who gave their lives in the name of space exploration, was dedicated on May 9, 1991. This **Space Mirror Memorial,** which has the astronauts' names brilliantly lit by reflected sunlight, sits beside a quiet lagoon on six acres of land.

Kennedy Space Center Visitor Complex is open from 9:00 A.M. to dusk every day except Christmas. Plan to arrive early. Lunch is available at either the Orbit Cafeteria or the Launch Pad restaurant. The Visitor Complex is less busy on weekends than weekdays. Located on Florida's Space Coast one hour east of Orlando, the Visitor Complex is off SR 405, NASA Parkway, 7 miles east of U.S. 1. Use exit 78 off I–95. Take SR 407 north if you're eastbound on the Beeline (SR 528). For visitor or launch information, call (407) 452–2121 or write DNPS, Kennedy Space Center; FL 32899. For Space Coast visitor information call (800) USA–1969; Web site: www.space-coast.com/Florida.

The Kennedy Space Center is flanked by the **Canaveral National Seashore** and the sprawling Merritt Island National Wildlife Refuge. All that's left of 600 years of fresh oyster dinners consumed by early Florida Indians is the 40-foot historic **Turtle Mound** at the northern tip of the National Seashore. Because this shell mound was the highest point of land for miles around, it served as an important landmark and appeared on sixteenth-century maps. Climb the boardwalk to the top for an impressive view of river and ocean. Turtle Mound is 10 miles south of New Smyrna Beach on SR A1A. Canaveral National Seashore is 7 miles east of Titusville.

Swimmers, surfers, and beachcombers head for Playalinda Beach at the south end of Canaveral, where sea oats and shifting dunes create a lovely seascape. The National Seashore is one of the last sections of undeveloped beach on the east coast of Florida. The beach, open during daylight hours (except when the road is closed due to NASA launch-related activities), is free. Call (904) 428–3384 for information.

The **Merritt Island National Wildlife Refuge** protects more endangered species of birds, mammals, and reptiles than any other area of the

OTHER ATTRACTIONS WORTH SEEING IN CENTRAL FLORIDA

Walt Disney World Resort, *Lake Buena Vista*

Universal Studios, *Orlando*

Sea World, *Orlando*

Splendid China, *Kissimmee*

Fantasy of Flight, *Winter Haven*

International Drive, *Orlando*

Cypress Island, *Kissimmee*

Busch Gardens, *Tampa*

continental United States. The Audubon Society has registered one of the highest counts of bird species in the country here. Gulls, terns, egrets, herons, ibis, and storks are a common sight. You may even be lucky enough to spot the pretty pink roseate spoonbill or the bald eagle. Open during daylight hours; (407) 861–0667. Free.

If you are intrigued by tropical foliage, you will want to see the **Botanical Garden** on the grounds of the Florida Institute of Technology in Melbourne with more than 300 species of palms, ferns, and other plants. The institute is on Country Club Road, a mile south of New Haven Avenue, Melbourne; (321) 674–8125.

Orlando Area

The **Maitland Art Center** is a special place. Originally designed to be a retreat for avant-garde artists, it is now an attractive complex housing a fascinating permanent collection and monthly rotating exhibits by contemporary artists. The buildings, adorned with murals and ornamental carvings in Aztec-Mayan motif, are well worth seeing, as is the tranquil garden and courtyard area. When you visit the Garden Chapel with its trellised walkway, you'll understand why this is such a popular place for weddings. Maitland Art Center, 231 West Packwood Avenue, Maitland, FL 32751. Open 9:00 A.M.–4:30 P.M. Monday through Friday and noon–4:30 P.M. on Saturday and Sunday. Call (407) 539– 2181. Free.

If you love birds you'll be very happy at the **Florida Audubon Center for Birds of Prey,** which includes a large collection of live birds in an aviary and a gift shop featuring books on birds and a variety of bird-related items. Its **Center for Birds of Prey** is one of the leading raptor rehabilitation centers in the state. You are encouraged to report injured or orphaned birds of prey to (407) 644–0190. The center is at 1101 Audubon Way, Maitland, FL 32751. Open Tuesday through Sunday 10:00 A.M.–4:00 P.M. Call (407) 644–0190.

The largest collection of Tiffany glass and jewelry in the world resides at the **Morse Museum of American Art** in Winter Park. This gallery features late-nineteenth- and twentieth-century art and decorative arts including leaded stained-glass windows, lamps, blown glass, pottery, paintings, and furniture. Open Tuesday through Saturday 9:30 A.M.–4:00

P.M., Friday evenings 4:00–8:00 P.M., and Sunday 1:00–4:00 P.M. The Morse Gallery of Art, 445 Park Avenue North, Winter Park, FL 32789; (407) 645–5311.

Winter Park's *Rollins College* has a beautiful campus with even more going for it than the attractive Spanish/Mediterranean architecture. The college's *Cornell Fine Arts Museum,* with three galleries of rotating art exhibits, is open to the public year-round 10:00 A.M.–5:00 P.M. Tuesday through Friday and 1:00–5:00 P.M. Saturday and Sunday; (407) 646–2526.

One fun way to really appreciate this lovely lake-dotted area is to take a *Scenic Boat Tour*. The boat leaves hourly between 10:00 A.M. and 4:00 P.M. from the eastern foot of Morse Boulevard on Lake Osceola in Winter Park. The one-hour narrated ride takes you through various Winter Park lakes and canals, by estates, the Isle of Sicily, Kraft Azalea Gardens, and Rollins College. Scenic Boat Tour, 312 East Morse Boulevard, Lake Osceola, Winter Park, FL 32789; (407) 644–4056.

Central Florida's major city, Orlando, was settled by soldiers who decided to stick around after the Seminole wars in the 1830s. It was little more than a cattle country trading post until the railroad's arrival brought an influx of people and business in 1880. Then the town eased into a string of unremarkable years as a shipping center for citrus fruits and vegetables.

Over the years Orlando capitalized on its best features—fifty-four lakes within the city limits and a year-round average temperature of 72 degrees. The community protected its venerable groves of live oaks by creating forty-seven parks. A loyal contingent of northerners who appreciated both the beauty and the climate enjoyed the town's relaxed pace each winter.

Those were the days before the nation's launch into space from nearby Cape Canaveral and before the coming of Walt Disney World. The city is still pretty with all its lakes and parks intact, but the relaxed pace is a memory. Orlando is one of the fastest growing metropolitan areas in the United States, and the face of central Florida has been forever changed.

Loch Haven Park in Orlando offers a cluster of quality attractions. Parking is easy and you may spend all day enjoying the *Orlando Museum of Art,* Orange County Historical Museum, and Orlando Science Center. The Art Center has a growing permanent collection of American art, pre-Columbian artifacts, African art, and changing exhibitions from internationally renowned museums and private collections.

Gallery hours are 9:00 A.M.–5:00 P.M. Tuesday through Saturday and noon–5:00 P.M. Sunday; (407) 896–4231.

The *Orange County Historical Museum* began in 1942 when a group of women set up a pioneer kitchen in the 1892 redbrick courthouse for a countywide centennial. It has evolved into a handsome museum that will take you on a trip down memory lane. Here you'll travel back to the time when Florida was a wilderness, learn about the Big Freeze of 1894–95 that destroyed the citrus industry, and ride the roller coaster real estate boom-and-bust days of the 1920s. On display are a 1,000-year-old Timucuan Indian canoe, a newspaper composing room in the hot-type tradition, a Victorian parlor, and the hide of a 15-foot alligator. Open Monday through Saturday 9:00 A.M.–5:00 P.M. and Sunday noon–5:00 P.M. Orange County Historical Museum, Loch Haven Park, 812 East Rollins Street, Orlando, FL 32803; (407) 897–6350.

On the premises you'll find Fire Station No. 3, *Orlando's oldest standing firehouse,* which operates as an extension of the Historical Museum. This captures the flavor of the early bucket brigade days and comes complete with a traditional sliding pole, an 1885 hose cart, and even a potbellied stove. It's open Monday through Saturday 9:00 A.M.–5:00 P.M. and Sunday noon–5:00 P.M.; (407) 897–6350.

Those who find their earth weight discouraging may take consolation in learning their moon weight, one of many neat things you can do at the *Orlando Science Center.* This is one of those places where you learn a great deal while having a good time, and it is especially good for families. Ask about the daily planetarium shows. Open Tuesday through Thursday 9:00 A.M.–5:00 P.M., Friday 9:00 A.M.–9:00 P.M., Saturday 9:00 A.M.–9:00 P.M., and Sunday noon–5:00 P.M. Orlando Science Center and John Young Planetarium, Loch Haven Park, 777 East Princeton Street, Orlando, FL 32803; (407) 514–2000; Web site: www.osc.org.

When the hustle and bustle of Orlando is too much for you, a walk through *Leu Gardens* provides a welcome tonic. More than fifty acres of trees, flowering shrubs, roses, camellias, orchids, and azaleas border Lake Rowena. Several floral varieties bloom most of the year, but the big show is from December to March, as this is primarily a winter garden. A museum house, which shows how a well-to-do Florida family lived at the turn-of-the-century, is open daily 10:00 A.M.–3:30 P.M. Tours are on the half hour. The garden is open 9:00 A.M.–5:00 P.M. daily except for Christmas. Leu House and Gardens, 1920 North Forest Avenue, Orlando, FL 32803; (407) 246–2620.

Camping sounds like fun, but you want a real vacation complete with daily maid service, cable TV, and air-conditioning. Surprise! You can have it all at **Walt Disney World's Fort Wilderness Campground.** More than 400 Fleetwood trailers are fully equipped with dishes and cooking utensils and dishwashers. Most sleep six. While enjoying all the comforts and conveniences of a fine hotel, you can also have the rustic beauty of the great outdoors.

Hearty fare and wholesome fun is close by. The *Hoop-Dee-Doo-Revue* at Pioneer Hall is the second-longest-running show at Walt Disney World. A cast of six "stagecoach passengers" keeps everyone in stitches for almost two hours. In between laughs fill up on fried chicken, barbecued ribs, corn on the cob, and strawberry shortcake. Afterward, it's home-sweet-home to your trailer under the trees. For information about Fort Wilderness, write Walt Disney World Central Reservations, P.O. Box 10100, Lake Buena Vista, FL 32830, or call (407) 934–7639.

Just in case you're in the mood for an early-morning hot air balloon ride over Orlando, Church Street Station is standing by. Start the day with coffee and orange juice, and polish off your aerial adventure with a champagne brunch at **Lili Marlene's Restaurant.** A day to store in the memory forever! Call (407) 422–2434.

Church Street Station also features Phineas Phogg's Balloon Works (purveyors of balloons, burgers, and boogie), Apple Annie's Courtyard, and Cheyenne Saloon and Opera House. Nickel beer night is Wednesday, and western and Indian antiques are available at Buffalo Trading Co. It's impossible to take advantage of all the excitement at Church Street Station, but you might as well try. This complete dining, shopping, and entertainment complex is open every day 11:00 A.M.–2:00 A.M. and features twenty live shows nightly. Church Street Station is at 129 West Church Street, Orlando, FL 32801; (407) 422–2434.

Gatorland should also be in your plans. Don't worry about the huge alligator jaws you walk through to enter. This isn't just another hokey attraction, but a fine zoo with more than 5,000 alligators and crocodiles (Gatorland claims to be the world's largest alligator farm attraction) and some rather exotic animals including snakes, birds, and monkeys. An interesting artificial insemination program for alligators is in full swing here.

Allow plenty of time to stroll the boardwalk through the eerie beauty of a cypress swamp. This sanctuary, lush with wild orchids and ferns, offers a welcome reprieve from the hectic pace some sight-seers set for themselves. Open daily 9:30 A.M. to dusk, Gatorland is on U.S. 441 next to Tupperware.

Mailing address: 14501 South Orange Blossom Trail, Orlando, FL 32837; (407) 855–5496.

A novel way to see the "real" Florida is by piloting your own airboat. Explore **wild cypress swamps,** where tall waterbirds stalk their supper and trees are festooned with Spanish moss. You'll get the hang of the steering bar right away. Just pull back if you want to go right and push forward to go left. Only ten minutes from Walt Disney World, this lovely natural spot can also be seen by electric boat and/or canoe. Boats and canoes can be rented at **Airboat Rentals U-Drive,** which is 6 miles east of I–4 on U.S. 192 in Kissimmee; (407) 847–3672.

*Some people love to be scared out of their wits. They should head for **Skull Kingdom,** a haunted family attraction promising 12,800 feet of fun and fright beginning at the Giant Skull Entrance. The spooky journey includes a walk-through, hands-on, interactive experience that culminates in the Ghoulish Face Painting Gallery and the Haunted Toy Shop. This attraction is NOT recommended for kids under seven. Located on International Drive across from Wet 'N Wild in Orlando. (407) 354–1564.*

Aaah, the romance of medieval times when brave knights defended their kingdoms and castles were scenes of great feasts and much revelry. This is now a possible dream thanks to **Medieval Times Dinner and Tournament.** Slip back to Europe in the eleventh century and admire valiant knights on richly attired horses. A "serving wench" brings a delicious four-course dinner, which you eat with your hands. (Remember, this is the year of grace 1092.)

Spectacular pageantry, splendid horses galloping at full tilt, and knights who duel to the death (well, almost) combine to make quite an evening. Just when you thought chivalry was dead, a knight shows up and throws you a flower. A knight to remember! Medieval Times is on U.S. 192 in Kissimmee. Medieval Times, P.O. Box 422385, Kissimmee, FL 34742; (800) 229–8300. The number for the castle in Kissimmee is (407) 396–1518.

Kissimmee had a long proud heritage as the capital of cattle country before being billed as the Gateway to Walt Disney World. Spanish explorers brought livestock to the New World, and when Florida became a United States territory in 1821, the open range and scrub cattle descended from Spanish cows lured homesteaders to the Florida frontier. South of Orlando's dazzle, hundreds of cattle ranches and a thriving beef and dairy industry prosper. The cowboy's own brand of excitement rears up twice a year at Florida's largest and oldest professional rodeo, **Kissimmee's Silver Spurs.** For information about these special events and a weekly Friday night rodeo at Kissimmee Sports Arena, contact the Kissimmee–St. Cloud Convention and

Visitors Bureau, P.O. Box 422007, Kissimmee, FL 34742–2007; (407) 847–5000 or (800) 831–1844; Web site: www.Floridakiss.com.

In Kissimmee don't forget to visit the **Monument of States,** made of stones from every state in the Union. The 50-foot structure was built by Kissimmee citizens in 1943 with 1,500 stones from every state and twenty-one foreign countries. Near the lakefront in downtown Kissimmee.

Kissimmee lies at the head of the 50-mile-long **Kissimmee Chain-of-Lakes,** and those who want to experience central Florida at its natural best should see it from the water. Far from the madding crowd are quiet lagoons and blue herons picking their way through water hyacinths. Besides being splendidly scenic, this is one of the country's best bass fishing grounds. The sunset is in living color, the view is multidimensional, and the big sound is a night chorus of tree frogs and cicadas. Houseboats and assorted other craft may be rented on Lake Tohopekaliga. Take U.S. 192 to SR 17-92 south, then at the second or third traffic light, turn left to lakefront. For information call Parks and Recreation; (407) 847–2388.

Originally founded in 1972 as a research center for the production and distribution of snake venoms, **Reptile World Serpentarium** now offers close-up views of poisonous snakes being milked. Time your visit to be on hand during one of the daily venom programs given at noon and 3:00 P.M. You'll see turtles and alligators as well as cobras, mambas, vipers, rattlesnakes, and nonvenomous giant pythons. The gift shop has an excellent selection of books on reptiles. Open Tuesday through Sunday 9:00 A.M.–5:30 P.M. Closed the month of September. Located 4 miles east of St. Cloud on U.S. 192. Reptile World Serpentarium, 5705 East Bronson Memorial Highway, St. Cloud, FL 34771; (407) 892–6905.

Central Heartland

The central heartland of Florida seems, from certain viewpoints, like a huge sprawling sea of orange trees. Tidy parallel rows of trees undulate off into the distance like dark green waves. In the midst of citrus country are modern packing plants and frozen juice processors well equipped to handle the huge harvest. Many highway fruit and juice stands cater to tourists intent on carrying some fresh Florida fruit home to their winterbound northern friends. At **Orange Ring** you can sample a free glass of orange juice and purchase any number of goodies including orange butter and chocolate alligators. The packing plant, behind the gift shop, gives brief tours during the week. Orange Ring, P.O. Drawer 2107, Haines City, FL 33845; (863) 422–2005. On U.S. 27 north of Haines City; Web site: www.orangering.com.

Watch citrus candy being made in copper kettles at *Davidson of Dundee Citrus Candy Factory* on U.S. 27 in Dundee. Open daily 8:00 A.M.–6:00 P.M., but candy is not made on weekends. Davidson of Dundee, P.O. Box 800, Dundee, FL 33838; (863) 439–1698; Web site: www.davidsonofdundee.com.

Cypress Gardens in Winter Haven has been a popular tourist destination for many years. The Pope family began extensive landscaping on the shores of Lake Eloise in the 1930s. In 1942 they enlivened the botanical beauty by adding water ski shows. Amateur and professional photographers as well as moviemakers are drawn to the gorgeous scenery, and spectators cheer the talented skiers' mastery of the newest tricks.

Today Cypress Gardens features, along with magnificent gardens and thrilling water ski shows, a variety of attractions including "Cypress Roots," a walk down memory lane complete with a display of cameras from the twenties to the seventies; Cypress Junction, an elaborate model railroad; a Russian ice-skating show; and "When Radios Were Radios," commemorating the nostalgic years of radio. Kids love the rides in "Carousel Cove" and the old-fashioned circus daredevil acts. Do not—repeat, *do not*—leave without experiencing Cypress Gardens' *Wings of Wonder,* the butterfly conservatory where visitors encounter more than fifty colorful species of butterflies from around the world. Cypress Gardens is open year-round 9:30 A.M.–5:00 P.M. with extended hours during special seasons. The gardens are off U.S. 27, 22 miles south of I–4 between Orlando and Tampa. Cypress Gardens, P.O. Box 1, Cypress Gardens, FL 33884; (863) 324–2111; Web site: www.cypressgardens.com.

Chalet Suzanne Country Inn and Restaurant, in Lake Wales, opens itself up like the petals of a flower. First you discover a tiny, whimsical pastel village with its thirty rooms each decorated in different combi-

Everywhere you look, striking vistas are highlighted by pretty young girls in hoop skirts carrying parasols. The addition of these Southern belles came about because of a winter freeze that killed the flowers at the entrance. Visitors would drive up, take one look at the dead plants and, thinking the rest of the park had been similarly stricken, drive on.

Julie Pope, wife of Cypress Gardens' founder Dick Pope, Sr., was in charge while her husband was away serving in the armed forces during World War II. She rounded up several women from the office staff, dressed them in the widest possible skirts to hide the dead flowers, and placed them at the entrance. Enchanted by this welcoming committee of Southern belles, visitors could hardly wait to see the rest of Cypress Gardens.

The Singing Tower

nations of Swedish tile, Spanish ironwork, and Moorish mosaics. Then sample some of the Chalet's famous romaine soup in the intimate Old World dining room. (No wonder this soup was chosen to go to the moon with the crew of Apollo 15.) Each place is set with fine china, perhaps German porcelain or elegant Limoges, and your view overlooks a private lake.

Then you come upon the Chapel where you can buy all manner of fine glassware and antiques, the Wine Dungeon, the Wreck Room, the Soup Cannery, and a ceramic salon where Lilliana and Boz Birvis are turning out treasures. Chalet Suzanne is one surprise after another, and that, and the good taste with which everything is done, accounts for its success as well as its charm.

Gourmet Magazine labeled Chalet Suzanne food "glorious" and surely it is, but be warned that the prices are also glorious. If a glance at the lunch menu withers your wallet, ask for the soup and sandwich du jour (unlisted). That way you can treat yourself to a fine meal without taking out a new mortgage. Owned and operated by the Hinshaw family since 1931, Chalet Suzanne is between Cypress Gardens and Bok Tower Gardens just off U.S. 27 and 17A. Or come by plane and land on the 2,450-foot private airstrip! Chalet Suzanne, 3800 Chalet Drive, Lake Wales, FL 33853; (863) 676–6011 or (800) 433–6011. Expensive.

The 128-acre **Bok Tower Gardens** in Lake Wales have been devoted to peace and beauty since 1928. Listed in the National Register of Historic Places, the gardens and tower were dedicated to the American people because Edward Bok, a Dutch immigrant, wanted to make America "a bit more beautiful" because he had lived here. The hushed atmosphere of the surroundings is interrupted only by a daily bell serenade (3:00 P.M.) from the 205-foot "singing" tower, which has been called one of the world's great carillons. Enjoy the azaleas, camellias, magnolias, and many birds. Surrounded by citrus orchards, this is the place to come in the spring when the air is heavy with the scent of orange blossoms. The gardens are open every day 8:00 A.M.–5:00 P.M. Located 3 miles north of Lake Wales off CR 17A (Burns Avenue). Bok Tower Gardens, 1151 Tower Boulevard, Lake Wales, FL 33853; (863) 676–1408; Web site: www.Boktower.org.

Lake Kissimmee State Park is way off the beaten path, but worth it.

The park consists of more than 5,000 acres bordered by lakes Kissimmee, Tiger, and Rosalie. The lakes, floodplain prairies, marshes, and pine flatwoods are home to a variety of wildlife, including the rare Florida panther. (Don't count on seeing a panther; they're very shy.) This is a fine spot to boat, hike, picnic, and camp. For an excellent view of Lake Kissimmee, try the top of the observation platform.

One of the best features of the park is a reconstructed *1876 Cow Camp* with scrub cows and "cow hunters." (They will quickly tell you they do not care to be called cowboys.) Here you can learn firsthand about the bustling cattle business on the south Florida frontier and see one of the few remaining herds of scrub cows in existence.

Bok Tower

As you walk down the trail to the camp, you travel back to the year 1876. The cow hunter may be having a cup of coffee near his campfire or perhaps is rounding up cows for the long cattle drive to the west coast of Florida. The cattlemen were paid in gold Spanish doubloons. The cow hunter welcomes your questions, but don't bother asking about anything that happened after 1876. He will just look very puzzled and won't know what you're talking about.

The cow camp is only open on weekends and holidays 9:30 A.M.–4:30 P.M. The park is open daily 7:00 A.M. to sunset year-round. Lake Kissimmee State Park, 14248 Camp Mack Road, Lake Wales, FL 33853. The park is 15 miles east of Lake Wales, off Camp Mack Road. Call (863) 696-1112.

Follow nature trails and boardwalks through the jungles, cypress swamps, and tropical wilderness of *Highlands Hammock State Park.* Your stroll will be rewarded with glimpses of sunning alligators and rare orchids. You'll also want to visit the C.C.C. museum and ride the park's "trackless train" on regularly scheduled wildlife tours. A good place to bike (rentals available), picnic, and camp. Highlands Hammock is open daily 8:00 A.M. until sunset. Located 6 miles west of Sebring, off U.S. 27–CR 634; (863) 386–6094.

Florida Southern College, in Lakeland, boasts the world's largest concentration of architecture by Frank Lloyd Wright. Wright's design for these seven unconventional buildings called for steel for strength, sand for Florida, and glass to bring the outdoors in. The steeple of the *Annie Pfeiffer Chapel,* designed as a chime resonator, casts shifting shadows into the interior. Tinted glass squares filter colored light in during the day. The low esplanade, a sheltered walkway, was obviously not designed with today's basketball players in mind; no ceiling or doorway is much over 6 feet tall! The Science Building, more than 400 feet long with a planetarium at the southern end, is the largest structure, and some say the most magnificent.

The lakeside campus is open to the public 8:00 A.M.–5:00 P.M. weekdays. The Frank Lloyd Wright Visitors Center is open Tuesday to Friday 10:00

Highlands Hammock State Park

*H*ere thrives the Florida of old—the lush, swampy salad bar, which in prehistoric times quelled the hunger of huge mastodons. This is the jungle primeval, the primitive pre-condo Florida that enchants nature lovers and is today in such scarce supply. We could easily envision disillusioned Spanish explorers clanking through the dense undergrowth, steaming under the weight of their armor, as they uncovered only alligators, elegant birds, and exquisite natural beauty where they had hoped to find gold.

One of Florida's most valuable state parks, Highlands Hammock is a biologically rich mix of hammocks, pine flatwoods, sand pine scrub, cypress swamps, bayhead, and marsh. The great diversity of habitats—resulting from interaction of water level, soil,

and climate—has created a fertile area for bird watchers (177 species have been identified in the 2,800–acre park) as well as a marvelous maze of hiking trails.

After a looping drive through the park to get our bearings, we set out to explore. Surely, these are some of the best trails in Florida. The United States Champion Sabal Palm appeared fairly regal at 90 feet, and on Big Oak Trail we admired 1,000-year-old oak trees. Wild fruit perfumed the air on Wild Orange Trail. Hickory Trail, Ancient Hammock Trail, and Fern Garden Trail all offered different versions of untamed beauty. But our favorite was Cypress Swamp Trail, a boardwalk meandering through the swamp and along Little Charley Bowlegs Creek.

A.M.–4:00 P.M., Saturday 10:00 A.M.–2:00 P.M. and Sunday 2:00–4:00 P.M., (863) 680-4597. Florida Southern College, 111 Lake Hollingsworth Drive, Lakeland, FL 33801–5698; (863) 680-4111; Web site: www. flsouthern.edu. From Orlando, go west on I–4 to the U.S. 98 south exit 18. Turn left. Travel into town and turn left onto McDonald Street. The college is on the right.

Tampa–St. Petersburg Area

Spanish explorers discovered Tampa in the sixteenth century. They also discovered the resident Indians who resisted being converted to Catholicism and resented the European urge for conquering. The resulting clash of interests led frequently to bloodshed over the years.

One of those early Spanish explorers, Hernando DeSoto, discovered the mineral springs of Safety Harbor, which he named the "Springs of the Holy Spirit," on May 18, 1539. He was not the first to be attracted by the springs. Various Indian tribes, inhabiting the area as long as 12,000 years ago, believed the springs had curative powers.

During a fight with the Seminoles, Colonel William J. Bailey captured a sick Indian who volunteered to be a guide if the colonel would take him to the healing springs. The colonel bought the springs and surrounding land from the government in the 1850s, the first person to own the springs after the United States acquired Florida from the Spanish.

In the early 1900s five different springs were identified that "cured" a variety of ailments from dropsy to psoriasis. Before long Northerners were visiting the spa to "take the waters." In 1964 Safety Harbor Resort was officially listed as a historical landmark by the U.S. Department of the Interior.

All well and good, but what's going on at the springs today? The answer is plenty, and in keeping with tradition, it's all very healthy and restorative to both body and spirit. The *Safety Harbor Resort and Spa* offers more than fifty rejuvenating, relaxing, and pampering spa and salon services ranging from deep tissue sports massages, facials, loofah salt glows, and herbal wraps to aromatherapy. Lifestyle and fitness classes, tennis clinics, and golf on nearby courses are also featured. One of America's oldest spa resorts, Safety Harbor is Florida's only spa resort featuring natural mineral springs. On arrival, guests find a carafe of specially filtered mineral water in their rooms from the springs beneath the hotel.

The resort's spa menu offers nutritious, low-fat, low-calorie, gourmet cuisine. A full-fare menu is also offered with emphasis on naturally grown fresh Florida fruits and vegetables and regional seafood specialties.

Located on the shores of Old Tampa Bay, Safety Harbor Resort is twenty minutes from two major international airports—Tampa International Airport and St. Petersburg/Clearwater International Airport—and is easily reached from I–75 and I–4. Call for directions. Safety Harbor Resort and Spa, 105 North Bayshore Drive, Safety Harbor, FL 34695; (727) 726–1161 or (888) BESTSPA (237–8772); Web site: www.safetyharbor.com.

Safety Harbor Museum of Regional History, a tiny gem of a museum featuring rare treasures of prehistoric Indians and other exhibits of local interest, is a short walk from the resort. Fascinating dioramas enlighten visitors to the rich history of this area as well as the evolution of the American Indian throughout the Southeast.

Located in Safety Harbor on Old Tampa Bay, the museum is on a Tocabaga shell mound site. Open Tuesday through Friday 10:00 A.M.–4:00 P.M.; Saturday 1:00–4:00 P.M.; closed Sunday and Monday. The Safety Harbor Museum of Regional History, 329 South Bayshore Boulevard, Safety Harbor, FL 34695; (727) 726–1668.

Tampa's real development began in 1883 when Henry B. Plant linked Tampa with Jacksonville by a combination of railroad and steamship connections. Henry Plant, competing with East Coast railroad tycoon Henry Flagler, erected the ostentatious Moorish-style *Tampa Bay Hotel* in 1891. Sporting silver Turkish minarets, the palatial hotel ushered in Tampa's era as a fashionable winter resort for well-heeled Northerners. Costing a cool $3.5 million, it was regarded in its day as the most elegant and most expensive hotel in the world.

Today it is a National Historic Landmark, considered the finest example of Moorish architecture in the Western Hemisphere, and is home to the *University of Tampa.* To see some of the furniture and art of the late Victorian era, visit the *Henry B. Plant Museum* in a wing of the main university building. Open Tuesday through Saturday 10:00 A.M.–4:00 P.M. and Sunday noon–4:00 P.M. The museum/university is at 401 West Kennedy Boulevard, Tampa 33606, at the Hillsborough River; (813) 254–1891; Web site: www.plantmuseum.com.

Today Tampa is a major industrial metropolis and busy shipping center for a great variety of products including phosphates, citrus fruits, and cattle. At day's end you may be interested in watching shrimp boats unload their catch at the *shrimp docks* on the Twenty-second Street Causeway. Free.

Citizens have worked hard to preserve Tampa's heritage. The Hispanic community centered in **Ybor City** has been largely returned to its late-nineteenth-century appearance. Cigar makers demonstrate the art of hand rolling in restored **Ybor Square,** a complex of shops and restaurants. Ybor City, which is a National Historic District, is bounded by Columbus Drive, Fifth Avenue, Nebraska Avenue, and Twenty-second Street.

Around the turn of the century, the Ferlita Bakery flourished along with Ybor City and the cigar industry. In the "Cigar Capital of the World" workers lived very well indeed, and a boomtown atmosphere prevailed. The bakery (listed on the National Register of Historic Sites) has now been transformed by the state of Florida into a museum where you can learn about Tampa's Latin community and see old photos, cigar industry artifacts, and the original 1896 bakery oven. The **Ybor City State Museum,** 1818 Ninth Avenue, Tampa, FL 33605. Open 9:00 A.M.–5:00 P.M. every day; (813) 247–6323; Web site: www.ybormuseum.org.

Tampa's distinct Latin flavor is retained in its Spanish shops, restaurants, and the general ambience of the community. You may see long loaves of Cuban bread rolled out by hand at **La Segunda Central Bakery** if you arrive before 9:00 A.M. Go around to the back door and watch as bakers shape the dough and place a single strand of palmetto leaf on each yard-long loaf. The bakery is at 2512 North Fifteenth Street in Ybor City.

You may buy a fresh loaf from the store or order a Cuban sandwich (looking for all the world like a sub) for lunch at a number of Spanish restaurants on East Seventh Street in Ybor City. If you choose **La Tropicana,** you'll notice one table in the back that looks different from all the rest. It even has its own old-fashioned upright phone used to gather news for the local scandal sheet. If you have something to contribute, stop in at La Tropicana at 1822 East Seventh Street. Those who don't go for subs might like the deviled crab or potato stuffed with meat.

There's always a possibility you'll get caught in a hurricane, but then that's all part of the fun (and learning) going on at MOSI, the **Museum of Science and Industry.** The museum has tripled in size to become the largest science center in the Southeast with Florida's only IMAX Dome Theater. Take part in all kinds of fascinating experiments in this hands-on center, and be sure to see BioWorks Butterfly Garden and the planetarium. Exhibits and demonstrations explain the major scientific phenomena— energy, weather, electricity, water, flight and space, and the environment. Don't miss the "Amazing You," a tour of the human body from DNA cells to organs to individuals. The museum is in North Tampa, 3 miles east of

I–275 and is open 9:00 A.M.–5:00 P.M. Sunday through Thursday and 9:00 A.M.–7:00 P.M. Friday. Museum of Science and Industry, 4801 East Fowler Avenue, Tampa, FL 33617; (813) 987–6100.

Get out your skateboard. Put on your jogging shoes or your roller skates. Tampa boasts nothing less than the longest continuous sidewalk in the world. *Bayshore Boulevard*'s 6½-mile sidewalk is the focus of much activity as folks take advantage of this scenic stretch bordering one of the city's oldest and finest residential areas. During a hurricane this is where the water comes ashore, and daring surfers replace joggers and skaters. You don't have to be quite that adventurous, but this just might be a good time to find out what it feels like to walk half a dozen miles.

One of the interesting things you'll see along Bayshore Boulevard is the *Jose Gasparilla,* the world's only fully rigged pirate ship. The ship stars during the annual *Gasparilla Invasion* held each February when businessmen-turned-buccaneers take over. The ensuing month-long festivities include torchlight parades, marathons, and fancy dress balls. For information: Tampa/Hillsborough Convention and Visitors Association, 111 East Madison Street, Tampa, FL 33602; (813) 353–8070.

You'll enjoy a "wild" safari on the *Serengeti Plain at Busch Gardens.* Four hundred head of exotic big game including giraffes, zebras, elephants, gazelles, and Cape buffalo roam at will as you cross the veldtlike plain via monorail, steam locomotive, or skyride. Much more than an amusement park, Busch Gardens, with its African motif and more than 3,000 animals, is regarded as one of the top four zoos in the country. Be sure to pay your respects to the rare white Bengal tigers and see Eagle Canyon, a natural habitat display for American bald eagles and golden eagles located at the entrance to the *Anheuser-Busch Brewery;* 3605 East Bougainvillea Avenue, Tampa, FL 33612; (800) 372–1797.

Bern's Steak House is as much an experience as it is a restaurant. The menu looks like an engineering spec sheet, the place is ornate (to put it mildly), and the emphasis is on doing things differently. Perhaps that explains why the gargantuan wine list is almost too heavy to lift. (To have your own copy, you'll have to part with more than $20.)

From their own organic farm to the world's largest wine cellar, the emphasis at Bern's is on putting together the perfect meal. Waiters train a minimum of one year working in every station in the restaurant before being permitted in the dining room. Cress seeds from London are sprouted right in the kitchen, and caviar is flown in daily. Your steak is cut, trimmed, and weighed only after you have placed your order. Coffee beans are roasted and hand-sorted, and the whole operation is coordinated by computer.

All this information (and much more) is on your menu, but is it all true? Yes. Bern's encourages tours of the kitchen and wine cellar throughout the evening. Between courses, diners take advantage of this offer to inspect the immaculate facilities and cavernous (and cold—take a sweater) wine cellar. They even get to see the sprouts sprouting.

The final course of coffee and dessert is served in your own private room upstairs, which comes complete with numerous selections of music to choose from—including Bern's pianist who will play favorites on request. You may dance if you wish or simply spend the rest of the evening trying to select the perfect drink from a list of 1,000 dessert wines. The choice of dessert is not so overwhelming. Besides, you can't go wrong ordering the house specialty—Chocolate, Chocolate, Chocolate. Bern's Steak House, 1208 South Howard Avenue, Tampa, FL 33606; (813) 251–2421. In Florida: (800) 282–1547. Expensive.

Take the scenic drive on Dunedin Beach Causeway to *Honeymoon Island State Recreation Area* and notice the large pines on the island's northern loop trail. This is one of a very few virgin slash pine stands in south Florida, as well as an important nesting site for the threatened osprey. A wide variety of plants and birds, including several endangered species, call this lovely island home. You may want to picnic, swim, fish, or catch the ferry to Caladesi Island. Honeymoon Island is at No. 1 Causeway Boulevard, Dunedin, FL 34698, west of U.S. 19A; (727) 469–5942.

Caladesi Island, located off Dunedin, is one of Florida's few unspoiled barrier islands. Catch the ferry (which leaves hourly, weather permitting) from Dunedin Beach on Honeymoon Island and spend some time at this attractive state park. Accessible only by boat, this is a good place to swim, skin dive, boat, picnic, or beachcomb for shells. The park has almost 3 miles of sandy beach, a ridge of virgin pine flatwoods, and a mangrove swamp. A 60-foot observation tower offers views of the area and of vessels in the Gulf. The island is north of Dunedin off U.S. 19A. For information call the ferry (727) 734–1501 or the park (727) 469–5917.

Remember the old sugarcane mill, the railroad depot, and the bandstand in the middle of the park? Open-air *Heritage Village* has these and more. Travel back in time to the early days of Pinellas County while browsing the old barn, church, cottage, loghouse, and other structures. A guide in period dress will show you around, or you can poke about on your own. How did those early settlers manage? At least some of the answers are here in this pretty pine and palmetto park. Open Tuesday through Saturday 10:00 A.M.–4:00 P.M., Sunday 1:00–4:00 P.M. Closed Monday. Heritage Village, 11909 125th Street North, Largo, FL 33774; (727) 582–2123. Free.

The **Suncoast Seabird Sanctuary** is dedicated to the rescue, repair, recuperation, and, hopefully, the release of rehabilitated wild birds. It all began when Ralph Heath nursed an injured cormorant back to health in 1971. Word spread and soon people were leaving injured birds on his doorstep. Today the sanctuary is home to more than 500 birds, and as many as twenty injured birds are brought daily. Unfortunately more than 90 percent of these injuries are directly or indirectly related to human beings, who seem adept at throwing the delicate balance of nature out of kilter.

This nonprofit organization (supported entirely by donations) has a full-time staff of fifteen, a hospital complete with intensive-care room, and an annual budget of $700,000. So far nearly 35,000 birds have been returned to the wild.

A recent success story involved the release of a Southern bald eagle. Some permanently injured birds become full-time residents. You may watch brown pelicans building nests with branches and rearing young in captivity. Notice the contingent of perfectly well birds perching on top of the aviary. Isn't it thoughtful of them to visit their hospitalized friends?

Bring a camera and leave a donation or, better yet, fill out an application to adopt a bird. The sanctuary is open seven days a week 9:00 A.M. until dark. Suncoast Seabird Sanctuary, 18328 Gulf Boulevard, Indian Shores, FL 33785; (727) 391–6211. Free.

A couple of sea turtle hunters returning from the Gulf were the first to see **John's Pass** in Madeira Beach. (It didn't exist until the hurricane of 1848.) Juan Levique was the one who spotted the changed coastline, so naturally it came to be known as John's Pass. Today an early Florida fishing village atmosphere prevails. Boutiques and shops cater to tourists' whims. Choose from a large selection of beachwear, jewelry, stained glass, or handcrafted items. This is a fine place to fish, charter a boat, or just walk the boardwalk with an eye out for playful dolphins.

An excellent way to start the day is at the *Friendly Fisherman Seafood Restaurant* with a Boardwalk Breakfast. You can't miss with a basket of hot corn fritters. Later in the day, you can stop in and munch on grouper cheeks (no bones!). The Friendly Fisherman is on the boardwalk at John's Pass in Madeira Beach. Inexpensive.

St. Petersburg was the birthplace of scheduled commercial aviation on New Year's Day 1915. Pilot Tony Jannus flew a Benoist airboat across the bay to Tampa with former mayor Abe Phiel along as the first passenger. The historic flight captured the world's attention, and the airline capitalized on the novelty during its brief, three-month term of operation. A replica of the Benoist is on exhibit at the St. Petersburg Museum of History.

No wonder folks flock to St. Petersburg with its exquisite beaches and 361 days of sunshine each year. Settled in the 1840s, St. Petersburg came to life in 1885 when Peter Demens extended his Orange Belt Railroad into the peninsula and named the settlement for his Russian birthplace. Imagine a place so confident of its sunshine that one of its newspapers gives away all the street editions if the weather remains cloudy for the entire day.

The world's largest collection of art by Spanish surrealist Salvador Dali can be found in St. Petersburg. The $35 million collection features oil paintings, watercolors, drawings, graphics, and sculptures. The fascination here is to see Dali's development from 1914 to 1980. The *Salvador Dali Museum* is open Monday through Saturday 9:30 A.M.–5:30 P.M. and Sunday noon–5:30 P.M. It is located on the waterfront in south St. Petersburg at 1000 Third Street South, St. Petersburg, FL 33701; (727) 823-3767.

If you want a touch of history in your vacation itinerary, you will delight in the grand wedding cake of a hotel known as the *Don Ce Sar.* Take off your rose-colored glasses and it's still pink—really pink, as in flamingos, Easter eggs, and bubble gum.

Unfortunately a glorious opening night in January 1928 was followed by the stock market crash of 1929. Despite the patronage of such prominent guests as Scott and Zelda Fitzgerald, Clarence Darrow, and Babe Ruth, the dismal days of the 1930s took their toll. Tourism had all but disappeared when the army bought it during the war for a song and turned it into a hospital. (The Bistro served as the morgue.) Deterioration and neglect pointed toward the Don's demise until a Save the Don committee worked a near miracle and rescued it during the 1970s.

The National Archives in Washington, D.C., lists the Don as a historical monument, and it is one of three building landmarks used by the National Maritime Association on its maps and navigational aids for sailors. In

The Don Ce Sar

April 1975 the Don was named to the National Register of Historic Places. An extensive renovation has been completed, and the palatial hotel glows throughout its ten stories with all its original elegance. (It has received a Mobil four-star rating since 1978.)

The Don Ce Sar is at the southern end of the island of St. Petersburg Beach directly on the Gulf of Mexico. You can't miss it. It's the only thing around that is both huge and pink. The Don Ce Sar Beach Resort and Spa, 3400 Gulf Boulevard, St. Petersburg Beach, FL 33706; (727) 360–1881.

Directly south of St. Petersburg Beach is sprawling *Fort DeSoto Park,* a great place to get away from it all and spend some quiet time with the pelicans and great white herons. Its 900 acres, with more than 7 miles of waterfront and almost 3 miles of fine swimming beaches, ramble over five islands: Madeline Key, St. Jean Key, St. Christopher Key, Bonne Fortune Key, and the main island—Mullet Key.

Ponce de Leon anchored off Mullet Key during the summer of 1513 to clean the barnacles off the bottom of his ship. He was interrupted by Indians who thought he had no business in their territory. In the skirmish that followed, the first white soldier known to be killed in North America died. Apparently Ponce de Leon didn't get the message that he was not welcome in the area. When he returned in 1521, he again fought with the Indians, this time receiving the wound that later caused his death in Havana, Cuba.

Construction of Fort DeSoto began in 1898 and was completed two years later. Its eight 12-inch mortars never fired a single shot at any enemy. The remains of this old fort graphically illustrated the then popular concept of harbor defense. Today it is an interesting relic of history, a good place to climb for a view of the surrounding sea.

Two islands provide a haven for campers, ancient oaks on the northern end of *Mullet Key* shade a lovely picnicking area, and lifeguards are on duty at the swimming beaches during the summer. There is a boat-launching ramp, two fishing piers, and a small restaurant and gift shop near the fort.

By car you can get to Fort DeSoto Park only by two toll bridges. This county park wants you to know, however, that the money goes to the State Road Department and not to the park. Fort DeSoto Park, 3500 Pinellas Bayway South, Tierra Verde, FL 33715; (727) 866–2484.

Western Interior

*Y*ou'll get your exercise if you cover all forty acres of canopies, stalls, and sheds at **Webster Flea Market,** one of the largest flea markets in the Southeast. It's hard to believe this all started in 1937 as a one-shed farmers' produce auction. More than 1,700 vendors await you and your spare change. It's all here—from fine antiques, clothes, fresh produce, and homemade sausage to just plain junk. You'll be exhausted if you try to see everything there is to see, but you'll surely find at least one item you cannot live another day without. Open every Monday 6:00

Sea Cows

*T*he manatee has been hunted for centuries for its meat, bone, hide, and fat. Florida Indians regularly hunted manatees and sold excess meat to the Spanish. Hides were made into leather shields, cords, and shoes, and the ivorylike bones were believed to be of medicinal value. Pioneers arriving in the nineteenth century shot manatees for food. Cowpens Key in the Florida Keys is believed to be so named because manatees were once penned in a small cove there as a food supply.

The West Indian manatee, or sea cow, is Florida's official marine mammal. Only about 1,000 of these harmless, fascinating creatures now remain, living their peaceful lives in Florida waters. Manatees can live in fresh or saltwater, but apparently need to drink fresh water periodically. They are vegetarians subsisting entirely on aquatic plants. Huge, gentle, and slow-moving,

manatees are distantly related to elephants and more closely to dugongs. An adult manatee averages between 10 and 12 feet long and may weigh from 1,000 to more than 2,000 pounds.

The species is listed as endangered by the U.S. Fish & Wildlife Service. For nearly a decade, more than one hundred manatees have died each year. Many manatee deaths are people related, and most of these occur from collisions with watercraft. Other problems include pollution, the ingestion of fish hooks and monofilament line, and their being crushed in canal locks and becoming tangled in crab trap lines. Vandalism and harassment by boaters, divers, and anglers can force manatees to leave preferred habitats and lead to the separation of mother and calf. Ultimately, loss of habitat is the most serious threat facing the manatee today.

A.M.–3:00 P.M. Webster Flea Market is located at Rt. 478 and Northwest Third Street in Webster; (352) 793–9877.

The **Dade Battlefield State Historic Site** is the picture of serenity now, but it was once drenched in blood. Here Indians, who were not pleased at the prospect of being evicted from their land, ambushed more than one hundred soldiers under the command of Major Francis L. Dade. The Dade Massacre, as it came to be known, touched off the Second Seminole War, a war that dragged on for seven years and became the country's costliest Indian war. While visiting the small museum and reading the markers along the nature trail, you'll have a chance to ponder the events of December 28, 1835. Dade Battlefield Historic Site, 720 CR 603, Bushnell, FL 33513. Located southwest of Bushnell off U.S. 301; exit 63 on I–75; (352) 793–4781.

Gulf Coast

I f you haven't looked a manatee in the eye lately, you'll never have a better opportunity than at **Homosassa Springs Wildlife Park.** You may pay a visit to these gentle mammals while walking under water (and staying nice and dry) in the underwater observatory.

Besides the lovable manatees, you'll see more than thirty-four varieties of fish, both saltwater and freshwater species. Three educational programs—on alligators, manatees, and native Florida reptiles—are offered seven times daily. Be sure to take the nature cruise and stroll the trails. Open 9:00 A.M.–5:30 P.M. Located just west of U.S. 19. Homosassa Springs, 4150 South Suncoast Boulevard, Homosassa Springs, FL 34446; (352) 628–5343.

Yulee Sugar Mill Ruins State Historic Site was once part of a thriving sugar plantation, the area's first known settlement made by a white man. David Yulee, a former U.S. senator, operated the mill for thirteen years beginning in 1851. He supplied the Confederate Army with sugar products until 1864, when a Union naval force burned Yulee's home to the ground. Interpretive signs will guide you through the partially restored sugar mill, the only antebellum structure of its kind in the country. Located in Homosassa on SR 490 southwest of U.S. 19. Write to Yulee Sugar Mill Ruins, c/o Crystal River State Archaeological Site, 3400 North Museum Point, Crystal River, FL 34428; (352) 795–3817.

And you thought Christmas came only once a year. Not at **Roger's Christmas House and Village,** which is open every day except December 25. You're welcome to browse the five houses of Christmas, which overflow with trees, wreaths, gifts, and the widest selection of ornaments in the country. Before long you are feeling festive. Next to the original house are Country Cottage, Magnolia House, Little House Under the Oak Tree, and Storybook Land with animated display figures. Open daily 9:30 A.M.–5:00 P.M. One block from the intersection of U.S. 98, SR 50A, and U.S. 41. Roger's Christmas House, 103 Saxon Avenue, Brooksville, FL 34601; (352) 796–2415.

Weeki Wachee Springs is home to live mermaids as well as more traditional denizens of the deep. The unusual theater is 16 feet below the surface of the spring (which is more than 137 feet deep) with glass windows for your viewing pleasure. Walk through lush tropical gardens and ride a **Wilderness River Cruise Boat**. Weeki Wachee Springs, 6131 Commercial Way, Weeki Wachee, FL 34606. The theme park is on U.S. 19 south at the junction of SR 50; (352) 596–2062 or (800) 678–9335.

Tarpon Springs' famous sponge industry began in the 1890s when John K. Cheyney launched his first sponge-fishing boat and began hooking sponges. In 1905 John Cocoris, a recent immigrant from Greece, introduced the diving techniques used to harvest sponges in the Mediterranean. The first Tarpon Springs sponger to try this method emerged after a ten-minute dive thoroughly convinced that these sponge beds could supply the whole world.

Word of the bountiful beds off Tarpon Springs spread to Greece, and soon whole families were packing up their lives and moving to the west coast of Florida. From their homeland they brought the colorful customs and traditional cuisine of the rich Hellenic culture.

The village prospered during the first forty years of the twentieth century as sponging grew to be a multimillion-dollar business. Auctions held at the Sponge Exchange were lively affairs, and Tarpon Springs soon surpassed Key West as the country's main sponging center. But in the 1940s a mysterious disease known as the red tide decimated the sponge beds, and consumers began turning to synthetic sponges.

Today visitors fascinated by this Greek community stroll the *sponge docks,* which have been designated a National Historic Landmark. The Sponge Exchange has been taken over by boutiques and gift shops, but a few boats still return from sea with ropes of sponges drying in the rigging. Lining the docks are many Greek coffeehouses and restaurants where a meal of pastitso and baklava may be washed down with a glass of retsina wine. Information on Tarpon Springs is available at the Greater Tarpon Springs Chamber of Commerce, 11 East Orange Street, Tarpon Springs, FL 34689; (727) 937–6109.

The Big Scrub

Ocala National Forest, covering more than 430,000 acres, is known locally as the "Big Scrub." Ocala is the oldest national forest east of the Mississippi River as well as the southernmost in the country. This forest preserve, bounded by the St. Johns and the Oklawaha Rivers, contains central highlands, coastal lowlands, swamps, springs, and literally hundreds of lakes and ponds, as well as a great variety of vegetation and wildlife. Our only national forest with subtropical vegetation, Ocala boasts the world's largest stand of sand pine, the only tree capable of growing to usable size in dry sand. The forest is home to one of the state's largest deer herds, as well as such Florida rarities as the Southern bald eagle and black bear.

The community still revolves around the church. *St. Nicholas Greek Orthodox Cathedral,* a fine example of neo-Byzantine architecture with icons, stained glass, and sculptured marble, was named for the patron saint of ships and seafaring men. The celebration of Epiphany, held each January 6, is a study in pomp and pageantry. The archbishop leads the colorful procession from the church to Spring Bayou, the site of the original settlement. There he releases a dove and tosses a large gold cross into the water. Young men dive for the sacred trophy, and the successful one receives a blessing, which is supposed to bring him a year of good luck. The community then funnels all its energies into singing and dancing. Especially during this Old World festival, Tarpon Springs seems more like a Mediterranean community than a Floridian one. The church, open 9:00 A.M.–5:00 P.M. Monday to Friday, is at 36 North Pinellas Avenue; (727) 937–3540.

Ocala Area

The Ocala area is a land of gently rolling hills, massive oaks bearded with Spanish moss, and sleek thoroughbreds gamboling in neatly fenced paddocks. This is the fastest-growing thoroughbred community in the world and is responsible for Florida's development, in less than half a century, as a major force in international racing and breeding.

The racing world sat up and took notice when Needles became the first Florida-bred to win the Kentucky Derby in 1956. Since then what started as a few converted cattle farms has grown to nearly 500 thoroughbred facilities. Marion County is now second only to Lexington, Kentucky, in concentration of *thoroughbred farms*.

Central Florida offers ideal conditions for raising superior thoroughbreds. Year-round sunshine, mineral-rich water, and fertile pastureland have turned out to be a winning combination. Mild weather, with cold snaps rarely lasting more than a few days, plays an important role. Central Florida's extended springs and autumns flank a long summer. The absence of a harsh winter means that, rather than standing idle in their stalls, horses run free all year. Unlike its northern counterpart, a new Florida foal is usually out romping with its dam within hours of its birth.

The area is wonderfully scenic and many horse farms welcome visitors for self-guided tours, but the hours vary. Visitors are encouraged to pick up information at the Ocala/Marion County Chamber of Commerce on

Bubbling Sands

*J*uniper Springs *is a jewel. Rimmed by a circular stone wall and surrounded by dense semitropical forest, this swimming hole is a real stunner. For a while we watched as intrepid teenagers dropped from the limbs of a huge tree into the brilliant cobalt-blue depths. Thunderous splashes as the kids cannonballed into the pool punctuated the rhythmic sounds of an undershot waterwheel almost hidden by foliage.*

Two springs in this area, Juniper and nearby Fern Hammock, produce a combined flow of about twenty million gallons of 72-degree water every day of the year. But statistics don't even hint at their true beauty. Water boils up through clean white sand, creating ever-changing formations resembling creamy cumulus clouds. The billowing sand in this watery kaleidoscope never rests.

Water temperature may remain constant, but the weather changes with the season. According to the woman at the snack counter, Northerners enthusiastically plunge in year-round, but Floridians wouldn't dream of swimming during the winter. The local population shows up during the cooler months, but it is usually to camp, hike, and canoe. Temperatures in this national forest during the dry months between November and February range from 50 degrees to 72 degrees. Summer is warmer, between 70 degrees and 95 degrees, and wetter.

Passing close to Juniper Springs, the Ocala Trail (a portion of the Florida Trail) runs the 66-mile length of Ocala National Forest. We were content to stroll the lush ³/₄-mile nature trail, passing numerous small springs along the way. Our brief encounters with turtles and birds in this idyllic setting whetted our appetites for more. Exploring by canoe proved a satisfying answer. Because this is a one-way trip from Juniper Springs to the bridge on SR 19 (about 7 miles), an early start is recommended.

Juniper Creek begins as a swift, narrow stream almost completely hidden from the sun by dense foliage. After ducking overhanging branches and negotiating many twists and turns, we were glad to have the stream gradually widen and slow so we could relax and absorb some of the sights. A pair of otters followed us for about a mile, their heads popping up from time to time. Cormorants and ibis flew overhead, and herons stalked the shallows. After catching glimpses of both alligators and snakes, we understood why rafts, floats, and inner tubes aren't allowed on this pretty stretch of water. We stopped for a picnic along the way, felt eyes on us, and turned to find a deer watching.

Silver Springs

"There is nothing on earth comparable to it. We seemed floating through an immense cathedral where white marble columns meet in vast arches overhead and are reflected in the grassy depths below. The dusky plumes of palmetto . . . looked like fine tracery of a wondrous sculptured roof. . . . Clouds of fragrance were wafted to us from orange groves along the shore; and the transparent depth of the water gave the impression that our boat was moving through the air."—Harriet Beecher Stowe, on her 1873 visit to Silver Springs, Florida.

110 East Silver Springs Boulevard, Ocala, FL 34470, or call (352) 629–8051; Web site: www.ocalacc.com.

Just east of Ocala is the ***Ocala National Forest*** with more than 300,000 acres of untamed springs, winding streams, and natural lakes. The southernmost national forest in the continental United States, Ocala is a popular recreation area for canoeing, swimming, camping, hiking, picnicking, and hunting. Detailed maps of the forest may be obtained at the ranger station. USDA Forest Service, 325 John Knox Road, Suite F100, Tallahassee, FL 32303; (352) 625–2520. Visitors center on SR40; (352) 236–0288.

Although this is the largest area of sand pine in the world, with one of the largest deer herds in Florida, it is the clear, clean springs that steal the show. ***Alexander Springs*** pumps out seventy-six million gallons of 72-degree water each day of the year. The spring here is so large that local scuba experts use it for new diver certification tests. Canoers use this run for an excursion into the unspoiled forest, and swimmers and sunbathers make good use of the large sand beach. Located in Ocala National Forest off CR 445; 49525 County Road 445, Altoona, FL 32702; (352) 669–3522.

Another favorite, ***Juniper Springs,*** contributes twenty million gallons to the local water supply. Besides swimming, the most popular activity is canoeing the 7-mile spring run. This campground is in such demand that reservations are not accepted, and accommodations are handled on a first-come basis. Located in Ocala National Forest on SR 40 just west of SR 19; 26701 East Highway 40, Silver Springs, FL 34488; (352) 625–3147.

Salt Springs Recreation Area is on the shores of a beautiful natural spring, which empties into Lake George, the state's second-largest lake. The 5-mile spring run is ideal for canoeing, boating, and fishing; the spring boil is a mecca for swimmers and snorkelers. Located in Ocala National Forest on SR 19 about 21 miles north of SR 40, Salt Springs has complete camping facilities; 14151 Highway 19 north, Salt Springs, FL 32134; (352) 685–2048.

Silver Glen Springs is a beautiful 1,000-acre camping area bordering a crystal clear spring. A good place to bird-watch, swim, boat, or fish. Located in Ocala National Forest off SR 19, 6 miles north of SR 40; 5271 North State Road 19, Salt Springs, FL 32134; (352) 685–2799.

Although Ocala's waterworks are impressive, they are literally just a drop in the region's overflowing bucket. Of the country's seventy-eight major springs, twenty-seven are in Florida. Its central section is literally riddled with them. Springs are classified according to volume—a major spring, one of first magnitude, produces 100 cubic feet of water a second, or more than sixty-four million gallons daily. The combined output from all 300 of Florida's known springs is eight billion gallons of water a day!

Silver Springs, near Ocala, is the largest limestone artesian spring formation in the world. With an average output of 800 million gallons a day, the springs have the greatest long-term measured average flow of any freshwater group in Florida. No wonder early Indians considered them sacred and paid homage to them with elaborate ceremonies. Scientists have discovered evidence of human activity dating back a hundred centuries. Certainly this is one of Florida's oldest attractions.

Most of the earliest sight-seers came by boat, although the 136-mile trip from Palatka involved several weeks poling along the tortuous Ocklawaha River. By the 1880s steamboats began regular trips from Palatka to the Springs carrying such notables as Mary Todd Lincoln, Harriet Beecher Stowe, and William Cullen Bryant. The expedition, a real breeze, took only two nights and a day.

Visitors are rarely disappointed by this natural wonder. The limestone-filtered water in the deep blue pool inspired one early journalist to describe the springs as shining "like an enormous jewel." Phillip Morrell, a young man living at Silver Springs, invented the glass-bottom boat to provide passengers their first fish-eye view of the aquatic world. Watching this ever-changing panorama while gliding over the pellucid springs is still a favorite activity. Numerous movies and television shows, attracted by the extraordinary clarity, have done underwater filming in this location.

The luxuriant gardens and subtropical scenery on the 350-acre site add to the viewing pleasure. Other diversions include a Jungle Cruise, Lost River Voyage, and a Jeep Safari. You'll see giraffes, ostriches, camels, and a colony of monkeys descended from those used in the old Tarzan movies. Located just off I–75, 1 mile east of Ocala on SR 40. Open daily 10:00 A.M.–5:00 P.M. Florida's Silver Springs, 5656 East Silver Springs Boulevard, Silver Springs, FL 34488; (352) 236–2121 or (800) 234–7458.

Eastern Interior

The endangered manatees have long made **Blue Springs State Park** their winter home. These large mammals congregate in Blue Springs Run between November and March because the year-round 72-degree water offers a refuge from the chilly St. Johns River. You may view these large "sea cows" (adults weigh about a ton) from observation platforms along Blue Springs Run. Once common from the Carolinas to Texas, these gentle giants now survive only in Florida, and this is one of the few places you may observe them in their native habitat. A two-hour boat ride explores the St. Johns River and the area around Hontoon Island.

In 1872 the Thursby family built a big frame house on the top of an ancient snail shell mound. The house and grounds have been restored to look as they did in the 1880s when oranges grew in the yard and the family sent their crops to Jacksonville by steamboat. The park is a fine place to camp (six family vacation cabins available), canoe, swim, fish, picnic, snorkel, and scuba dive. Located 2 miles west of Orange City off I–4 and U.S. 17-92, the park opens at 8:00 A.M. and closes at sunset year-round. Blue Springs State Park, 2100 West French Avenue, Orange City, FL 32763; (904) 775–3663.

The only way to reach **Hontoon Island State Park** is by boat. Luckily a daily ferry crosses the St. Johns River between the parking lot and the island. Of special interest is a 300-foot-long Timucuan Indian ceremonial mound. No vehicles are allowed. Besides being a sanctuary for the bald eagle, this is a good place to fish, picnic, and camp in either tents or cabins. The park is open 8:00 A.M. to sunset daily year-round. Six miles west of DeLand off SR 44; 2309 River Ridge Road, Deland, FL 32720; (904) 736–5309.

Between Sanford and Longwood keep an eye out for the **Big Tree** marker. The country's largest bald cypress tree is less than a mile up the cutoff road. "The Senator" is 126 feet high with a diameter of 17½ feet and an estimated age of more than 3,000 years. Impressive! Big Tree Park is on General Hutchinson Parkway, Longwood, Florida. The Seminole County Parks and Recreation Department closes the gates at sunset. Free.

You are not going to believe there are this many cacti in the world until you tour the greenhouses at **Florida Cactus, Inc.,** in Plymouth. Is your idea of a cactus green? Take a good long look at the endless rows of red, yellow, and pink cacti.

You may buy (or just admire) dish gardens, colorful grafted cacti, cactus books, and a special fertilizer called cactus juice. The mailing address is Florida Cactus, Inc., P.O. Box 2900, Apopka, FL 32704. The greenhouse, at South Peterson Road in Plymouth, Florida, is off U.S. 441. Turn off 441 south onto Boy Scout Boulevard. Follow the Florida Cactus signs to South Peterson Road. Open 7:30 A.M.–5:00 P.M. Monday through Friday and 7:30–11:30 A.M. on Saturday; closed Sunday; (407) 886–1833. Free.

STATE PARKS OF CENTRAL FLORIDA

Anclote Key State Preserve (727) 469–5918

Blue Spring State Park (904) 775–3663

Caladesi Island State Park (727) 469–5918

Crystal River State Archaeological Site (352) 795–3817

Dade Battlefield State Historic Site (352) 793–4781

DeLeon Springs State Recreation Area (904) 985–4212

Egmont Key State Park (727) 893–2627

Fort Cooper State Park (352) 726–0315

Fort Pierce Inlet State Recreation Area/Avalon State Recreation Area (561) 468–3985

Highlands Hammock State Park (863) 386–6094

Hillsborough River State Park (813) 987–6771

Homosassa Springs State Wildlife Park (352) 628–5343

Honeymoon Island State Recreation Area (727) 469–5942

Hontoon Island State Park (904) 736–5309

Lake Griffin State Recreation Area (352) 360–6760

Lake Kissimmee State Park (863) 696–1112

Lake Louisa State Park (352) 394–3969

Lake Manatee State Recreation Area (941) 741–3028

Little Manatee River State Recreation Area (813) 671–5005

Lower Wekiva River State Preserve (407) 884–2009

Paynes Creek State Historic Site (863) 375–4717

Rainbow Springs State Park (352) 489–8503

Rock Springs Run State Reserve (407) 884–2009

Savannas State Reserve (561) 468–3985

Sebastian Inlet State Recreation Area (407) 984–4852

Silver River State Park (352) 236–1827

Tomoka State Park (904) 676–4050

Tosohatchee State Reserve (407) 568–5893

Wekiwa Springs State Park (407) 884–2009

Ybor City State Museum (813) 247–6323

Yulee Sugar Mill Ruins State Historic Site (352) 795–3817

PLACES TO STAY IN CENTRAL FLORIDA

DAYTONA BEACH
Super 8 Speedway, 2992 West International Speedway Boulevard; (904) 253–0643

Hilton–Daytona Beach, 2637 South Atlantic Avenue; (904) 767–7350

Palm Plaza Oceanfront Resort, 3301 South Atlantic Avenue; (904) 767–1711

Holiday Inn–Indigo Lakes, 2620 West International Speedway Boulevard; (904) 258–6333

TITUSVILLE
Comfort Inn–Kennedy
Space Center,
3810 South Washington
Avenue; (407) 267–9111

Ramada Inn, 3500 Cheney
Highway; (407) 269–5510

La Cita Country Club,
777 Country Club Drive;
(407) 383–2582

ORLANDO
Delta Orlando Resort,
5715 Major Boulevard;
(407) 351–3340

Hampton Inn at Universal,
5621 Windhover Drive;
(407) 351–6716

Adam's Mark, 1500 Sand
Lake Road; (407) 859–1500

Peabody Orlando,
9801 International Drive;
(407) 352–4000

Courtyard at Lake Lucerne,
211 North Lucerne Circle
East; (407) 648–5188

Meadow Marsh,
940 Tildenville School
Road, Winter Garden;
(407) 656–2064

KISSIMMEE
Days Inn,
7980 West Irlo Bronson
Memorial Highway;
(407) 396–1000

Holiday Inn Express,
2145 East Irlo Bronson
Memorial Highway;
(407) 846–4646

Ramada Limited
2407 West Irlo Bronson
Memorial Highway;
(407) 933–2400

Doubletree Guest Suites
Resort–Maingate,
4787 West Irlo Bronson
Memorial Highway;
(407) 397–0555

The Inn at Maingate,
7501 West Irlo Bronson
Memorial Highway;
(407) 396–1400

The Unicorn, 8 South
Orlando Avenue;
(407) 846–1200

OCALA
Courtyard by Marriott,
3712 Southwest
Thirty-eighth Avenue;
(352) 237–8000

Holiday Inn,
3621 West Silver Springs
Boulevard; (352) 629–0381

Seven Sisters,
820 Southeast Fort King
Street; (352) 867–1170

TAMPA
La Quinta Inn,
2904 Melbourne
Boulevard; (813) 623–3591

Tahitian Inn,
601 South Dale Mabry
Highway; (813) 877–6721

Best Western Resort at
Busch Gardens,
820 East Busch Boulevard;
(813) 933–4011

Hyatt Regency Westshore,
6200 Courtney Campbell
Causeway; (813) 874–1234

Behind the Fence,
1400 Viola Drive, Brandon;
(813) 685–8201

Saddlebrook Resort,
5700 Saddlebrook Way,
Wesley Chapel;
(813) 973–1111

ST. PETERSBURG
Comfort Inn Central,
1400 Thirty-fourth Street
North; (727) 323–3100

Holiday Inn Sunspree
Resort–Marina Cove,
6800 Sunshine Skyway
Lane; (727) 867–1151

Hilton, 333 First Street
South; (727) 894–5000

Renaissance Vinoy Resort,
501 Fifth Avenue Northeast;
(727) 894–1000

ST. PETERSBURG BEACH
Colonial Gateway Inn,
6300 Gulf Boulevard;
(727) 367–2711

Trails End,
11500 Gulf Boulevard,
Treasure Island;
(727) 360–5541

Sandpiper Beach Resort,
6000 Gulf Boulevard;
(727) 562–1212

Trade Winds,
5500 Gulf Boulevard;
(727) 562–1212

Don Cesar Beach Resort &
Spa, 3400 Gulf Boulevard;
(727) 360–1881

CLEARWATER
Residence Inn by Marriot,
5050 Ulmerton Road;
(727) 572–4446

Holiday Inn Select,
3535 Ulmerton Road;
(727) 577–9100

Belleview Biltmore Resort Hotel, 25 Belleview Boulevard; (727) 442–6171

Safety Harbor Resort and Spa, 105 North Bayshore Drive, Safety Harbor; (727) 726–1161

CLEARWATER BEACH
Clearwater Beach Hotel, 500 Mandalay Avenue; (727) 441–2425

Holiday Inn Sunspree, 715 South Gulfview Boulevard; (727) 447–9566

HOMOSASSA SPRINGS
Homosassa Riverside Resort 5297 South Cherokee Way, Homosassa; (352) 628–2474

Crown, 109 North Seminole Avenue, Inverness; (352) 344–5555

WEEKI WACHEE SPRING
Best Western, 6172 Commercial Way, Weeki Wachee; (352) 596–2007

TARPON SPRINGS
Best Western Tahitian Resort, 2337 U.S. 19 North, Holiday; (727) 937–4121

Tarpon Shores Inn, 40346 U.S. 19 North; (727) 938–2483

Westin Innisbrook Resort, 36750 U.S. 19 North, Palm Harbor; (727) 942–2000

SILVER SPRINGS
Holiday Inn, 5751 East Silver Springs Boulevard; (352) 236–2575

Sun Plaza, 5461 East Silver Springs Boulevard; (352) 236–2343

DELAND
Quality Inn, 2801 East New York; (904) 736–3440

Holiday Inn, 350 International Speedway Boulevard; (904) 738–5200

WINTER HAVEN
Days Inn Cypress Gardens, 339 U.S. 27, North, Dundee; (941) 439–1591

Florida Garden, 2345 Eighth Street Northwest; (863) 294–3537

LAKE WALES
Chalet Suzanne, 3800 Chalet Suzanne Drive; (863) 676–6011

River Ranch, 24700 FL 60 East; (863) 692–1321

LAKELAND
Comfort Inn, 1817 East Memorial Boulevard; (941) 688–9221

Holiday Inn–South, 3405 South Florida Avenue; (863) 646–5731

SEBRING
Quality Inn 6525 U.S. 27 North; (863) 385–4500

Inn on the Lakes, 3100 Gulfview Road; (863) 471–9400

DUNEDIN
Best Western Yacht Harbor Inn and Suites, 150 Marina Plaza; (727) 733–4121

Inn on the Bay, 1420 Bayshore Boulevard; (727) 734–7689

PLACES TO EAT IN CENTRAL FLORIDA

DAYTONA BEACH
Aunt Catfish's, 4009 Halifax Drive; (904) 767–4768

Down the Hatch, 4894 Front Street, Ponce Inlet; (904) 761–4831

Park's Seafood, 951 North Beach Street; (904) 258–7272

ORLANDO
Bergamo's (Italian), 8445 International Drive; (407) 352–3805

The Crabhouse, 8291 International Drive; (407) 352–6140

Dux, Peabody Orlando Hotel, 9801 International Drive; (407) 345–4550

Devino's Italian Restaurant, 8445 International Drive; (407) 345–0883

Visitor Information for Central Florida

Bradenton Area Convention & Visitors Bureau,
P.O. Box 1000, Bradenton 34206; (800) 462–6283;
Web site: www.floridaislandbeaches.org

Central Florida Visitors & Convention Bureau,
P.O. Box 61, Cypress Gardens 33884; (800) 828–7655;
Web site: www.sunsational.org

Citrus County Tourist Development Council,
801 Southeast U.S. Highway 19, Nature Coast Trail, Crystal River 34429; (800) 587–6667

Clearwater Regional Chamber of Commerce,
1130 Cleveland Street, Clearwater, FL 33755; (727) 461–0011;
Web site: www.clearwaterflorida.org

Clay County Chamber of Commerce,
1724 Kingsley Avenue, Orange Park 32073; (904) 264–2651;
Web site: www.claychamber.org

Cocoa Beach Area Chamber of Commerce/Convention and Visitors Bureau,
400 Fortenberry Road, Merritt Island 32952; (407) 459–2200;
Web site: www.cocoabeachchamber.com

Daytona Beach Area Convention & Visitors Bureau,
126 East Orange Avenue, Daytona Beach 32114; (800) 854–1234;
Web site: www.daytonabeach.com

Dunnellon Area Chamber of Commerce,
P.O. Box 868, Dunnellon 34430; (352) 489–2320 or (800) 830–2087

Florida's Space Coast Office of Tourism,
8810 Astronaut Boulevard, #102, Cape Canaveral 32920; (800) USA–1969;
Web site: www.space-coast.com/florida

Greater Clearwater Chamber of Commerce,
1130 Cleveland Street, Clearwater 33755; (727) 461–0011;
Web site: www.clearwaterflorida.org

Greater Hernando Chamber of Commerce,
101 East Fort Dade Avenue, Brooksville 34601; (352) 796–0697;
Web site: www.hernandochamber.com

Greater Sanford Chamber of Commerce,
400 East First Street, Sanford 32771; (407) 322–1408;
Web site: www.sanfordchamber.com

Gulf Beaches of Tampa Bay Chamber of Commerce,
6990 Gulf Boulevard, St. Pete Beach 33706; (727) 360–6957 or (800) 944–1847;
Web site: www.gulfbeaches-tampabay.com

Visitor Information for Central Florida

Hernando County Tourist Development Council,
31170 Cortez Boulevard, Brooksville 34602; (800) 601–4580;
Web site: www.co.hernando.fl.us/tourdev/

Highlands Hospitality, Inc.,
P.O. Box 2001, Sebring 33871; (800) 255–1711;
Web site: www.sebringflchamber.com

Indian River County Chamber of Commerce,
1216–21st Street, Vero Beach 32960; (561) 567–3491 or (800) 338–2678, ext. 17802;
Web site: www.indianriverchamber.com

Kissimmee–St.Cloud Convention & Visitors Bureau,
1925 East Irlo Bronson Highway, Kissimmee 34744; (800) 327–9159;
Web site: www.floridakiss.com

Lake County Convention & Visitors Bureau,
20763 U.S. Highway 27, Groveland 34736; (352) 429–3673 or (800) 798–1071;
Web site: www.lakecountyfl.com

Lake Wales Area Chamber of Commerce,
340 West Central Avenue, Lake Wales 33853; (863) 676–3445

Lakeland Area Chamber of Commerce,
P.O. Box 3607, Lakeland 33802; (941) 688–8551;
Web site: www.lakelandchamber.com

Melbourne/Palm Bay Area Chamber of Commerce,
1005 East Strawbridge Avenue, Melbourne 32901; (407) 724–5400 or (800) 771–9922;
Web site: www.melpb-chamber.org

New Smyrna Beach Resort Area,
115 Canal Street, New Smyrna Beach 32168; (800) 541–9621;
Web site: www.sevchamber.com

Okeechobee County Tourist Development Council,
55 South Parrott Avenue, Okeechobee 34974; (800) 871–4403

Orlando/Orange County Convention & Visitor Bureau,
6700 Forum Drive, Suite 100, Orlando 32821; (800) 551–0181;
Web site: www.goflorida.com/orlando

Pasco County Office of Tourism,
7530 Little Road, Suite 140, New Port Richey 34654–5522; (800) 842–1873;
Web site: www.//pascocounty.com/govt

Sebastian River Area Chamber of Commerce,
700 Main Street, Sebastian 32958; (561) 589–5969

Visitor Information for Central Florida

Seminole County Convention and Visitors Bureau,
105 International Parkway, Heathrow 32746; (800) 800–7832;
Web site: www.visitseminole.com

St. Lucie County Chamber of Commerce,
P.O. Box 8209, Port St. Lucie 34985; (888) 785–8243;
Web site: www.stluciechamber.org

St. Lucie County Tourist Bureau,
2300 Virginia Avenue, Fort Pierce 34982; (800) 344–TGIF

St. Petersburg/Clearwater Convention & Visitors Bureau,
14450–Forty-sixth Street North, Suite 108, Clearwater 33762; (800) 345–6710;
Web site: www.floridasbeaches.com

Tampa/Hillsborough Convention & Visitors Association,
400 North Tampa Street, Suite 1010, Tampa 33602; (800) 44–TAMPA;
Web site: www.gotampa.com

Ybor City Chamber of Commerce,
1800 East Ninth Avenue, Tampa 33605; (813) 248–3712;
Web site: www.ybor.org

Lili Marlene's Aviators
Restaurant & Pub,
129 West Church Street;
(407) 422–2434

Passage to India (Indian),
5532 International Drive;
(407) 351–3456

Vivaldi, 107 Pine Street;
(407) 423–2335

KISSIMMEE
Charley's Steak House,
2901 Parkway Boulevard;
(407) 396–6055

Pacino's (Italian),
5795 West FL 192;
(407) 396–8022

OCALA
Carmichael's,
3105 Northeast Silver
Springs Boulevard;
(352) 622–3636

TAMPA
Bern's Steak House,
1208 South Howard
Avenue; (813) 251–2421

Columbia,
2117 East Seventh Avenue,
Ybor City; (813) 248–4961

Mise En Place,
442 West Kennedy
Boulevard, Hyde Park;
(813) 254–5373

Donatello (Italian),
232 North Dale Mabry
Highway; (813) 875–6660

ST. PETERSBURG
Basta's,
1625 Fourth Street South;
(727) 894–7880

The Keystone Club,
320 Fourth Street North;
(727) 822–6600

Native Seafood & Trading
Company, 5901 Sun Boule-
vard; (727) 866–8772

Pepin,
4125 Fourth Street North;
(727) 821–3773

ST. PETERSBURG BEACH
Brunello,
3861 Gulf Boulevard;
(727) 367–1851

The Lobster Pot,
17814 Gulf Boulevard,
Redington Shores;
(727) 391–8592

Maritana Grille,
Don Cesar Beach Resort,
3400 Gulf Boulevard;
(727) 360–1882

Wine Cellar,
17307 Gulf Boulevard,
North Redington Beach;
(727) 393–3491

CLEARWATER
Marco Polo,
2516 McMullen Booth
Road; (727) 791–7979

CLEARWATER BEACH
Alley Cat's Cafe,
2475 McMullen Booth
Road; (727) 797–5555

Bob Heilman's
Beachcomber,
447 Mandalay Avenue;
(727) 442–4144

Julie's Seafood and Sunsets,
351 South Gulfview
Boulevard; (727) 441–2548

HOMOSASSA SPRINGS
Churchill's, Crown Hotel,
109 North Seminole
Avenue, Inverness;
(352) 344–5555

TARPON SPRINGS
Louis Pappas' Riverside
(Greek/American),
10 West Dodecanese
Boulevard; (727) 937–5101

DELAND
Pondo's,
1915 Old New York Avenue;
(904) 734–1995

WINTER HAVEN
Christy's Sundown,
U.S. 17 South at Avenue K
and Third; (941) 293–0069

LAKE WALES
Chalet Suzanne,
3800 Chalet Suzanne Drive;
(941) 676–6011

Vinton's (French),
229 East Stuart Avenue;
(941) 676–8242

LAKELAND
Red Fox Grill,
1239 Memorial Boulevard;
(941) 683–5500

DUNEDIN
Bon Appetit,
148 Marina Plaza,
(813) 733–2151

Southwest Florida

I f you want to move around southwest Florida in a hurry, then I–75 is the way to go. A more pleasurable route for your wanderings is U.S. 41, which tries to get as close to the Gulf as it can. It often succeeds, with glorious sunset-over-the-water views.

To access the tempting islands just offshore, you'll have to cross a bridge (often complete with toll) or arrange for boat transportation. Be patient with both options, and remember that getting off the beaten path has its own built-in rewards.

To reach the Peace River, head inland to Arcadia either by SR 70, SR 72, or U.S. 17. The bonus for using SR 72 is that it takes you through the heart of verdant Myakka River State Park.

You'll find Corkscrew Swamp by heading east of Naples on CR 846. To explore Big Cypress Swamp take either Alligator Alley (I–75) or Tamiami Trail (U.S. 41), routes connected by SR 29 that will eventually take you to Fort Lauderdale or Miami if you stay on them long enough.

Big Cypress Swamp is a vast wilderness area featuring a range of habitats including sandy islands of slash pine, wet and dry prairies, hardwood hammocks, and dense forests of cypress trees. You would do well to exercise caution in this undeveloped area, especially on unpaved roads.

Thirty miles south of Naples are the Ten Thousand Islands, a maze of mangrove islands teeming with wildlife. Stick with conducted tours, or at the very least, have a guide with you.

Everglades City is quite literally the jumping-off place. Access to the wilderness is strictly by water from here on in. Take mosquito repellent and a guide and discover a haunting environment like none other on Earth.

Sarasota Area

A ficionados of the arts feel right at home in Sarasota, which offers the appealing combination of sandy beaches and

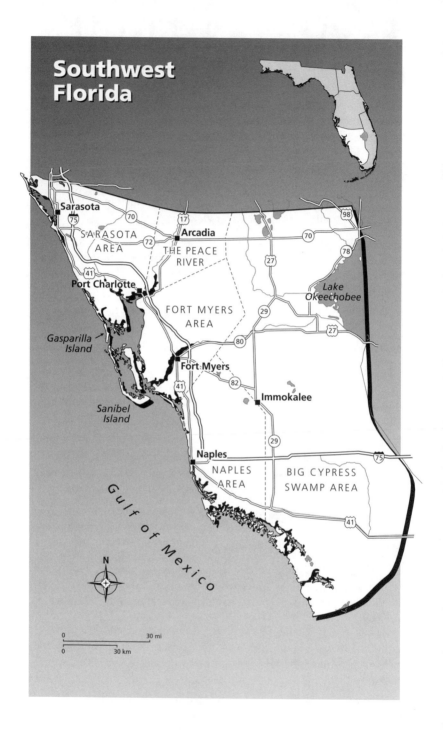

Southwest Florida

Sarasota

SARASOTA AREA

Arcadia

THE PEACE RIVER

Port Charlotte

FORT MYERS AREA

Gasparilla Island

Lake Okeechobee

Fort Myers

Sanibel Island

Immokalee

Naples

NAPLES AREA

BIG CYPRESS SWAMP AREA

Gulf of Mexico

N

0   30 mi
0   30 km

TOP EVENTS IN SOUTHWEST FLORIDA

Mullet Festival & Craft Fair, Goodland, January, (941) 394–3041

Sarasota Medieval Fair, Sarasota, February, (941) 957–1877

Southwest Florida Fair, North Fort Myers, February, (941) 543–8368

Marco Art, Marco Island, February, (941) 394–4221

Swamp Cabbage Festival, LaBelle, February, (863) 675–2995

Desoto County Fair, Arcadia, March, (863) 494–5678

Sarasota Jazz Festival, Sarasota, March, (941) 366–1552

Annual Sanibel Shell Fair, Sanibel Island, March, (941) 472–2155

Suncoast Offshore Grand Prix, Sarasota, July, (941) 957–1877

Fifth Avenue Oktoberfest, Naples, October, (941) 472–2155

sophistication. Settled in 1842, the city's attributes were not really appreciated until it was "discovered" by a Chicago socialite in 1910. Wealthy and influential Northerners followed, and in 1927 John Ringling decided this would be the ideal winter quarters for his circus. John and Mable Ringling were instrumental in making Sarasota what it is today.

"The Greatest Show on Earth" made a fortune for Ringling, who knew just what he wanted to do with his money. He built his dream mansion, poured millions into his art collections, and invested heavily in civic improvements for Sarasota. The Ringling enthusiasm was contagious, and the city became known as a mecca for the arts.

Today's proliferating art galleries and theaters are direct descendants of the circus king's munificence. *The John and Mable Ringling Museum of Art* gives visitors a chance to see a cultural complex that puts Florida on the fine arts map. Included are a museum of art with one of the most distinguished collections of Baroque art in the hemisphere, the *Asolo Theatre* (an eighteenth-century theater imported in its entirety from Asolo, Italy), the *Circus Galleries,* and *John Ringling's Home.*

To call *Ca'd'Zan* (meaning House of John) simply Ringling's home doesn't quite do it justice. The thirty-two-room mansion on Sarasota Bay, patterned after the Doge's Palace on the Grand Canal in Venice, is one of America's great historic houses. Built in the 1920s at a cost of more than $1,500,000, this stately residence features a huge crystal chandelier from the lobby of New York's Waldorf Astoria Hotel and is elaborately furnished with art objects from around the world.

Although the home is officially known as the House of John, Mable Ringling had a lot to say about the design. She insisted on including the tower of the old Madison Square Garden (where the circus regularly appeared) in the plans. The architects had some problems with the tower in combination with the Venetian Palace idea, but they gave in when Mable declared, "It is my house. I know what I want and that is that."

Circus King's Mansion

"Chandeliers with crystals the size of oranges hang in the galleries. Painted panels of Arcadia adorn one room. There are antique columns of every size and description, and gold galore—gold tables, gold Madonnas, gold reliquaries, enough to put King Tut to shame. John Ringling didn't think big; he thought tremendous."

Saturday Review
Magazine

The Ringling Complex is open daily 10:00 A.M.–5:30 P.M. A restaurant is located near the Circus Museum. The complex is located on U.S. 41, 3 miles north of downtown Sarasota. The John and Mable Ringling Museum of Art, The State Art Museum of Florida, 5401 Bay Shore Road, Sarasota, FL 34243; (941) 359–5700; Web site: www.ringling.org.

Did you know that at least twenty-seven species of sharks inhabit the Gulf of Mexico off Sarasota? Were you aware that more than 600 species of fish and even more invertebrates live in Sarasota's Gulf and Bay waters? If you'd like to know more about these creatures of the deep, stop in at the **Mote Marine Science Center.** Guides will introduce you to the residents of thirty-six aquaria, including "nibbles" the nurse shark and two West Indian manatees. The sea horses and sea turtles are especially popular, as is the extensive shell collection. The Research Exhibits provide the inside scoop on current scientific projects and explain how this research applies to our lives. Board the **Sarasota Bay Explorers** for an ecotour of Sarasota's waterways. A marine biologist on board will help you get firsthand experience with the fascinating creatures living in local grass flats. From downtown Sarasota follow CR 780 to St. Armands Circle, continue to New Pass Bridge Area, and look for directional signs. Open 10:00 A.M.–5:00 P.M. daily. Mote Marine Science Center, 1600 City Island Park, Sarasota, FL 33577; (800) 691–MOTE or (941) 388–4441; Web site: www.mote.org.

Orchid lovers should spend some time browsing the extensive collection of tropical plants at the **Marie Selby Botanical Gardens.** This is the only public garden in the United States focusing on epiphytes, which are plants that grow on other plants. The research done here is vitally important because the tropical forests and jungles of the world are fast disappearing, and with them are going many rare and beautiful plants.

Eight and a half bayfront acres on the slender peninsula between Sarasota Bay and Hudson Bayou contain more than 20,000 colorful plants, including more than 6,000 orchids. Besides being a magnificent floral display, Selby is an internationally recognized center for botanical research and plant identification.

Don't miss any of the twenty garden areas, especially the Tropical Display House, the Bamboo Pavilion, the Waterfall Garden, the Banyan Grove, the

Cactus and Succulent Garden, the Shoreline Restoration Garden, the award-winning Hibiscus Garden, and the Palm Grove. Also, be sure to visit the former Christy Payne Mansion, a unique example of eclectic Southern Colonial architecture, now serving as the Gardens' Museum of Botany and the Arts, where eighteenth- through twentieth-century botanical prints are on display.

You'll enjoy strolling through the waterfront gardens and seeing the greenhouse abloom with elegant air plants. The gift and bookshop has tropical plants for sale along with books on everything you ever wanted to know about gardening. The gardens are located at U.S. 41 and South Palm Avenue, 4½ miles south of the Sarasota-Bradenton Airport. Open 10:00 A.M.–5:00 P.M. every day of the year except Christmas. The Marie Selby Botanical Gardens, 811 South Palm Avenue, Sarasota, FL 34236. If you wish to have a guided tour, be sure to call ahead: (941) 366–5731; Web site: www.selby.org.

Myakka River State Park—28,000 acres of river, lakes, marsh, hammocks, and prairies—is one of the country's outstanding wildlife sanctuaries and breeding grounds. A 7-mile drive through this scenic park will acquaint you with the overall features of the area, but to really experience its incredible diversity, why not rent a bike or, better yet, a canoe. Camping opportunities range from rustic cabins to a backpack trail that leads to six primitive camping areas.

Bird-watchers will feel that their time on the lakeshore birdwalk and observation platform has been well spent when they catch sight of a majestic bald eagle, great blue heron, sandhill crane, egret, or ibis.

Some 200 species of birds have been spotted in the park, and there are large rookeries. Board **Gator Gal,** the world's largest airboat, or the special *Safari Tram* (open December through June) for a scenic cruise. Both excursions are narrated by knowledgeable guides. The park is 14 miles east of Sarasota on SR 72; 13207 State Road 72, Sarasota, FL 34241. Open daily 8:00 A.M. to sunset; (941) 361–6511.

Basket lovers beware! *Basketville* boasts the largest selection of baskets in the world, a claim you're sure to believe when you try to make up your mind about what to purchase. You'll be swamped with choices that range from handcrafted baskets of white ash and red oak to a

Gator Gal at Myakka River State Park

tremendous variety of permanent flowers, buckets, woodenware, wicker furniture accessories, and handmade imports from all over the world. Basketville is on U.S. 41, 4 miles south of Venice (4411 South Tamiami Trail, Venice, FL 34293). Open every day 8:30 A.M.–7:00 P.M. during the winter, 6:00 P.M. during the summer; (941) 493–0007.

Because they are near the longest sloping continental shelf in the world, the **beaches around Venice** are a fertile fossil hunting area, especially for shark teeth. Some of the teeth being washed ashore belong to creatures that have been extinct for millions of years. Put on your swimsuit and start scooping up sand in the shallow water. Keep a sharp eye out. Some teeth are very tiny. Free.

Folks who want to get off the beaten path love islands, but they especially love bridgeless islands, islands without cars that are approached the way an island should be—by boat. That's one reason they love Palm Island.

This is the place for those who want to get away from the crowds, stroll the beach at sunrise, let the kids run free, snooze after lunch, and watch the evening sun sink into the Gulf of Mexico.

Palm Island is a find! South of Sarasota on Florida's Southwest Gulf Coast, this 7-mile barrier island is north of Fort Myers and the islands of Sanibel and Gasparilla. The resort covers $2^1/_2$ miles of this pristine island and consists of 200 individually owned beach villas and cottages, many available for rental. Minimum stay is two nights; the resort does not allow day-trippers.

If you have your own boat, fine. Palm Island is on the Intracoastal Waterway south of Lemon Bay, a few minutes north of Gasparilla Pass near Charlotte Harbor. The channel entrance is midway between green marker "7" and red marker "8."

If you're yachtless, never fear. Park your car at the Palm Island Resort Reception Center's full-service marina and shift your mental gears to "no hassle." A bellman will take your bags and deliver them to your island villa. The resort launch leaves hourly for a twelve-minute cruise to Palm Island.

Born to a poor German immigrant family, John Ringling and his brothers toured the Midwest countryside as musicians. They billed their act as the "Ringling Brothers Moral, Elevating, Instructive & Fascinating Concert and Variety Performance." Over the years this eventually evolved into the "Greatest Show on Earth," and John became the vastly rich king of the circus.

Step onto the island and feel the stress evaporate. Now your transportation is by island tram (which makes hourly runs around the resort), bike or electric golf cart (both available for rent), or footpower.

After you've beachcombed the glistening 2-mile beach for rare shells and prehistoric sharks' teeth, what is there to do? You may watch the dolphins play, bike or walk the resort's winding trails, go for a swim (five pools or the entire Gulf of Mexico), relax in the hydro spa, fish (rental boats, charter, or surf fishing), play tennis (eleven courts, lessons from the pro), watch the birds, snorkel, windsurf, waterbike, or explore Rum Bay by kayak or canoe.

The island recreation team keeps everyone (who wants to) jumping. There are playgrounds, displays, and programs at the nature center. An Island Kids Club sponsors activities ranging from nature walks, Kids' Movie Night, Kids' Olympics, sand castle construction, crafts and cooking classes, to shell and treasure hunts. Activities for adults run the gamut from nature walks to family bingo.

If being on Palm Island isn't off the beaten path enough, rent a bike and head south to Don Pedro Island State Recreation Area. Connected to Palm Island by two wooden bridges, Don Pedro is an easy 2-mile bike ride. The reward for your effort is a mile-long stretch (usually deserted) of gleaming white sandy beach.

This is where loggerhead sea turtles come ashore during the summer to nest and lay eggs. The turtle nesting season is the reason you are asked to keep beach lights (including flashlights and beach fires) off from May 1 to October 31. Newborn turtles head for the brightest light, which in a natural state would be the Gulf of Mexico. If they head for artificial light inland, they become lost and eventually perish.

Florida beaches host the largest gathering of nesting sea turtles in the United States. Although these docile reptiles have been severely threatened by human activities in the past, enlightened citizens would like to see their numbers increase. For more information on sea turtles, contact the Florida Department of Natural Resources, Division of Marine Resources, Florida Marine Research Institute, 100 Eighth Avenue, Southeast, St. Petersburg, FL 33701; (727) 896–8626; Web site: www.fmri.usf.edu.

Accommodations in the Palm Island Resort are fully equipped one-, two-, or three-bedroom Old Florida–style villas with full kitchen, living and dining room, washer, dryer, and screened porch overlooking the Gulf of Mexico.

If your idea of a vacation does not include getting too well acquainted with the kitchen, saunter on down to the Rum Bay Restaurant, which is open for lunch and dinner. The chef serves a variety of burgers, salads, and sandwiches until 3:00 P.M. Dinner is another story. You might want to whet your whistle with a Green Dolphin cocktail (vodka, blue Curacao, and sour mix) before diving into fresh chargrilled grouper. For those with hearty appetites, the island seafood sampler (crab cake, grilled shrimp, broiled freshwater snapper, and calamari rings) or the combination filet and lobster tail (two tails and a 5-ounce filet) will surely satisfy. The ribs are sensational, or, for a quick pick-me-up, try the shrimp pizza. Key lime pie provides the perfect finale.

Near the southern tip of the Cape Haze peninsula just south of Englewood, Palm Island is an easy ninety-minute drive from Fort Myers Airport. Those traveling south from Tampa should follow the signs for I–75 south to exit 34 (Englewood, North Port). Turn right on River Road. After crossing U.S. 41 continue about 7 miles to the traffic light at Pine Street. Turn left on Pine and continue for another 7 miles. Palm Island Resort will be on the right side of CR 775.

Those traveling north from Fort Myers should follow signs for I–75 north to exit 32 (Toledo Blade Boulevard). Turn west on Toledo Blade, cross RT 41, and continue to the stop sign; turn right onto SR 776. Go across El Jobean Bridge to first traffic light. Turn left onto CR 771 and continue to Palm Island Resort on the left.

Palm Island Resort, 7092 Placida Road, Cape Haze, FL 33946; (941) 697–4800 or (800) 824–5412.

As you leave Palm Island and pull out of the marina parking lot, turn right. Just down CR 775 (on the right) in Placida, you'll find the Fishery Restaurant with an expansive view of Gasparilla Sound. The family business has blended Old Florida with the new and put the emphasis where it should be—on fresh seafood.

Start with Gator Bites, tender fried alligator with key lime mustard, or try the famous Fishery Gumbo, a "mess of shrimp, crab, tomato, and okra." You can't miss with a Thunderation Platter (broiled grouper, shrimp, oysters, and scallops) or a Snapper Melt with tomato and honey mustard on marble bread. Finish your feast off with Key Lime Cheesecake or Orange (!) Key Lime Pie. Chocoholics will be totally happy with the Ultimate Turtle Haagen-Dazs Ice Cream Pie. The Fishery Restaurant, P.O. Box 39, Placida, FL 33946; (941) 697–2451.

If you enjoyed the hand-painted silks in the Fishery Restaurant, drop by the Margaret Albritton Gallery next door to browse more of this artist's original paintings and crafts. Greg Albritton did the wooden fish you saw in the restaurant. His work is in the Placida Cove (the pink and green building) along with crafts, clothing, jewelry, and other fun things.

Gasparilla Island

P ristine shell-strewn beaches, fragrant tropical flowers, and not a single traffic light on the entire island. Year-round sunshine tempered by breezes from the Gulf. Best tarpon fishing in the world. Streets that make a statement: Damn If I Know, Damn If I Care, and Damn If I Will. Welcome to *Gasparilla Island* or, as it is better known (for its main community), *Boca Grande.*

Gasparilla, approximately an hour's drive south of Sarasota, is one of a string of barrier islands scattered along southwest Florida's coast between Tampa and Fort Myers. Bordered on the west by the Gulf of Mexico, on the north by Little Gasparilla Pass, on the east by Charlotte Harbor, and on the south by Boca Grande Pass, the island is accessible by toll bridge or boat.

Boca Grande (Spanish for "big mouth") Pass, one of Florida's deepest natural inlets, accounts for its early history. Calusa Indians were drawn to its rich fishing grounds. Railroads that once carried phosphate mined in central Florida to the island's deep water harbor later transported distinguished guests for the winter season.

Today Boca Grande's population of nearly 800 more than triples during winter and spring. Visitors come for their own reasons, which range from exhilarating angling to somnolent afternoons under a palm tree.

No wonder Katharine Hepburn adores the ice cream in Boca Grande. At one time a handwritten note of hers posted in the **Loose Caboose** declared: "That ice cream is perfect—Wow!" Of course, you might not see it amidst the general accumulation of stuff—the fuzzy alligator wearing sunglasses, the antique vacuum cleaner on the wall, or the sign: STOP—LOOK—LISTEN—PROCEED WHEN TRAIN IS COMING.

Not to worry. There hasn't been a train here in years. The preferred transportation is by bicycle, and the bike path extends the length of this lush, 7-mile sliver of land. Lots of folks prefer parking their cars and relying solely on pedal power. Better for the blood pressure. Come to think of it, the entire island of Gasparilla is good for the blood pressure. Stash the alarm clock. You'll know when the sun emerges and when it slips into the Gulf. If you must know how long it takes to reach tournament-size tarpon, the answer is "not long." Listen up: The major sounds on this tranquil island are gulls calling or maybe the soft whisper of a dolphin breathing.

The Boca Grande Chamber of Commerce consists of a personable woman in the Chamber of Commerce office who'll give you a map and offer to "tell you anything you want to know." Where can you get the best breakfast in town? **Loons on a Limb.** Best undiscovered art gallery? Next to the Theater Restaurant. Best place to have your *Wall Street Journal* delivered? Fugates. Best local news source? The *Boca Beacon* ties with the local librarian.

The best grouper sandwich? **Millers Marina.** The best onion rings? Also at Millers. The best clams? The killer Cajun Clam Strips at—where else?—the **Casual Clam Cafe.** The best dinner? Local sentiment favors the **Temptation,** with **The Pink Elephant** (islanders call it "The Pink") a close second.

Apparently, the folks staying in the grand old **Gasparilla Inn** are quite happy with their fare, or they wouldn't return with such astonishing regularity. In 1911 when the twenty-room inn was newly opened and so empty it echoed, the first inquiry came from a socially prominent Bostonian. Before granting a reservation, the manager asked her to wire both a social and a bank reference. When the word got around that this hostelry catered to the "right" people, the right people appeared and stayed the season.

There are still two seasons on the island: the social season from November to April and the tarpon season from mid-April to July. The Gasparilla

Inn, open from mid-December to June, has expanded to 150 rooms (with the addition of cottages) and boasts the only golf course (private) on the island.

Our Lady of Mercy Chapel

What to do on Boca Grande? True beach lovers don't need anything more than dazzling white sand, a view of the distant horizon, and the gently lapping, Perrier-clear Gulf. Others enjoy shelling, birding, and all manner of water sports from fishing to sailboarding.

Grab your bike (rentals available) and wander the back roads. Island architecture, blessedly free of high-rises and time-shares, is an eclectic mix of Spanish-style stucco (note the community center and the Catholic church), elegant walled mansions of the rich and famous, and the more humble dwellings of fisherfolk.

Be sure to include the library—a distinctive pink stucco affair with coquina-rock walls, oversized cypress doors, and an intimate courtyard—in your ramblings. Browse the library's **shell collection** (donated by Henry Francis duPont) and ask for *Walking Tours on Boca Grande* or buy a copy at **Books in the Sand.**

A good place to walk is through the winding pathways of **Boca Bay** with its luxuriant landscaping, bridges, gazebos, and low-slung, generously latticed, wooden homes. This was the last residential community that could be built on the island, thanks to the conservation-minded 1980 Gasparilla Island Act, and it's satisfying to see its turn-of-the-century look blending so naturally into the island's easygoing style.

Explore at your own pace. If you're looking for local color, **Whidden's Marina** offers a double dose. Stop in **Our Lady of Mercy Chapel** to see the sixteenth-century Icon of Our Lady of Perpetual Help and other Old World treasures. Stroll down lanes canopied by banyans or hedged by scarlet hibiscus, and pause to admire a century-old gumbo-limbo tree. Breathe deeply of air perfumed by plumeria blossoms.

At day's end saunter down to Millers Marina and watch the fishing boats unload their catch, or head for the restored 1890 lighthouse on the island's southern tip for a show that's always in season—a luminous bronze sun slipping into the Gulf of Mexico. For more information contact the Boca Grande Chamber of Commerce, Box 704, Boca Grande, FL 33921; (941) 964–0568; Web site: www.bocagrandechamber.com.

The Peace River

More shark teeth, some as large as your hand, can be found in the *Peace River.* In fact, a canoe trip down the pristine Peace can provide you with one of your very best off-the-beaten-track experiences in the entire state. Florida's most uninhabited waterway winds its tranquil way (too shallow for motorboats) from a source in central Florida's Green Swamp to the Gulf of Mexico. Once the Peace marked the boundary between Indian territory to the east and white settlers' land to the west.

Every bend in the river is a movie set of palmettos, pine, cypress knees, and long strands of gray Spanish moss hanging from the gnarled limbs of live oaks. Wildflowers line the banks and large waterbirds stand in the shallows. You may spot armadillos, alligators, and deer. You will surely see cows that belong to the cattle ranches you paddle past. The perfectly clear water makes fossil finding easy, and there are many lovely spots to camp along the riverbanks.

Tailor your trip length to your own whims. Half-day trips are fun, but to really get in tune with this beautiful river, plan to spend several days. Put your canoe in at the bridge in Ft. Meade, Bowling Green, Wauchula, Zolfo Springs, Gardner, Brownsville, Arcadia, or Nocatee.

The friendly folks at **Canoe Outpost** will help select the right trip for you, answer all your questions, and provide whatever you need to be comfortable and safe. They can furnish either transportation upstream or pickup downstream, canoes, paddles, life cushions, all camping gear, coolers, and ice. Open year-round. Canoe Outpost (a mile northwest of Arcadia on CR 661), 2816 Northwest CR 661, Arcadia, FL 34266; (800) 268–0083; Web site: www.canoeoutpost.com.

Fort Myers Area

It's hard to resist such a huge collection of shells and coral. Pick out your own oyster (complete with pearl), examine rare shells from the seven seas, or select just the right piece of precious black coral. The **Shell Factory** has more than 70,000 square feet of temptations, which include a year-round Christmas shop, imported gifts, beachwear, and handmade moccasins. Quite a display! Located on U.S. 41 (North Tamiami Trail) 4 miles north of Fort Myers. Open seven days a week 10:00 A.M.–9:00 P.M. 2787 North Tamiami Trail, North Fort Myers, FL 33903; (941) 995–2141.

Sanibel Island's fortunate location enables it to snare some of the ocean's most beautiful treasures. This pretty island has a well-deserved reputation as one of the three best shelling beaches on Earth. (The others are in Africa and the Southwest Pacific.) Beachcombers take their hobby very seriously, pacing the shoreline with bodies bent in a position known locally as the "Sanibel Stoop."

Nearly half of the land on Sanibel and the adjoining island of Captiva

Mammoth Pleasures of the Peace River

I looked down river where my husband had been wading a few moments before. A few bubbles. Nothing more.

Alligators! My mind somersaulted. There are alligators in this river.

He had been walking in waist-deep water. I started wading toward him but the river slowed me. He surfaced, grabbed a breath, and submerged, obviously not in the clutches of a reptilian wrestler.

Still, the man does not usually go underwater without provocation. Just then he exploded from the water.

"They aren't tires," he shouted jubilantly between gasps. Sloshing toward me, he proclaimed, "They're teeth!" He held two large rocks out for us to see. "They looked like tires under water. See the tread." It did indeed look like tread. "So I kicked one and almost broke my toe," he explained cheerfully.

Later, we verified his find with a museum expert. Sure enough, he was holding the molars of some prehis-

toric elephant that had tromped Florida's steaming jungles many thousands of years before. The "tread" turned out to be the grinding surface this huge vegetarian used to chew up his dinner. Each tooth weighed in at fourteen pounds.

Bill had begun thinking in terms of teeth after we stopped in a tiny one-room museum near our canoe launch site at Zolfo Springs. There we'd seen a mammoth tooth still attached to the jaw and studied a series of photographs of a dig conducted by the Smithsonian Institute. A Boy Scout troop canoeing down the river had come upon a tusk sticking out of the bank. Some exploratory probing revealed the tusk was still very much attached to a complete mammoth skeleton that was later exhumed by geologists.

Central Florida's Peace River is a fertile bed for fossil collectors. Each of our kids came away with a pocketful of shark teeth, some as large as their palms. But Bill, with his two mammoth teeth, was the clear winner.

With their beautiful beaches and delightful seaside setting, both Sanibel and Captiva seem ideal island havens for the peace-and-quiet crowd. In fact, it was from Captiva Island that Anne Morrow Lindbergh drew inspiration to write her best-selling book, A Gift from the Sea.

Actually, these serene islands have seen their share of violence. Seafaring Indians, rampaging pirates, saltwater floods, and hurricanes all have left their marks on these sandy isles. According to legend, pirates once imprisoned a band of women on Isla de las Captivas, which explains why it is now known as Captiva Island.

has been preserved in its natural state. The most frequented sanctuary is the J. N. *"Ding" Darling National Wildlife Refuge,* named for a Pulitzer Prize–winning political cartoonist. Darling was an ardent conservationist before anyone ever heard the word *ecology.* This mangrove wilderness at the southern end of the Atlantic flyway is a way station for migrating ducks and shelters more than 200 varieties of birds including the endangered brown pelican. Viewing is best at sunrise or sunset. Visitors can drive, bike, or paddle winding canoe trails through the 6,000-acre refuge, which is laced with fishing streams and hiking trails. Visitors center open 9:00 A.M.–5:00 P.M., 9:00 A.M.–4:00 P.M. during summer. Closed on Friday. U.S. Fish and Wildlife Service, 1 Wildlife Road, Sanibel, FL 33957; (941) 472–1100.

Useppa Island has a beach that looks like it was yanked from the South Pacific and a swimming pool, tennis court, three-hole golf course, and deepwater marina. Best of all, it has a profusion of lush tropical vegetation—palms, royal poinciana, and massive banyans.

Useppa is considered the most beautiful island in the chain of islands in Pine Island Sound, but its air of serenity hides a tempestuous past. The Calusa Indians apparently found it appealing. Archaeologists claim this is the oldest continuously occupied landmass on the western Florida coast. (The Indians started piling up oyster shell mounds in 3500 B.C.)

For a while the notorious pirate Jose Gaspar held his favorite female captive here. (The run-of-the-mill ladies were kept in a group on the nearby island named for these unsavory goings on—Isle de las Captivas, now known as Captiva Island.) Joseffa was a headstrong sixteen-year-old who never did take to Gaspar. He found this so withering to his ego that he chopped off her head. As you can imagine, this place has its share of ghost stories. (Local dialect changed *Joseffa* to *Useppa.*)

Streetcar tycoon John Roach bought Useppa in 1894, and publisher Barron Collier purchased it in 1912. Lots of rich and famous folks liked the combination of beauty and privacy that this tiny half-mile-long island afforded. Theodore Roosevelt, the Vanderbilts, the Rockefellers, Zane Grey, and Mae West stopped in from time to time, and the Izaak

SOUTHWEST FLORIDA

Walton Fishing Club was founded here. More recently Useppa served as the training ground for the Bay of Pigs invasion.

Neglect and deterioration threatened to scuttle the island's charm, but Gar Beckstead arrived just in time. In 1976 he purchased Useppa, moved his family there and started the long process of restoration. In his mission to recapture the past, Gar uncovered one historic treasure after another, including a bathtub full of signed tarpon scales. To stroll the east ridge's pink pathway to the old *Collier Inn* is to return to the era of the 1920s. Architecture is strictly controlled; new cottages are all white frame with latticework and wide, screened porches to match their restored counterparts. No cars intrude on the quiet.

OTHER ATTRACTIONS WORTH SEEING IN SOUTHWEST FLORIDA

Broadway Palm Dinner Theatre, Fort Myers

Caribbean Gardens, Naples

Naples CityDock, Naples

Naples Trolley Tours, Naples

Victor Alexander Glass Museum/Factory, Naples

Babcock Wilderness Adventures, Punta Gorda

Bailey–Matthews Shell Museum, Sanibel Island

Today the island is run as a private club, but nonmembers are welcome to stay as long as a week on an "investigatory" visit. (Members arrive by boat or seaplane.) A wide range of rental accommodations are available; (941) 283–1061.

If you prefer a day trip, sign up to cruise on the *Lady Chadwick.* This 150-passenger, double-decked excursion boat takes passengers through scenic Pine Island Sound while the captain points out leaping dolphins and baby ospreys peering from nests on the channel markers. Choose from the Island Cruise, Sight-seeing Cruise, or Sunset Cruise; (941) 472–5300.

If your yacht is less than 100 feet, the marina can accommodate it. Useppa Island lies just 2 miles south of Boca Grande Pass at Marker 63 on the Intracoastal Waterway, midway between Naples and Sarasota on the southwest coast of Florida. Useppa Island Club, P.O. Box 640, Bokeelia, FL 33922; (941) 283–1061.

Cabbage Key was once home of playwright and mystery novelist Mary Roberts Reinhart. Her house, built in 1938 on the highest point of the island, has been converted into *Cabbage Key Hide-Away Inn and Restaurant.* One memorable feature of the inn is its "wallpaper" worth more than $22,000. Somewhere along the way, the guests started tacking one dollar bills to the walls, and signing them. Today these bills cover the ceilings, walls, and beams. Visitors get a kick out of locating "their" dollar when returning to Cabbage Key.

Cabbage Key is a popular watering hole with excellent docking facilities.

You might want to explore the nature trails before dining on one of the outdoor porches. Accessible only by boat or seaplane, Cabbage Key is at Channel Marker 60 on the Intracoastal Waterway. Boats from three areas make the run to Cabbage Key. In the Charlotte Harbour area call (941) 639–0969. In the Fort Myers area call (941) 283–0015. In the Captiva area call (941) 472–7549. Cabbage Key is 5 miles south of Charlotte Harbour on the Intracoastal Waterway near Marker 60. Cabbage Key Hide-Away Inn, P.O. Box 200, Pineland, FL 33945. To reach the inn call (941) 283–2278.

Fort Myers got its start as a military post during the Seminole Indian wars. Abandoned after a brief occupation by Federal troops during the Civil War, the fort became the center of a tiny village reached, in those days, by boat. Majestic palm-lined avenues and a profusion of exotic flowers and fruit trees contribute to Fort Myers' tropical good looks.

Thomas Edison, who made his winter home here, imported 200 royal palms from Cuba in 1900, starting Fort Myers on its way to being known as a "City of Palms." Edison was a great promoter of Fort Myers and wanted to bestow the fruits of his genius on the local citizenry. Soon after perfecting the electric lamp, he offered to provide the

Enlightenment

Since Southwest Florida is blessed with a fine year-round climate, it makes sense that Thomas Edison came to Fort Myers on his doctor's orders. At thirty-eight he was seriously ill, his health suffering from years of overwork. If he wanted to live, his doctor warned him, he would have to escape the brutal northern winters.

Edison investigated Fort Myers, liked its warm tropical climate and gulf breezes, and proceeded to lead an enormously productive life to the age of eighty-four. The annual trip was not an easy matter in those days. It involved, among other things, a ten-hour sail from Punta Gorda 52 miles to the north. The prescient inventor, who obviously believed the area's attributes far outweighed these inconveniences, declared, "There is only one Fort Myers and 90 million people are going to find it out."

Edison, who spent nearly fifty winters in Fort Myers, is considered the most inventive man who ever lived, but he was also an accomplished horticulturist. His riverfront garden contains more than a thousand varieties of plants imported from all over the world.

Edison's genius is evident throughout his fourteen-acre Caloosahatchee River estate. Here the visitor will find Florida's first modern swimming pool, the couch where Edison took his famous catnaps, the inventor's unique Model-T Ford, and Florida's largest banyan tree.

entire city with electric streetlights. The town voted against the proposal when many expressed fear that the lights would keep the cows from getting a good night's sleep.

Thomas Edison's winter residence, complete with chandeliers still burning with their original carbon filament bulbs, is open to the public. Edison held 1,096 patents, and many of his inventions are on display in the adjoining museum. You cannot help being impressed and inspired by this inventor's philosophy and achievements. Unusual plants and trees from the far corners of the globe flourish on his fourteen-acre homesite on the Caloosahatchee River. Open 9:30 A.M.–5:30 P.M. Monday through Saturday and noon–5:30 P.M. on Sunday; 2350 McGregor Boulevard, Fort Myers, FL 33901; (941) 334–3614.

Those who want to talk to the manatees should head for the **Florida Power and Light Park** on SR 80 east of Fort Myers. The best viewing times are cold mornings, when these endangered "sea cows" are toasting their flippers in the warm waters of the power plant discharge. You may park your car alongside the lagoon south of SR 80. Open daily during daylight hours. Free.

The world is not flat, but round. Columbus proved it and you're sure, right? But can you really be sure that the earth isn't hollow, that life doesn't cover its inner walls, and that the sun isn't actually in the center of this round sphere? If you find these thoughts intriguing, you should stop in at the **Koreshan State Historic Site.**

Dr. Teed, a physician from Chicago, founded a **utopian commune** here

Swamp Buggy Races

*H*unters originally designed swamp buggies to provide access to the boggy Everglades. In fact, these races were first run in 1949 to signal the opening of the Everglades hunting season. Racing these souped-up buggies is the local version of a tractor pull, but, they claim, a lot more fun. The race course is flooded with water for two weeks before the race to assure it is in the worse possible condition. If you want to see these hardy vehicles tackle the celebrated "Mile o' Mud" and the perilous "Sippy Hole," don't miss the Swamp Buggy Races each March, May, and October. Contestants compete in various classes, and at the end of the races the Swamp Buggy Queen is taken for a victory ride around the track and given a royal dunking. The races are held at the Florida Sports Park off SR 951 near Rattlesnake Hammock Road in Golden Gate, Naples; (941) 793–0086.

in the later 1800s. The doctor brought a group with him from Chicago, but the movement never caught on, though some of his followers still publish a newspaper and magazine. For one thing, there were no children to carry the banner for Dr. Teed because he insisted everyone practice celibacy. You may visit the tropical garden and restored village of this pioneer settlement and learn how Dr. Teed went about proving his theories in the museum. This is also a good place to camp and canoe. Open daily 8:00 A.M. to sunset. Guided tours given according to seasonal demand. Take I–75, exit 19. Go 2 miles on Corkscrew Road to Junction 41, Estero, FL 33928; (941) 992–0311.

Naples Area

The city of Naples caters to the upper crust with all the amenities money can buy, but it has not forgotten the less-well-heeled folk who have the run of its splendid 7-mile public beach and *1,000-foot fishing pier.* Shoppers will look a long time before finding such a marvelous assortment of shops. If your credit cards are suffering from lack of use, don't worry. Shopping in Naples is guaranteed to get them back in the swing of things.

Browsers are more than welcome at the *Old Marine Market Place,* better known as Tin City. A carefully preserved part of Naples' past, now restored, awaits right on Naples Bay at 1200 Fifth Avenue South. This old-fashioned shopping bazaar was created from historic boat buildings connected by cobbled and planked river walks and comes complete with waterfront dining and open air markets. Don't miss the chic stores on Third Street and those marvelously posh emporiums on Fifth Avenue.

Longtime Naples resident Michael Watkins, general manager of the landmark Naples Beach Hotel and Golf Club, contends the best way to see this attractive area is by bike. His suggested route includes stops at Lowdermilk Park, the Conservancy Nature Center, Tin City, the restored historic Naples Depot, Cambier Park, Naples Fishing Pier, and the shops on Fifth Avenue and Third Street. In the process you'll pass through some gorgeous residential real estate. Bikes are available for rent at the hotel's front desk, along with complimentary bicycle maps. For information or reservations contact The *Naples Beach Hotel and Golf Club,* 851 Gulf Shore Boulevard North, Naples, FL 33940; (941) 261–2222 or (800) 237–7600.

The *Conservancy of Southwest Florida's Naples Nature Center* is, surprisingly, on a wooded fourteen-acre site right in the middle of Naples. The *Conservancy Museum of Natural History* contains natural history, animal and marine displays, and participatory exhibits. Visitors can touch a snake, count an alligator's teeth, and explore southwest Florida's underwater world through seven different marine aquariums. Be sure to stroll the two nature trails and visit the recuperating animals and birds (mostly eagles, hawks, and owls) in the *Wildlife Rehabilitation Center.* Most are successfully released back into the wild. Naturalist-guided trail walks are offered daily at 11:00 A.M. and 2:00 P.M. Guided electric boat trips run from November through March.

This private, nonprofit organization is dedicated to environmental protection, conservation, wildlife rehabilitation, nature education, and ecological research. The Conservancy of Southwest Florida's Naples Nature Center, 1450 Merrihue Drive, Naples, FL 33942 (1 block east of Goodlette Road). Open Monday through Saturday 9:00 A.M.–4:30 P.M. year-round. January through March open 1:00–5:00 P.M. on Sunday. Nature Center grounds open 9:00 A.M.–4:30 P.M., closed Sunday; (941) 262–0304; Web site: www.conservancy.org.

For casual waterfront dining (on outdoor picnic tables, if you wish), you should seek out the *Lighthouse Restaurant.* While peeling your shrimp and sipping a cold beer, you can watch the water-skiers zip by and the seagulls hover. (Please, heed the sign that asks you NOT to feed the birds. There's a very good reason for it.) The atmosphere is relaxed, the service friendly, and the jumbo sandwiches excellent. Open Wedneday through Sunday 8:00–11:00 A.M. for breakfast, Tuesday through Sunday 11:30 A.M.–9:00 P.M., closed Monday. Lighthouse Restaurant, 9180 Gulf Shore Drive North, Naples, FL 34708; (941) 597–2551. Inexpensive to moderate.

Thirty miles to the south of Naples are the *Ten Thousand Islands.* This maze of mangrove islands teeming with fish and bird life is best approached with a guide. Conducted tours leave from the ranger station, the entrance to the western portion of Everglades National Park. This is literally the jumping-off place, because access to the wilderness is by water.

One of the most satisfying ways to explore these islands, if insect repellent

First inhabited 1,000 years ago by Calusa Indians, Everglades City became a hideout for outlaws, gun and rum runners, and those seeking a simpler life. Unlivable conditions, hordes of mosquitoes, and the threat of attacks from Seminole and Miccosukee Indians thwarted the pioneering spirt of the first American settlers. However, Everglades City experienced economic rebirth when the city was named county seat for Collier County in 1923. Seen as a center of commerce and possible rival to Miami, Everglades City dominated the financial life of lower southwest Florida. That hopeful period came to an end in 1960 when Hurricane Donna swept away the community's chances for a golden future, and the government seat was moved to higher ground.

is at hand, is by canoe. To glide quietly by an egret rookery, to listen to the beat of many wings as flocks pass overhead, and to watch the evening sun beam a path of orange across a silent sea is to know Florida at its very best.

Sight-seeing tours into the Ten Thousand Islands region and the mangrove swamps of the northwestern Everglades leave from the Gulf Coast Ranger Station. For information about boat tours (available year-round) and boat rentals at the Gulf Coast Ranger Station, write the concessioner at Everglades National Park Boat Tours, P.O. Box 119, Everglades City, FL 34139, or call Everglades National Park at (941) 695–2591. Open 9:00 A.M.–4:30 P.M.

Big Cypress Swamp Area

Corkscrew Swamp Sanctuary, maintained by the National Audubon Society, is an 11,000-acre preserve with a dwindling population of wood storks. These rare large birds, dangerously close to extinction, are definitely worth the trip. The most interesting time to visit is from December through March, when the storks nest and breed. Their breeding is timed so that young storks are raised when food is plentiful (which depends entirely on receding water levels to concentrate the fish). An unexpected rainstorm at the wrong time of year can mess up the whole process. (A single family of wood storks requires 440 pounds of food per breeding season!) The frantic activity of the nesting season is something to see. The male gathers the sticks for the nest, the female arranges them, and young storks kick up quite a racket.

The sanctuary also protects the largest stand of virgin bald cypress trees in the country. A boardwalk trail (2¼ miles long) winds through this primeval forest of huge trees, some more than 700 years old! An illustrated self-guiding tour booklet describes plants and animals, and there are members of the staff along the way to answer questions. You'll see lots of birds, turtles, and alligators along with a variety of lush plant life.

Take a lunch to eat in the pleasant picnic area or buy a snack at the lunch concession (open December to April). The sanctuary is located 21 miles east of Naples, 14 miles from Immokalee and 21 miles from U.S. 41. Go east on Immokalee Road (CR 846). Look for Sanctuary Road. The entrance is at the end of Sanctuary Road. No pets admitted, and overnight camping is not permitted within sanctuary boundaries or in parking area. The visitor center and boardwalk are open daily 8:00 A.M.–5:00 P.M.; 7:00 A.M.–5:00 P.M. December through April. For information write: Chief Naturalist, Corkscrew Swamp Sanctuary, 375 Sanctuary Road, Naples, FL 34120, or call (941) 348–9151.

Corkscrew Swamp Sanctuary is at the northern end of **Big Cypress Swamp,** a vast wilderness area administered by the National Park Service. You may explore the swamp by car on Alligator Alley (I–75) and Tamiami Trail (U.S. 41), which are connected by SR 29. The fascinating Loop Road (CR 94) from 40-Mile Bend to Monroe Station is only paved for 8 miles. Be careful on unpaved roads as they can be dusty and rough or, worse, muddy—as in stuck-in-the-mud.

Approximately one-third of Big Cypress is covered by cypress and the rest is given over to prairies of saw grass, mixed hardwood hammocks, marshes, and estuarine mangrove forests. You may also see alligator, wild turkey, deer, mink, bald eagle, ibis, heron, egret, and wood stork. The Big Cypress Visitor Center is 55 miles east of Naples on U.S. 41 in the Preserve. For information write: Park Superintendent, Big Cypress National Preserve, HCR 61, Box 110, Ochopee, FL 34141, or call (941) 695–2000.

Those continuing north on SR 29 will eventually come to Palmdale and the **Cypress Knee Museum.** Tom Gaskins experiments in controlled cypress knee growth, and some of his creations are not to be believed. You'll be fascinated by the museum, which is built around the world's largest transplanted cypress tree. Save the best for last—a $1/2$-mile catwalk stroll through a cypress swamp, cabbage palm and oak hammock, and bayhead.

The sign in front of the museum assures visitors that it was built by a "selfish reactionary" without any help from "city, county, state or federal government" and that it contains "souvenirs of a time before civilization covered the United States." Cypress Knee Museum is 1 mile south of Palmdale, near the junction of U.S. 27 and SR 29, 6870 Highway 27 North, Palmdale, FL 33944. Open daily 8:00 A.M. to sundown; (863) 675–2951.

STATE PARKS OF
SOUTHWEST FLORIDA

Cayo Costa State Park
(941) 964–0375

Collier–Seminole
State Park
(941) 394–3397

Delnor–Wiggins Pass
State Recreation Area
(941) 597–6196

Don Pedro Island
State Recreation Area
(941) 964–0375

Fakahatchee Strand
State Preserve
(941) 695–4593

Gasparilla Island
State Recreation Area
(941) 964–0375

Koreshan State
Historic Site
(941) 992–0311

Lovers Key State
Recreation Area
(941) 463–4588

Myakka River State Park
(941) 361-6511

Oscar Scherer State Park
(941) 483-5956

PLACES TO STAY IN
SOUTHWEST FLORIDA

SARASOTA
Best Western Midtown,
1425 South Tamiami Trail;
(941) 955-9841

The Cypress B & B, 621
Gulfstream Avenue South;
(941) 955-4683

Holiday Inn Express,
6600 South Tamiami Trail;
(941) 924-4900

Wellesley Inn, 1803 North
Tamiami Trail;
(941) 366-5128

Hyatt,
1000 Boulevard of the Arts;
(941) 953-1234

Timberwoods Vacation
Villas, 7964 Timberwood
Circle; (941) 923-4966

FORT MYERS
Hampton Inn, 13000 North
Cleveland Avenue;
(941) 656-4000

Wellesley Inn and Suites,
4400 Ford Street;
(941) 278-3949

Radisson Inn,
12635 Cleveland Avenue;
(941) 936-4300

Sanibel Harbor,
17260 Harbour Pointe
Drive; (941) 466-4000

FORT MYERS BEACH
Best Western Pink Shell,
275 Estero Boulevard;
(941) 463-6181

Sandpiper Gulf Resort,
5550 Estero Boulevard;
(941) 463-5721

Santa Maria,
7317 Estero Boulevard;
(941) 765-6700

The Grand View,
8701 Estero Boulevard;
(941) 765-4422

Visitor Information for Southwest Florida

Charlotte County Visitors Bureau,
1600 *Tamiami Trail, Port Charlotte 33948;*
(941) 743-1900;
Web site: www.pureflorida.com

Lee Island Coast Visitor and Convention Bureau,
2180 West First Street, Suite 100, Ft. Myers 33901;
(800) 237-6444;
Web site: www.leeislandcoast.com

Marco Island Area Chamber of Commerce/Marco Island,
1102 North Collier Boulevard, Marco Island 34145;
(941) 394-7549 or (800) 788-6272;
Web site: www.marco-island-florida.com/chamber

Naples Area Chamber of Commerce,
895 Fifth Avenue South, Naples 34102; (941) 262-6141;
Web site: www.naples-online.com

Sanibel and Captiva Islands Chamber of Commerce,
1159 Causeway Road, Sanibel 33057; (941) 472-1080;
Web site: www.sanibel-captiva.org

Sarasota Convention & Visitors Bureau,
655 North Tamiami Trail, Sarasota 34236;
(800) 522-9799;
Web site: www.sarasotafl.org

Visit Naples, Inc.,
1400 Gulf Shore Boulevard North, Suite 218,
Naples 34102;
(941) 403-2015 or (800) 605-7878;
Web site: www.visitnaples.com

SANIBEL AND CAPTIVA ISLANDS
'Tween Waters Inn,
15951 Captiva Drive,
Captiva Island;
(941) 472-5161

West Wind Inn,
3345 West Gulf Drive,
Sanibel Island;
(941) 472-1541

South Seas Plantation,
13000 Captiva Road,
Captiva Island;
(941) 472-5111

Sundial Beach
& Tennis Resort,
1451 Middle Gulf Drive,
Sanibel Island;
(941) 472-4151

NAPLES
Red Roof,
1925 Davis Boulevard;
(941) 774-3117

Vanderbilt Inn on the Gulf,
9225 Gulf Shore Drive
North; (941) 597-3151

Registry Resort Naples,
475 Seagate Drive;
(941) 597-3147

The Ritz-Carlton, Naples,
280 Vanderbilt Beach Road;
(941) 598-3300

La Playa Beach Resort,
9891 Gulf Shore Drive;
(941) 597-3123

VENICE
Best Western Sandbar
Beach Resort,
811 The Esplanade North;
(941) 488-2251

Holiday Inn,
455 North U.S. 41 Bypass;
(941) 485-5411

Inn at the Beach Resort,
101 The Esplanade South;
(941) 484-8471

MARCO ISLAND
The Boathouse,
1180 Edington Place;
(941) 642-2400

Eagle's Nest Beach Resort,
410 South Collier
Boulevard; (941) 394-5167

Marco Island Hilton Beach
Resort, 560 South Collier
Boulevard;
(941) 394-5000

EVERGLADES CITY
On the banks of the
Everglades, a Bed-
and-Breakfast Inn,
201 West Broadway;
(941) 695-3151

**PLACES TO EAT IN
SOUTHWEST FLORIDA**

SARASOTA
Michael's on East,
1212 East Avenue South;
(941) 366-0007

Bart's Bayside
230 Sarasota Quay;
(941) 954-3839

FORT MYERS
Peter's La Cuisine,
2224 Bay Street;
(941) 332-2228

The Veranda, Second Street
and Broadway;
(941) 332-2065

FORT MYERS BEACH
Anthony's on the Gulf,
3040 Estero Boulevard;
(941) 463-2600

Mucky Duck,
2500 Estero Boulevard;
(941) 463-5519

**SANIBEL AND
CAPTIVA ISLANDS**
The Bubble Room,
15001 Captiva Road,
Captiva; (941) 472-5558

Chadwick's, South Seas
Plantation, 5400 South Seas
Plantation Road;
(941) 472-5111

NAPLES
Chardonnay (French/
Continental),
2331 Tamiami Trail North;
(941) 261-1744

Opus,
5200 Tamiami Trail North;
(941) 261-2555

VENICE
Landmark,
133 South Tamiami Trail;
(941) 485-0668

Sharky's on the Pier
(seafood),
1600 West Harbor Drive;
(941) 488-1456

MARCO ISLAND
Vito's Waterfront,
1079 Bald Eagle Drive;
(941) 394-7722

Southeast Florida

I t's not easy to get off the beaten path in Southeast Florida, but here and there you can do it by seeking out A1A (the closest road to the ocean) rather than I–95, the Florida Turnpike or, heaven forfend, U.S. 1. Try to avoid traveling on major roads in this congested area during rush hours (7:30–9:30 A.M. and 4:30–7:00 P.M. weekdays). A1A will present wonderful seascapes from time to time and is less crowded than U.S. 1. You would be wise to avoid U.S. 1 entirely as it is neither swift nor scenic—merely frustrating.

To reach the Everglades and its grand expanse of saw grass, either U.S. 41, better known locally as Tamiami Trail (for northern access via Shark Valley), or SR 9336 (the road to Flamingo in the south) will take you into the wilderness. Vast prairies of sedge are punctuated by hammocks, stands of pine, and palmetto and freshwater sloughs. Note: If you continue on Tamiami Trail, you'll end up in Tampa. The name is a combination of Tampa and Miami, a historic route completed in 1928 that opened the Everglades to travelers.

Atlantic Coast

S ebastian Inlet State Recreation Area is now an ocean playground, but you would have a hard time telling that to the survivors of the fleet of ships that went down here in 1715. Spanish galleons, loaded with gold and silver, were pummeled by a terrible storm before they sank to the bottom of the sea. At the *McLarty Museum* you'll see artifacts of the Ais Indians, as well as exhibits and dioramas on the Spanish treasure. The salvage efforts, both historic and recent, are a story in themselves.

Located in Sebastian Inlet on SR A1A about midway between Melbourne and Vero Beach, the area offers outstanding fishing and camping. The time to beachcomb for ancient pieces of eight is right after a storm. You'll need a lot of luck, but it's not impossible. Sebastian Inlet State Recreation Area, 9700 South A1A, Melbourne Beach, FL 32951;

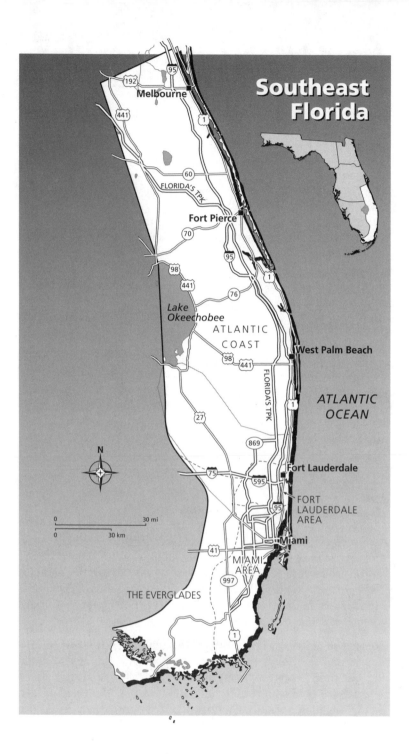

Southeast Florida

192
95
Melbourne
441
1
60
FLORIDA'S TPK
Fort Pierce
70
95
1
98
441
76
Lake
Okeechobee
ATLANTIC
COAST
98
441
West Palm Beach
FLORIDA'S TPK
1
ATLANTIC
OCEAN
27
869
N
75
595
Fort Lauderdale
95
FORT
LAUDERDALE
AREA
0   30 mi
0   30 km
41
Miami
MIAMI
AREA
997
THE EVERGLADES
1

Top Events in Southeast Florida

Art Deco Weekend Festival, Miami Beach, January, (305) 672–2014

Carnival Miami/Calle Ocho, Miami, March, (305) 644–8888

Fort Lauderdale Seafood Festival, Fort Lauderdale, April, (954) 463–4431

Sunfest, West Palm Beach, May, (561) 659–5992

Coconut Grove Goombay Festival, Miami, June, (305) 372–9966

Bon Festival, Delray Beach, August, (561) 495–0233

King Orange Jamboree Parade, Miami, December, (305) 539–3034

(561) 589–2147. For camping reservations call (561) 589–9659. The museum is open 10:00 A.M. to 5:00 P.M. daily year-round.

The **Elliott Museum** is a well-kept secret with many collections. There are shops and rooms representing the 1890s to the 1950s. Also, there are antique automobiles, motorcycles, Seminole artifacts, a baseball memorabilia collection and an art gallery. The museum was built in 1960 by Sterling Elliott's son to house his father's inventions, which included the first addressing machine, a knot-tying machine, and the original quadracycle. On Hutchinson Island's East Ocean Boulevard near Stuart; 825 Northeast Ocean Boulevard, Hutchinson Island, Stuart, FL 34996. Open daily 10:00 A.M.–4:00 P.M.; (561) 225–1961.

The **Gilbert's Bar House of Refuge** (1875) is the last of ten lifesaving stations built by the U.S. Treasury Department in 1875 along the east coast of Florida. Listed on the National Register of Historic Places, the house is furnished with antiques from the 1890s. The site was one of the first living history museums in south Florida. From Stuart take East Ocean Boulevard and turn right at the first stop light on Hutchinson Island. Follow the road through the Indian River Plantation, Marriott Resort, $1^3/_{10}$ miles to the entrance. Open daily 10:00 A.M.–4:00 P.M.; 301 Southeast McArthur Drive, Stuart, FL 34996; (561) 225–1875.

If you'd like to view water traffic negotiating the 14-foot St. Lucie Locks, drive 8 miles southwest of Stuart on SR 76 for a look.

Bass fishermen should head for **Lake Okeechobee,** about 40 miles inland, which is the second-largest lake wholly within the United States. It might encourage you to know that more than 3,500,000 pounds of fish (including both sport and commercial catches) are caught here every year. Take your pick of fishing camps; they are all over the place.

Back on the coast, **Blowing Rock Preserve** on Jupiter Island is worth a ten-minute walk through a pine forest. When a stiff wind is coming out of the northeast, the surf surges through holes in the rocks to create spectacular geysers.

It's only 85 feet high, but in Florida they call it a mountain even if it is only an overgrown sand dune. Add a 25-foot observation tower to Hobe Mountain in *Jonathan Dickinson State Park* and you have a good view of ocean and the surrounding woodlands.

The park was named for a Quaker who was shipwrecked nearby in 1696, discovered by Indians, and who survived all sorts of traumas before getting his wife and baby safely home to Philadelphia. His journal provides valuable insight into early Florida.

An exciting way to see the park is a trip down the Loxahatchee River to Trapper Nelson's camp. The Loxahatchee is the only National Wild and Scenic River in the state of Florida, and you really ought to experience it. Take the thirty-passenger pontoon boat, **Loxahatchee Queen,** or rent a canoe and paddle past the alligators and bald eagles to Trapper Nelson's. The boat ride takes almost two hours; if you paddle yourself, count on three hours. Alas, the legendary Trapper Nelson is no longer with us, but a ranger will fill you in on some of his eccentricities.

A wide range of activities includes fishing (both saltwater and freshwater), boating, camping, and bicycling. The park, on U.S. 1, 6 miles north of Jupiter, is open 8:00 A.M. to sunset year-round, but call if you're interested in the boat trip, because it does not go every day. Jonathan Dickinson State Park, 16450 Southeast Federal Highway, Hobe Sound, FL 33455; (561) 746–1466.

In Jupiter, the 105-foot redbrick *Jupiter Lighthouse* is one of the oldest (1860) lighthouses on the Atlantic coast. Still functioning, it is operated by the Coast Guard as a navigational aid. The lighthouse, beside Jupiter Inlet, provides a fine view of the Gulf Stream. Open 10:00 A.M.–5:00 P.M. Tuesday to Friday, noon–5:00 P.M. Saturday and Sunday. Call (561) 747–6639.

The Palm Beach area was developing slowly until Henry Flagler pushed his famous railroad south. With the railroad's arrival in 1894 and the grand hotels that Flagler built, Palm Beach quickly established, and still holds, a reputation as an enclave for the ultra wealthy. When Flagler planned his own Palm Beach home, he chose the architectural firm that had built the New York Public Library and the U.S. Senate Office Building. Described in the press as "more wonderful than any palace in Europe" and costing $4 million to build and furnish in 1901, Whitehall is a showcase that has been marvelously refurbished as the *Henry Morrison Flagler Museum.* The multimillionaire's private railroad car is on display, as are treasures collected from all over the world. The mansion provides a glimpse into the era before income taxes and sets a new standard for the term opulent. The museum is on Whitehall Way, off Coconut Row, in Palm Beach. The Henry Morrison Flagler Museum,

P.O. Box 969, Palm Beach, FL 33480. Open Tuesday through Saturday 10:00 A.M.–5:00 P.M. and Sunday noon–5:00 P.M.; (561) 655–2833; Web site: www.flagler.org.

The **Norton Museum of Art** has a reputation as one of the foremost small museums in the United States. The museum features a world-renowned permanent collection of European, American, Chinese, and contemporary art, with works by Monet, Picasso, Gauguin, Stuart Davis, and Georgia O'Keefe as well as an ever-changing schedule of special traveling exhibitions. Enjoy lunch in the cafe and shop in the museum store. The gallery is at 1451 South Olive Avenue, West Palm Beach, FL 33401. Open Monday through Saturday 10:00 A.M.–5:00 P.M. and Sunday 1:00–5:00 P.M.; (561) 832–5196; Web site: www.norton.org.

You may never have heard of George Morikami, but you will be impressed with his life story and the **Morikami Museum and Japanese Gardens** he donated. This humble pineapple farmer lived in a modest trailer and never stopped working his fields even though he amassed considerable wealth. You will be asked to remove your shoes (paper slippers provided) before entering the museum, where individual rooms are devoted to the tea ceremony, depict a traditional Japanese bedroom, or contain photographs of George Morikami and the twentieth-century Japanese farming community. The Morikami is the only museum in the United States dedicated exclusively to the living culture of Japan. Explore modern and traditional Japanese culture as well as permanent and changing exhibitions in two museum buildings, a 200-acre park, Japanese gardens and ponds, bonsai gardens, and nature trails. Visit the museum store and the Cornell Cafe, which specializes in Asian foods. Picnicking is permitted in the park. Allow four hours, one hour minimum. The Morikami Museum of Japanese Culture, 4000 Morikami Park Road, Delray Beach, FL 33446. Open Tuesday through Sunday 10:00 A.M.–5:00 P.M.; (561) 495–0233.

Did Architect Addison Mizner ever leave his mark on Boca Raton! In 1918 the forty-five year old, suffering from heart and lung ailments, came to Florida to die. As restless as he was eccentric, he became bored with dying and began designing homes for the super rich. He parlayed his profits into a fortune by wheeling and dealing in real estate and then tackled his real ambition—building a dream city.

Boca Raton Hotel

Construction crews working on the Boca Raton Hotel were appalled at architect Addison Mizner's instant aging techniques. He stomped on beautiful wood floors in hobnailed boots and broke new tiles, then cemented them back together. Frank Lloyd Wright once remarked that many architects had imagination but only Mizner had the courage to let it out of the cage.

He designed *The Cloister* to be a hotel worthy of being the centerpiece for this splendid project and held a grand opening in February 1926. At the time it was the most expensive hundred-room hotel ever built; the style of architecture has been summed up as "Bastard-Spanish-Moorish-Romanesque-Gothic-Renaissance-Bull-Market-Damn-the-Expense." But Florida went quickly from boom to bust and the hotel closed after a single season. Mizner's extravagant vision fizzled, but his pink wedding-cake hotel was destined to play many roles over the years, including one as a World War II barracks.

Today the *Boca Raton Resort and Club,* its original splendor intact, thrives in its reincarnation as a premier resort. The hotel is on Camino Real between U.S. 1 and SR A1A and is on the Intracoastal Waterway across from its seaside extension, the Boca Beach Club. Boca Raton Resort and Club, 501 East Camino Real, Boca Raton, FL 33432; (561) 447–3000; Web site: www.bocaresort.com.

Care to eat where Winston Churchill, Franklin D. Roosevelt, and the Vanderbilts once dined? If that list doesn't impress you, how about Casey Stengel and Jack Dempsey? Both notables and nonnotables have been flocking to *Cap's Place* for a long time because of its excellent fresh fish.

Back in the 1920s, this group of wooden shacks attached to an old barge was floated up the Intracoastal Waterway from Miami to its present location on Cap's Island. Once a center for rum-running and gambling, the restaurant has cleaned up its act, if not its ramshackle appearance, and serves dinner daily from 5:00 P.M.

The trick is knowing how to get there. In Lighthouse Point follow Northeast Twenty-fourth Street toward the ocean. Soon you'll see official looking signs leading the way to Cap's Place. You'll end up in a parking lot. If the boat isn't there, don't worry. It'll arrive soon. After a brief boat ride to the island, a WELCOME TO CAP'S sign hoves into view. The building looks pretty run-down, but say hello to the pelicans roosting in the nearby trees and press on.

Inside you'll find a rattlesnake skin on the wall measuring more than six feet and a sign that says HELP PRESERVE WILDLIFE, THROW A PARTY AT CAP'S. The floors are uneven, but the food is good. You can't miss with a stone crab appetizer (in season), hearts of palm salad, the catch of the day, and Key lime pie. Entrees range from moderate to expensive. The boat ride is free, but tips are appreciated on the return trip. Open seven days a week from 5:30 P.M. Call (954) 941–0418.

Fort Lauderdale Area

Pompano Beach Air Park is the winter home of the **Stars and Stripes,** one of four touring dirigibles in the world. The airship is 192 feet long, 55 feet wide, and 59 feet high. Powered by small engines, it has a cruising speed of 35 mph and can operate eight hours a day for a week on the same amount of fuel it takes to taxi a big jet out to the runway for takeoff. The visitor center is open to the public November through May. Sorry, you can't take a ride, but you will get a good close-up look at this huge flying machine. At 1500 Northeast Fifth Avenue on the west side of Pompano Air Park; (954) 946–8300.

One way to glimpse Fort Lauderdale's glittering Waterways is by cruising on the **Jungle Queen *Riverboat.*** Daily sight-seeing cruises at 10:00 A.M. and 2:00 P.M. (dinner cruise at 7:00 P.M.) go up New River and by Millionaires Row with a stop off at Indian Village to see birds, monkeys, and real live alligator wrestling. You'll learn something about the history of the area, where the cruise liners in Port Everglades are heading, who lives where, and how they made their money. Leaves from Bahia Mar Yachting Center, 801 Seabreeze Boulevard, Fort Lauderdale, FL 33316; (954) 462–5596.

Speaking of cruises, thousands of people cruise to exotic ports of call from *Port Everglades.* More than twenty cruise lines depart from six ultramodern terminals. This is the deepest port between Norfolk and New Orleans and serves more five-star cruise ships than any other port in the nation. You'll get a good view of Port Everglades activity from the Southeast Seventeenth Street Causeway Bridge.

You can watch manatees and tropical fish basking in the warmth of the Port Everglades Power Plant's water discharge from the parking and picnic area on Eisenhower Boulevard and Southeast Twenty-sixth Street.

One of Fort Lauderdale's worst-kept secrets is a restaurant that doesn't advertise and is appropriately named *By Word of Mouth.* Before you are seated, you are shown all the evening's selections and the host or hostess describes the ingredients and methods of preparation. You may select sun-dried tomato and pesto pâté, a salad of smoked turkey with dried cherries and hazelnuts, New Mexican cornbread salad, Key West lobster with Amaretto cream, and then top the whole thing off with chocolate raspberry cake, a house favorite.

By Word of Mouth is at 3200 Northeast Twelfth Avenue in Fort Lauderdale, FL 33334. The word is out. (Being featured in *Gourmet Magazine* took care of that.) Lunch starts at 11:00 A.M. Monday through Friday. Dinner starts at 5:00 P.M. Wednesday through Saturday. You'd better make a reservation; (954) 564–3663. Expensive.

The **Stranahan House** is a gem. When Frank Stranahan came to take charge of the New River overnight camp in 1893, it was the only outpost on a road between Lake Worth and Lemon City (now North Miami). By the late 1890s, Stranahan's trade with the Seminole Indians was at its peak and winter tourism was in its infancy.

Love and marriage entered his life when the first teacher arrived at the new settlement. The couple's restored store/home of classic Florida frontier design is the oldest existing structure in Broward County. The Stranahan House (off Las Olas Boulevard, at the New River tunnel) is at 335 Southeast Sixth Avenue, Fort Lauderdale, FL 33301. Open for tours Wednesday through Saturday 10:00 A.M.–3:00 P.M. and Sunday 1:00–3:00 P.M. Summer hours are Wednesday through Friday 10:00 A.M.–4:00 P.M. Tours begin on the hour. Call (954) 524–4736.

Ever dream of becoming an astronaut or a musical genius? The **Museum of Discovery and Science** provides the opportunity to explore these notions along with many other mysteries of science. Exhibit areas are displayed over two floors including Florida EcoScapes, a bilevel ecology mountain complete with live animal and plant species; Space Base, a simulation of the weightlessness of space on a Manned Maneuvering Unit; KidScience, featuring its own whimsical musical staircase; and Choose Health, an interactive examination of how nutrition and controlled substances affect the human body.

Play a game of virtual volleyball. Spin like a "human hurricane." Lift a 500-pound weight with a giant lever. Program a robot. You can do it all at Gizmo City, one of the museum's exciting permanent exhibits. One of the museum's most popular attractions is the five-story-high Blockbuster **IMAX® 3-D Theater** with a larger-than-life technique that allows viewers to "feel" the momentum of high-flying special effects. The Museum of Discovery and Science and its theater are at 401 Southwest Second Street on downtown Fort Lauderdale's historic Riverwalk, (33312). Exhibit hours are 10:00 A.M.–5:00 P.M. Monday through Saturday and noon–6:00 P.M. Sunday. It is the northern anchor of Broward

OTHER ATTRACTIONS WORTH SEEING IN SOUTHEAST FLORIDA

Museums of Science and Space Transit Planetarium, Miami

Miami Metrozoo, Miami

Miami Seaquarium, Miami

Fairchild Tropical Garden, Miami

Worth Avenue, Palm Beach

Lion Country Safari, Loxahatchee

Butterfly World, Coconut Creek

Everglades Alligator Farm, Homestead

County's Arts and Science District across from the Broward Center for the Performing Arts; (954) 467–6637; Web site: www.mods.org.

Fort Lauderdale's multimillion-dollar *Museum of Art* is a real prize. Some have called its astonishing twentieth-century collection "unsettling" and "disturbing," but none has denied its vitality. The impressive fan-shaped museum features six distinctive exhibition spaces, a sculpture terrace, gift shop, and art library. It contains the largest collection of ethnographic material in Florida encompassing Oceanic, West African, pre-Columbian, and American Indian art.

The museum is at One East Las Olas Boulevard, Fort Lauderdale, FL 33301. Open Tuesday through Sunday 10:00 A.M.–5:00 P.M., Friday 10:00 A.M.– 8:00 P.M.; closed Monday and all national holidays. Parking is available at the municipal parking facility on Southeast First Avenue that borders the museum on the east. Ask for hours of free public tours. Call (954) 525–5500.

The largest tree in Florida, a cluster fig 49 feet in circumference and 108 feet tall, keeps right on growing at *Flamingo Gardens.* That's just the beginning. There are also sixty acres of botanical gardens, an Everglades wildlife sanctuary, a tram ride through citrus groves, alligators, and peacocks. This is your chance to see a sausage tree, an African tulip tree, and a gumbo limbo, along with other exotic plants and trees. West of Hollywood off SR 84 at 3750 Flamingo Road, Fort Lauderdale, FL 33330. Open 9:30 A.M.–5:30 P.M. daily; (954) 473–2955.

Everglades Holiday Park is a gateway to the largest subtropical wilderness in the continental United States. One way to get acquainted with the Everglades is by a guided hour-long airboat ride. Tours run continuously from 9:00 A.M. to 5:00 P.M. daily. You'll see alligators, exotic birds, and an endless expanse of saw grass. The park is at the end of Griffin Road west of U.S. 27, about thirty minutes from Fort Lauderdale and Miami; 21940 Griffin Road, Fort Lauderdale, FL 33332. Call (954) 434–8111; Web site: www.introweb.com\Everglades.

In Fort Lauderdale when they refer to Davie, Florida, as "out west," they aren't just kidding. Davie is an authentic western town full of real live cowboys and cowgirls. If you'd like to look like they do, stop in at

Art Deco Dreaming

The Art Deco style became wildly popular during the decade following the 1925 Exposition Internationale des Arts Décoratifs et Industriels Modernes in Paris. The Art Deco hotels, along and near Ocean Drive in South Beach, were slated to be demolished to make way for modern high-rises when Barbara Capitman, vowing to protect them, founded the Miami Design Preservation League. Three years of intense effort resulted in a square mile of these architectural treasures being included on the National Register of Historic Places, the first twentieth-century district to qualify. Today visitors throng to the district, thanks to a revival of interest in this unique style of architecture and publicity generated by Gloria Estefan and other celebrities.

Grifs Western Store, which smells very leathery and sells all manner of boots, hats, shirts, jeans, and saddles. Even the Davie McDonald's sports a corral with salt licks, watering troughs, and hitching posts for your steed.

Come Wednesday night, folks gather in the domed **Davie Rodeo Arena** for some good old-fashioned steer wrestling, calf roping, and bull riding. This is, by the way, the only weekly jackpot rodeo between Key West and Maine. The rodeo, which begins at 8:00 P.M., is on Griffin Road at Davie Road in Davie, FL 33314; (954) 384–7075.

Miami Area

It's amazing what money can do. Publisher William Randolph Hearst wanted a Spanish monastery at his San Simeon castle in California, so he bought the **Cloisters of the Monastery of St. Bernard de Clairvaux** and had it shipped from Europe. Only it wasn't quite as simple as it sounds. The monastery arrived in this country in 10,751 crates, but Florida customs officers wouldn't release them because they were worried about hoof-and-mouth bacteria in the packing hay. The monastery was finally reassembled, one piece of stone at a time, after Hearst's death. Built in 1141, this is the oldest building in this hemisphere. You can still see the marks early stonemasons carved in the rock. Open Sunday 1:00–5:00 P.M. and 10:00 A.M.–4:00 P.M. Monday through Saturday. Located at 16711 West Dixie Highway in North Miami Beach, FL 33160; (305) 945–1462.

Some of the smaller hotels at the south end of Miami Beach have been getting face-lifts, and the heritage of old Miami is being preserved in the process. A square-mile area featuring the distinctive resort atmosphere of the late 1920s and 1930s is being restored. Officially known as the **Miami Beach Historic Architectural District** (fondly called the "Art Deco District"), this section contains the nation's largest collection of Art Deco structures. The buildings, totaling more than 800, are the first twentieth-century structures to be included on the National Register of Historic Places. The Art Deco District stretches from Sixth to Twenty-third Streets between Alton Road and the ocean in Miami Beach. Tours are available every Saturday and Thursday beginning at 10:30 A.M. on Saturday and 6:30 P.M. on Thursday, from the Art Deco Welcome Center (which is open every day 10:00 A.M.–6:00 P.M.) at 1001 Ocean Drive in Miami Beach 33119–0180; (305) 672–2014.

South Beach, a unique blend of glitz, glamour, and old-fashioned neighborhood, has become *the* trendy place to be. Young, old, black, white, straight, gay, Jewish, Christian, rich, and poor—they're all here and proud of it. At the south end of Miami Beach and barely a square mile in size, our very own "America Riviera" has become much more than an international playground. This world-class film and entertainment center, known for its ideal weather and fascinating mix of people, is home to a world-class ballet, symphony, opera, theaters, art galleries, dance clubs, jazz cafes, outdoor concerts, and an impressive collection of museums.

If you have time for only one South Beach museum, make it the **Wolfsonian.** This 70,000-piece, mixed-media museum showcasing the propaganda arts of the nineteenth and twentieth centuries is housed in an excellent example of Art Deco architecture. You will be intrigued by this investigation into the ways in which design shapes and reflects human experience. Open 11:00 A.M.–6:00 P.M. Tuesday through Saturday, noon–5:00 P.M. Sunday. The Wolfsonian, Florida International University, 1001 Washington Avenue, Miami Beach, FL 33139; (305) 531–1001.

Known for innovative New World cuisine, South Beach offers a variety of culinary adventures. The quintessential South Beach experience, however, is still alfresco dining at one of the popular outdoor cafes. The *News Cafe,* facing the great Atlantic Ocean, is a clear favorite. The idea was to create a pleasant environment where folks could hang out, read a paper over a leisurely cup of coffee, people watch, and listen to good music. Since its beginning in 1988, News Cafe has provided patrons with a variety of newspapers and magazines.

The original eight-seat ice cream parlor has evolved into a 350-seat cafe, and the news-

Art Deco District

The Dream City of Opa-Locka

Arabian-style architecture complete with pink minarets and golden domes mark Opa-Locka. Consisting of more than ninety Moorish buildings constructed during the 1920s' boom, this was once the dream city of aviator Glenn Curtiss. Inspired by the tales of The Arabian Nights, *Curtiss financed the construction of this modern-day "Baghdad of Dade County," but the area is now depressed. Visitors are cautioned not to wander far from the restored City Hall at Opa-Locka and Sharasad boulevards. Opa-Locka is at the junction of NW 27th and NW 135th St., 10 miles northwest of downtown Miami.*

stand has grown into a well-stocked news store. The food is excellent. Try the fried calamari, a cold cup of gazpacho, bruschetta (Italian bread, tomato, and herbs), or perhaps a tabouli salad of parsley and bulgar wheat. Still watching the world Rollerblade by? You might want to linger over a cappuccino with Frangelico. Open twenty-four hours a day. News Cafe is in South Beach at 800 Ocean Drive, Miami Beach 33139; (305) 538–6397.

Let's say you're a rock climber and find yourself in Florida. Poor choice of a place to be, you say? Not at all. You should head straight for the **Eden Roc Resort and Spa** on Miami Beach and check out the latest trend in fitness challenges—a rock climbing wall. This is the first such wall in the entire state. Here you can climb to your heart's content with other rock climbing buffs and enjoy the facilities of a first-class hotel in the process.

But the wall is just the beginning. The Eden Roc boasts the Spa of Eden, the largest oceanfront spa in the United States. This place has everything! Its new Lifestyles Wellness Center features programs that focus on inner health and well-being. The goal—nothing less than living life to the fullest. Think about it. When was your last Lavender Turkish scrub?

The spa's sports medicine complex comes complete with a resident exercise physiologist to conduct personal fitness and body fat evaluations. The physiologist can help determine the appropriate training level for each individual guest. An oceanfront cardiovascular theater provides the latest in computerized treadmills, cycling and stair-climbing equipment and a sixteen-channel personal audiovisual system so that you can tune into the music or TV program of your choice during your workout. A weight room featuring state-of-the-art equipment also enjoys a commanding view of the ocean.

A wide range of daily aerobics classes includes a variety of step, slide, and high- and low-impact choreography. Or you may prefer instruction in such innovative fitness techniques as yoga, ballet, and martial arts. Basketball courts, international squash courts, a racquetball court, an Olympic-size lap pool, an oceanside pool, and a private marina complete this extensive complex. A full complement of water sports and recreational activities offered daily from the beach includes SCUBA, kayaking, jet skiing, sailing, and parasailing.

OK, OK, but where do you eat? You have a choice. Harry's Grille is a Mediterranean-themed restaurant featuring Black Angus steaks, local seafood, and gourmet pizzas and pastas.

Prefer something more casual? Jimmy Johnson's Three Rings Bar & Grill is a sports bar with TVs (and enthusiastic fans) everywhere you look. The atmosphere of this seaside eatery is very casual, and you may eat inside or outside on the expansive deck.

No wonder this is such a popular watering hole for locals as well as resort guests. The cuisine is "Floribbean," a unique blend of Florida and Caribbean cuisine (be sure to try the sweet potato fries), but the menu ought to come with a generous-portion warning. Spa goers alert! If you kick off with the super nachos, you better have at least six friends to help polish them off. The mud pie is indeed the tallest north of the South Pole, as advertised. And the double fudge brownie packs enough caloric punch to erase a week of serious fitness training. Eden Roc Resort and Spa, 4525 Collins Avenue, Miami Beach, FL 33140; (800) 327–8337 or (305) 531–0000.

The **Sonesta Beach Resort** on Key Biscayne has a terrific "Just Us Kids" program for children ages five to thirteen. Well-trained counselors supervise a wide range of fun (as well as educational) activities. Kids are taken on excursions to Metro Zoo, The Science Museum, and Seaquarium. There are also beach and pool activities, contests, games, movies, and crafts classes. Kids can participate in any part of each day's activities. The program is offered to hotel guests at no extra charge with the exception of

The American Police Hall of Fame

*T*he morbidly curious may want to experience being strapped into an electric chair, without, of course, a jolt of the juice. Or maybe you'd like to inspect a gas chamber and imagine what it must be like to breathe deeply of lethal fumes. If you're into weapons and aren't allergic to gore, this may be a fine attraction for you. I hasten to add that not all the exhibits are gruesome, and it's hard not to be moved by the huge memorial to more than 5,000 American police officers killed in the line of duty. Let's just say that the American Police Hall of Fame is not everyone's cup of tea. Located at 3801 Biscayne Boulevard; (305) 573–0070.

the child's entrance fee to commercial attractions. Sonesta Beach Resort, 350 Ocean Drive, Key Biscayne, FL 33149; (305) 361–2021.

A distinctly Latin flavor permeates Miami, but it is most highly concentrated in its Cuban community. The Hispanic heart of the city is found in the colorful section of southwestern Miami known as *Little Havana.* This cluster of restaurants, nightclubs, cigar factories, fruit stands, and shops pulses with the energy of these lively, voluble people. Lingering over an aromatic cup of Cuban coffee and listening to Spanish may make you forget what country you're in. Little Havana is a 30-block strip on Southwest Eighth Street (known here as Calle Ocho), Miami.

Vizcaya Museum and Gardens is a must-see. Vizcaya is James Deering's Italian Renaissance palace, one of the finest homes ever built in America. Deering, vice president of International Harvester, spent twenty years collecting priceless treasures from around the world before beginning to build a home for them in 1914. After a global search, he selected Biscayne Bay as the ideal location for his winter retreat. The seventy-room villa was finished in 1916 and the formal gardens took five years to complete, with as many as a thousand artisans working at a time. The result is a magnificent achievement featuring an extraordinary collection of furnishings and art objects as well as gardens that have been called "the finest in the Western Hemisphere." 3251 South Miami Avenue, Miami, FL 33129. Open daily except Christmas Day 9:30 A.M.–4:30 P.M. Guided tours available. Call (305) 250–9133.

Be sure to take a leisurely drive through *Coral Gables,* one of the country's richest neighborhoods, to admire live oaks, Spanish-style homes, the Baroque-style Coral Gables Congregational Church, and the beautifully restored Biltmore Hotel.

If you overnight at the *Mayfair House Hotel,* you'll be in the heart of Miami's trendy Coconut Grove shopping and dining village, an enclave of exclusive boutiques, restaurants, and entertainment. A brief stroll in one direction takes you to CocoWalk, a lively open-air mall; walk the other way for the upscale shops and cafes of the Streets of Mayfair.

The Mayfair House Hotel is as much an experience as it is a place to spend the night. Each of 179 individually named suites has its own character and design and comes with a Japanese hot tub or marble Roman whirlpool bath, hand-carved mahogany furniture, and private terrace. Fifty rooms harbor antique British pianos!

And that's not all. In the midst of the largest orchid garden of any hotel in South Florida is the romantic, open-air Orchids Champagne Court.

CocoWalk

Ask someone to point out the Mayfair orchid, specially developed and named for the hotel's gardens. If weather is inclement, you may sip your bubbly indoors in romantic alcoves or at the marble Champagne and Wine Bar. Want something to nibble on? Ask to see the tapas menu. The Mayfair House, a Mobil Four-Star, AAA Four Diamond Hotel, is at 3000 Florida Avenue, Coconut Grove, FL 33133; (305) 441–0000.

For a memorable evening at the theater, check out the **Coconut Grove Playhouse,** nationally recognized for its original productions, or, if you prefer, settle into a leisurely dinner. Favorite restaurants include Ortanique on the Mile (the Miracle Mile in Coral Gables), Norman's (also in Coral Gables), and Mayfair Grill (Coconut Grove)—all renowned for their succulent New World Cuisine.

The historic pioneer home known as **The Barnacle** (1891) once belonged to one of Coconut Grove's earliest settlers, Ralph Middleton Munroe. This photographer and naval architect named the tiny village "Coconut Grove" and helped the settlement grow by encouraging his influential northern friends to visit. The resourceful Mr. Munroe first built a one-story building of wood salvaged from shipwrecks. Later, he jacked the house up on stilts and added a new first floor to make room for his growing family. Take note of Munroe's ingenious "air-conditioning" system and enjoy the lushly landscaped grounds. Guided tours are Monday, Friday, Saturday, and Sunday 9:00 A.M.–4:00 P.M. Barnacle State Historic Site, 3485 Main Highway, Coconut Grove, FL 33133; (305) 448–9445.

In 1895 early settlers to Coconut Grove built **Plymouth Congregational Church,** which is considered South Florida's finest example of Spanish Mission architecture. Vines cover the twin belfry towers, a peacock saunters about the grounds, and the church is surrounded by native flora. No wonder this is the most sought-after wedding chapel in Miami. It is located at Main Highway and Devon Road at 3400 Devon Road, Coconut Grove, FL 33133; (305) 444–6521.

Plymouth Congregational Church

The amazing thing about **Hotel Place St. Michel,** with its vaulted ceilings, graceful arches, Spanish tiles, and antique furnishings, is that you don't need a passport to get there. This small, European-style inn has mastered the little touches that mean so much to the traveler—a basket of fruit on arrival, a newspaper delivered to your door each morning, and a hearty continental breakfast (included in the price of the room) to get you going. (Their warm, flaky croissants are immense!)

The hotel (built in 1926) has been beautifully restored, and each of the thirty rooms has its own distinct personality. Along with all the charm, it's nice to have air-conditioning, a phone, a color TV, and a friendly face at the desk eager to help.

It's also wonderfully convenient to have a relaxing piano bar and elegant French restaurant (**Restaurant St. Michel**) just an elevator ride away. Breakfast is 7:00–9:30 A.M., lunch 11:00 A.M.– 2:30 P.M., dinner 5:30–10:30 P.M. (11:30 P.M. on weekends). Expensive. Sunday brunch is 11:00 A.M.–2:30 P.M.

Hotel Place St. Michel and Restaurant are on the corner of Ponce de Leon Boulevard and Alcazar Avenue at 162 Alcazar Avenue, Coral Gables, FL 33134. Hotel: (305) 444–1666 or (800) 848–4683; restaurant: (305) 446–6572.

Parrot Jungle will delight the entire family. This lush setting with brilliantly colored tropical birds flying freely among flowering plants and trees is unique. Parrot Jungle is the only natural subtropical jungle and gardens in the United States. Besides the abundance of natural beauty, trained parrots and macaws play poker, roller-skate, and ride bicycles in trained bird shows every one and a half hours. A wildlife show, presented four times each day, features indigenous south Florida wildlife.

Take time to stroll leisurely along the walkways through the gardens and cactus ravine; it's hard to miss the shocking-pink flamingos at Flamingo Lake. The cafeteria serves both breakfast and lunch. Open daily 9:30 A.M.–6:00 P.M.; 11 miles south of Miami, 2$\frac{1}{2}$ miles off U.S. 1. Parrot Jungle, 11000 Southwest Fifty-seventh Avenue, Miami, FL 33156; (305) 666–7834.

Here's a switch. At Monkey Jungle you're in the cage, and the monkeys run free. Hundreds of monkeys, gorillas, baboons, and trained chimpanzees swinging freely through a Florida rain forest obviously get a kick out of seeing you confined. Visitors enjoy performances daily in this unusual attraction that boasts the most complete collection of simians in the United States. Be sure to see the Wild Monkey Swimming Pool, the orangutan family, "King" the lowland gorilla, and the chimpanzee twins.

Monkey Jungle is also the site of one of the richest fossil deposits in southern Forida, including evidence linking the 10,000-year-old Paleo Indians to south Florida. More than 5,000 specimens have been unearthed from the limestone pit housing Florida alligators. Open 9:30 A.M.–5:00 P.M. Take Florida Turnpike's Homestead Extension (Highway 821) south to exit 11 (Cutler Ridge Boulevard/Southwest 216th Street). Once on 216th Street, go west 5 miles. Or take U.S. 1 south to 216th Street and go west 3 miles. Monkey Jungle, 14805 Southwest 216th Street, Miami, FL 33170; (305) 235–1611.

You shouldn't leave south Florida without spending some tranquil time amidst its lush foliage. *Fairchild Tropical Garden,* with its renowned collection of palms, cycads, and other plants, will fill the bill nicely. Tram tours, leaving from the Garden Shop on the hour, follow a path through informal groupings of plants and beside peaceful meadows and lakes. This eighty-three-acre garden's offerings include a rain forest, an endangered species garden, a Mayan fruit garden, and a palmetum housing a collection of some 900 of the world's 2,600 known species of palms. Guided walking tours of the palmetum, the arboretum, and the conservatory are offered seasonally. The garden is open 9:30 A.M.–4:30 P.M. every day except Christmas. Fairchild Tropical Garden, 10901 Old Cutler Road, Miami, FL 33156; (305) 667–1651; Web site: www.ftg.org.

A Park Is Born

Is there such a thing as a strawberryolic? If you're one (you know who you are), better hunker down beside **Burr's Strawberry Farm** because you'll never want to leave. Fresh strawberries are the main item here, but there are also tomatoes, pecans, strawberry ice, and ice-cream sundaes featuring pineapple, mango, coconut, and—surprise—strawberry. A strawberry milkshake is a must. Burr's is at 12761 Southwest 216th Street (near Homestead on the road to the Monkey Jungle). Open only during the winter months.

The folks at the **Knaus Berry Farm** make the best black bottom cake on the entire earth—not to mention outstanding cinnamon rolls, homemade breads (try the dilly bread), herb bread sticks, cookies, and, of course, berry pies, berry ice cream, and berry jellies. These folks know how to grow a strawberry.

The families who run this vegetable stand/bakery/ice-cream stand may look Amish with their long beards, black hats, bonnets, and shawls, but they're German Baptists. They believe in peace, brotherhood, temperance, and simple living. Because they are baptized by triple immersion, they are sometimes called Dunkers, which comes from the German *tunken,* meaning to immerse.

Their stand is open 8:00 A.M.–5:30 P.M. from mid-November to late April. Knaus Berry Farm, 15980 Southwest 248th Street, Coconut Palm Drive, Homestead, FL 33031; (305) 247–0668.

Brilliantly colored tropical fish dart among the reefs, and dense forests of exotic trees, ferns, vines, shrubs, and flowers cover the low-lying land of **Biscayne National Park,** a marine park and sanctuary for marine life, water birds, boaters, snorkelers, and divers. Since most of Biscayne National Park is underwater, the only way to really tour it is by boat. This, by the way, is the largest marine sanctuary administered by the National Park Service. Certainly the tiny Convoy Point Visitor Center exhibit and few nearby picnic tables are, in themselves, hardly worth the trip. However, a park concessionaire at Convoy Point offers **glass-bottom-boat tours** and **snorkeling trips** to the reefs, as well as island excursions for picnicking, camping, and hiking.

Biscayne has a subtropical climate that is warm and wet from May through October and mild and dry from November through April. Temperatures hover in the high 80s and low 90s in summer and range from the 60s to the low 80s in winter. High humidity and abundant sunshine are year-round features. Summer, the peak season for tropical storms and hurricanes, typically brings brief, torrential afternoon thunderstorms, but this is also the best time for diving and snorkeling because of the warmth and clarity of the water.

Convoy Point Visitor Center is 9 miles east of Homestead on North Canal Drive (Southwest 328th Street) adjacent to Homestead Bayfront Park. Access to park islands and most of the marine sanctuary is by boat only. Biscayne National Underwater Park, Inc., P.O. Box 1270, Homestead, FL 33030; (305) 230–1100.

> ### How the Alligator Got Its Name
>
> *Early Spanish settlers called this reptile "el largarto," the lizard. Alligator is the corruption by English settlers of the Spanish name.*
>
> *Crocodiles, much less common than alligators, are distinguished by their narrow snouts and greenish-gray color. The only crocodiles in the United States are found in southern Florida.*

The Everglades

here is no place like the Everglades anywhere on the planet. The Indians named it well. They called it *Pa-hay-okee,* which means grassy waters. Much of this unique wilderness consists of a shallow river percolating slowly toward the sea through a vast expanse of grass. Unlike any other river on earth, this one is 50 miles wide and a mere 6 inches deep. The water drops ever so gradually, only 15 feet over its entire 100-mile course. This is the country's largest remaining subtropical wilderness.

The river of grass seeps southward from Lake Okeechobee to the mangrove-lined rivers along the Gulf Coast through a transition zone where temperate climate blends with subtropic. The many different habitats along the way teem with life. Some plants and animals are tropical species native to the Caribbean Islands. Others are from the temperate zone.

Today the Everglades has generally come to mean all the various environments in the approximately one and a half million acres encompassed by **Everglades National Park.** Visitors reach the park by taking SR 9336 to the main park entrance, approximately $10\frac{1}{2}$ miles southwest of Homestead, Florida. The park road ends at Flamingo on the southern tip of the Florida mainland, a distance of 38 miles from the entrance.

The first thing a visitor will be aware of on the drive from the main entrance are vast prairies of 10-foot-high sedge, which make up the greatest concentration of saw grass in the world. But just as vital to the intricate balance of life are mounded islands called hammocks rising above the river of grass, stands of pine and palmetto, and fresh-water sloughs.

Labyrinthian mangrove forests, shallow offshore bays, and the many dollops of land known as the **Ten Thousand Islands** also are vital parts of this complex Everglades picture. Ten thousand is really just an approximation because new islands are being formed all the time, some consisting of only a few salt-tolerant mangrove trees. The area has a reputation as a fertile fishing ground, and the bird activity, especially at sunset, is impressive. This watery wilderness is easy to become lost in; it's a good idea to arrange for a guide or join a boat tour in Everglades City.

Everglades' Birthday

*W*e were houseboating in the Everglades to escape irritating interruptions that had been running roughshod over our lives. How was I to know it would be a week of constant interruptions. The first morning out I was drying a dish when Suzi squealed from the front deck. I raced through the houseboat like someone who had never seen a dolphin run and leap before the bow. (Which I hadn't.) The fifteen-minute dolphin show was, I hasten to add, well worth the run.

I was stowing blankets and pillows away when a tarpon showed his golden back not five feet from the boat. The fish cooperatively repeated his performance for me, to the extreme frustration of our son, who was casting right over it.

I was making up the beds for the night when they called me to the sundeck to watch the pelicans make their awkward landings on a nearby island.

Even the interruptions had interruptions. I was trying to photograph an osprey flying by with a fish in its talons when the dolphins popped right up in front of me.

If I had to be reminded of the passage of time by a birthday, a houseboat meandering through the Everglades proved a fine place for such a reminder. There were so many gifts—the sight of a bald eagle regally surveying his domain from atop a dead tree, hugs and kisses from everyone, a glimpse of a great blue heron making his dainty-footed way along the shoreline, and fresh trout for dinner.

Sitting on the deck thinking of the time going by, I felt that here it was easier. Here there was not so much emphasis on the accumulation of years as there was on the pleasure of being alive.

And isn't this the way life should be lived more of the time? Routine chores interrupted by the glimpse of a sunning alligator, a roseate spoonbill, or a spectacular sunset. A white ibis to watch while drying the dishes, a dolphin to guide the way.

And time . . . time to open oneself to the lure of the Everglades.

Pack the Repellent

*T*he Everglade's subtropical climate governs its life. The nearly uniform warm, sunny weather makes the park a year-round attraction, but there are two distinct seasons. Winter is dry, and summer is very wet. Heavy rains fall during intense storms from May through October. Rainfall can exceed 50 inches a year. Warm, humid conditions bring out hordes of mosquitoes, sand-flies, and other biting insects that are an important part of intricate food chains.

In the past, few comprehended the true value of the Glades in terms of sheer food production. This natural nursery ground supplies much of the Gulf with shrimp and the entire eastern seaboard, including New England, with fish. As a spawning ground, it is irreplaceable.

The value of the Everglades reaches far beyond a multimillion-dollar fishing industry. Few places anywhere offer greater variety of beautiful, rare, and interesting birds. About 300 species have been identified in the park, with large water birds—herons, egrets, ibises, and spoon-bills—getting the greatest share of attention. The sprawling mangrove wilderness, one of the world's most unusual plant communities, is refuge for panther, bobcat, deer, raccoon, diamondback terrapin, alligator, dolphin, and manatee as well as a wide variety of fish.

Visitors to the park who expect grand scenery in the tradition of soaring mountains or great canyons will be disappointed. Getting to know the Glades is like any worthwhile relationship. It takes time. The trick to appreciating this wilderness is to be able to absorb its subtleties, and that cannot be done from behind the windows of a car. Trails range from easy walks of less than half a mile to more strenuous 14-mile hikes. There is as much life per square inch as anywhere else on earth, but this is not the kind of environment that overwhelms. This is a place that whispers.

Park officials recommend that you begin your visit with a stop at the Main Visitor Center near the main park entrance on SR 9336. There you may view a short film explaining the interrelationships of man and nature in the Everglades and pick up information that will help you understand the environment and plan your time wisely. Natural-ists give hikes, talks, canoe trips, tram tours, and demonstrations throughout the year. Activities change daily. Campfire programs are offered during the winter months. One day there may be a sunrise bird walk or a paddle out into Florida Bay or a slough slog cross-coun-try or a moonlight tram tour. Ask at the visitor center for schedules.

The Cutting Edge

Saw grass in one of the oldest sedges known. Unlike regular grass, which has a hollow stem, sedge has a solid triangular stem. Blades of this plant are edged with razor-sharp, sawlike teeth.

Other entrances to the park are at Shark Valley on the Tamiami Trail (U.S. 41) and at Everglades City in the northwest corner of the park.

Whether you choose to canoe through the Ten Thousand Islands, cruise the **Wilderness Waterway** by outboard, take a swamp tromp with a naturalist, or explore the various trails on your own, you will be well rewarded. You'll soon discover that the Everglades is as much an experience as it is a place. It is the incomparable pleasure of watching a great blue heron make his dainty-footed way along the shoreline, of coming upon a flock of roseate spoonbills feeding, or of listening to a dolphin take a long, deep breath. To see egrets streaming across a sinking orange sun is to glimpse but a sliver of the abundant beauty in this mysterious, ancient land.

For motel or cabin reservations for the **Flamingo Lodge** write Flamingo Lodge, Marina and Outpost, Flamingo, FL 33034. (The food at Flamingo Lodge, by the way, is very good.) Motel and cabin reservations should be made well in advance by calling (941) 695–3101 or (800) 600–3813. Some facilities are closed between June 1 and October 31, so be sure to call ahead.

Park campgrounds—located at Long Pine Key, Flamingo, and Chekika—provide drinking water, picnic tables, grills, tent and trailer pads, and rest rooms. Flamingo has cold-water showers. Recreation vehicles are permitted, but there are no electrical, water, or sewage hookups. Campground stays are limited to fourteen days from December 1 to March 31. You may camp at other designated sites, on beaches, or in backcountry. Access is either on foot or by boat. You must first obtain a backcountry use permit.

You may explore well-marked canoe trails or chart your own course. Choose livery service or a complete camping outfit that meets the special requirements for canoeing in the Everglades.

The Wilderness Waterway, a well-marked inland water route runs from Flamingo to Everglades City. Sequentially numbered markers guide you over its 99 miles. Boats more than 18 feet long or with high cabins and windshields should not attempt the route because of narrow channels and overhanging foliage in some areas. The route requires a minimum of six hours with outboard motor or seven days by canoe. One-day round-trips are not recommended.

Campsites are available along the route. Be sure to notify a park ranger at either Flamingo or Everglades City both at the start and the end of your trip. The Flamingo marina, which can accommodate boats up to 60 feet long, rents houseboats, small powered skiffs, and canoes. Year-round boat tours at Flamingo travel through the mangrove wilderness and into Florida Bay.

Sight-seeing boats go into the Ten Thousand Islands region and the mangrove swamps of the northwestern Everglades. These concession-operated tours leave from the Gulf Coast Ranger Station. For information about boat tours and canoe rentals at the Gulf Coast Ranger Station, write the concessioner at Everglades National Park Boat Tours, P.O. Box 119, Everglades City, FL 33929. Open 9:00 A.M.– 5:00 P.M.; (941) 695–2591.

Shark Valley lies off U.S. 41, the Tamiami Trail. Here, along the 15-mile loop road, you may see a variety of wildlife that inhabits the wide, shallow waterway, which eventually empties into Shark River. Alligators, otters, snakes, turtles, and birds, including rare wood storks and the snail kite, are native to this watery expanse. Hardwood hammocks and other tree islands dot the landscape. The loop road is used for tram rides, biking, and walking. An observation tower along the road provides a spectacular view. Reservations are recommended for tram rides during the busy winter season. For further information contact the Everglades Park Superintendent, 40001 State Road 9336, Homestead, FL 33034–6733. For tram tours call (305) 221–8455. The park office number is (305) 221–8776.

It's hard to believe the *Miccosukee Indian Village* in the Florida Everglades is just 25 miles west of the gleaming towers of downtown Miami. Approximately 600 contemporary Miccosukees are descendants of some fifty tribespeople who escaped deportation from the United States during the Indian Wars of the nineteenth century.

Guided tours include the village of chickee huts where tribal members lived in traditional fashion. You may watch Indians wrestle alligators, take an adventurous airboat ride through the Everglades, or visit the Indian Museum, which features artifacts from various tribes.

Members of the Miccosukee tribe create and sell handmade dolls, wood carvings, beadwork, basketry, jewelry, and other crafts. The restaurant features authentic Miccosukee dishes along with standard American fare. Twenty-five miles west of Miami on U.S. 41 (Tamiami Trail), P.O. Box 440021, Miami, FL 33144. Open daily 9:00 A.M.–5:00 P.M.; (305) 223–8380.

Visitor Information for Southeast Florida

Bal Harbour Village,
655 Ninety-sixth Street, Bal Harbour 33154; (305) 866–4633 or (800) 847–9222;
Web site: www.balharbour@yahoo.com

Greater Boca Raton Chamber of Commerce,
1800 North Dixie Highway, Boca Raton 33432; (561) 395–4433;
Web site: www.bocaratonchamber.com

Greater Ft. Lauderdale Convention & Visitors Bureau,
1850 Eller Drive, #303, Ft. Lauderdale 33316; (800) 22–SUNNY;
Web site: www.sunny.org

Greater Hollywood Chamber of Commerce,
330 North Federal Highway, Hollywood 33020; (954) 923–4000 or (800) 231–5562;
Web site: www.hollywoodchamber.org

Greater Miami Convention & Visitors Bureau,
701 Brickell Avenue; Suite 2700, Miami 33131; (800) 283–2707;
Web site: www.tropicoolmiami.com

Greater Pompano Beach Chamber of Commerce,
2200 East Atlantic Boulevard, Pompano Beach 33062;
(954) 941–2940 or (800) 746–5708; Web site: www.pompanobeachchamber.com

Jensen Beach Chamber of Commerce,
1910 Northeast Jensen Beach Boulevard, Jensen Beach 34957; (561) 334–3444;
Web site: www.jensenchamber.com

Miami Beach Latin Chamber of Commerce,
235 Lincoln Road, Suite 216, Miami Beach 33139; (305) 674–1231;
Web site: www.miamibeach.org

Palm Beach County Convention & Visitors Bureau,
1555 Palm Beach Lakes Boulevard, Suite 204, West Palm Beach 33401;
(800) 554–7256; Web site: www.palmbeachfl.com

STATE PARKS IN
SOUTHEAST FLORIDA

*Barnacle State Historic
Site* (305) 448–9445

*Bill Baggs Cape Florida
State Recreation Area*
(305) 361–5811

*Hugh Taylor Birch State
Recreation Area*
(954) 564–4521

*John D. MacArthur
Beach State Park*
(561) 624–6950

*John U. Lloyd Beach State
Recreation Area*
(954) 923–2833

*Jonathan Dickinson
State Park*
(561) 546–2771

*Oleta River State
Recreation Area*
(305) 919–1846

*St. Lucie Inlet State
Preserve/Seabranch*
(561) 744–7603

Visitor Information for Southeast Florida

South Beach Marketing Council/Tourist Information,
1001 Washington Avenue (Bridgetender's House at The Wolfsonian Museum);
(305) 672–9100 or (800) 443–7372; Web site: http://www.southbeach.org

Stuart/Martin County Chamber of Commerce,
1650 South Kanner Highway, Stuart 34994; (561) 287–1088, ext. 101;
Web site: www.goodnature.org

Tropical Everglades Visitor Center,
160 U.S. Highway 1, Florida City 33034; (800) 388–9669
Web site: www.tropicaleverglades.com

Vero Beach Chamber of Commerce,
1216 Twenty-first Street, Vero Beach 32960;
(561) 567–3491 or (800) 338–2678, ext. 17802;
Web site: www.indianriverchamber.com

**PLACES TO STAY IN
SOUTHEAST FLORIDA**

STUART
Holiday Inn-Downtown,
1209 South Federal
Highway; (561) 287–6200

Howard Johnson, 950 South
Federal Highway;
(561) 287–3171

PALM BEACH
Howard Johnson,
2870 South Ocean
Boulevard; (561) 582–2581

The Four Seasons,
2800 South Ocean
Boulevard; (561) 582–2800

The Ritz-Carlton, Palm
Beach, 100 South Ocean
Boulevard; (561) 533–6000

WEST PALM BEACH
Days Inn
600 Northpointe Parkway;
(561) 848–8661

Days Inn Airport North,
2300 Forty-fifth Street;
(561) 689–0450

PGA National Resort &
Spa, 400 Avenue of the
Champions, Palm Beach
Gardens; (561) 627–2000

BOCA RATON
Best Western University Inn,
2700 North Federal
Highway; (561) 395–5225

Marriott, 5150 Town Center
Circle; (561) 392–4600

Boca Raton Resort & Club,
501 East Camino Real;
(561) 395–3000

POMPANO BEACH
Holiday Inn, 1350 South
Ocean Boulevard;
(954) 941–7300

Super 8,
2300 Northeast Tenth
Street; (954) 943–3500

FT. LAUDERDALE
Wellesley Inn,
13600 Northwest Second
Street, Sunrise;
(954) 845–9929

Riverside, 620 East
Las Olas Boulevard;
(954) 467–0671

Hyatt Regency Pier 66,
2301 Southeast
Seventeenth Street,
Causeway; (954) 525–6666

HOLLYWOOD
Clarion Intracoastal,
4000 South Ocean Drive;
(954) 458–1900

Holiday Inn, 2905 Sheridan
Street; (954) 925–9100

MIAMI
Fairfield Inn by Marriott,
3959 Northwest
Seventh-ninth Avenue;
(305) 599–5200

Quality Inn South,
14501 South Dixie
Highway; (305) 251–2000

Wellesley Inn at
Miami Lakes,
7925 Northwest
154th Street;
(305) 821–8274

Wyndam Grand Bay,
2669 South Bayshore Drive,
Coconut Grove;
(305) 858–9600

Mayfair House,
3000 Florida Avenue,
Coconut Grove;
(305) 441–0000

Doral Golf Resort and Spa,
4400 Northwest Eighty-
seventh Avenue; (305)
592–2000

Turnberry Isle Resort &
Club, 19999 West Country
Club Drive, Aventura;
(305) 932–6200

MIAMI BEACH
Beacharbour Resort,
18925 Collins Avenue;
(305) 931–8900

Eden Roc Resort,
4542 Collins Avenue;
(305) 531–0000

Fontainebleau Hilton
Resort and Towers,
4441 Collins Avenue;
(305) 538–2000

Bay Harbor Inn,
9660 East Bay Harbor
Drive; (305) 868–4141

CORAL GABLES
Hotel Place St. Michel,
162 Alcazar Avenue;
(305) 444–1666

Biltmore, 1200 Anastasia
Avenue; (305) 445–1926

Hyatt Regency,
50 Alhambra Plaza;
(305) 441–1234

Omni Colonnade,
180 Aragon Avenue;
(305) 441–2600

HOMESTEAD
Best Western,
1 Strano Boulevard,
Florida City;
(305) 246–5100

Hampton Inn,
124 East Palm Drive,
Florida City;
(305) 247–8833

Ramada Limited
990 Homestead Boulevard;
(305) 247–7020

**PLACES TO EAT IN
SOUTHEAST FLORIDA**

STUART
The Ashley, 61 Southwest
Osceola Street;
(561) 221–9476

PALM BEACH
Bice (Italian),
313½ Worth Avenue;
(561) 835–1600

Chuck & Harold's,
207 Royal Poinciana Way;
(561) 659–1440

The Florentine Dining
Room (Mediterranean),
The Breaker's Resort,
1 South Country Road;
(561) 659–8480

WEST PALM BEACH
Randy's Bageland
(Jewish deli),
911 Village Boulevard,
Village Commons;
(561) 640–0203

BOCA RATON
La Vieille Maison (French),
770 East Palmetto Park
Road, (561) 391–6701

The Board Room
1 Boca Place;
(561) 994–2201

Pete's Boca Raton,
7940 Glades Road;
(561) 487–1600

POMPANO BEACH
Flaming Pit, 1150 North
Federal Highway;
(954) 943–3484

Cafe Arugula,
3150 North Federal
Highway, Lighthouse Point;
(954) 785–7732

FT. LAUDERDALE
Brasserie La Ferme
(French), 1601 East Sun-
rise Boulevard; (954)
764–0987

Burt & Jacks, Berth
23; (954) 522–5225

Mango's, 904 East Las Olas
Boulevard; (954) 523–5001

Moonraker, 3001 East
Oakland Park Boulevard,
on Intracoastal Waterway;
(954) 561–4400

HOLLYWOOD
Bavarian Village
(German/American),
1401 North Federal
Highway; (954) 922–7321

Martha's Supper Club on
the Intracoastal;
(954) 923–5444

MIAMI

East Coast Fisheries
(seafood), 360 West
Flagler Street;
(305) 372–1300

The Fish Market (seafood),
Crowne Plaza Hotel,
1601 Biscayne Boulevard;
(305) 374–0000

Shula's Steak House,
7601 Northwest 154th
Street, Miami Lakes;
(305) 820–8102

Chef Allen's,
19088 Northeast 29th
Avenue, Aventura;
(305) 935–2900

MIAMI BEACH

Astor Place Bar and Grill,
956 Washington Avenue;
(305) 672–7217

Joe's Stone Crab (seafood),
227 Biscayne Street;
(305) 673–0365

Yuca (Cuban), 501 Lincoln
Road; (305) 532–9822

Blue Door, Delano Hotel,
1685 Collins Avenue;
(305) 674–6400

Pacific Time, 915 Lincoln
Road; (305) 534–5979

Island Cafe Waterfront
Tavern, Bay Harbor Inn,
9660 East Bay Harbor
Drive, Bay Harbor Islands;
(305) 867–8883

Lemon Twist,
908 Seventy-first Street;
(305) 868–2075

CORAL GABLES

John Martin's (Irish),
253 Miracle Mile;
(305) 445–3777

La Bussola Ristorante
(Italian), 264 Giralda
Avenue; (305) 445–8783

Caffe Abbracci (Italian),
318 Aragon Avenue;
(305) 441–0700

Bangkok Bangkok II
(Thai), 157 Giralda Avenue;
(305) 444–2397

HOMESTEAD

Capri, 935 North Krome
Avenue, Florida City;
(305) 247–1544

Chez Jean Claude (French),
1235 Krome Avenue;
(305) 248–4671

The Keys

The Overseas Highway (U.S. 1) begins at Florida City, but the Card Sound Road (SR 997) is a more scenic and less congested way to connect to it. Since there is only one road to Key West, you aren't in any danger of getting lost. Also, keeping track of your progress is a cinch. Small green mile markers on the right side of the road begin with number 126 a mile past Florida City on U.S. 1 and end with a Mile Marker 0 in Key West. These markers, used instead of addresses, make it easy to locate places.

The Overseas Highway is really spectacular, especially after the 7-mile bridge, where the islands are less developed. In fact, the seascapes on both sides of the highway seem to blossom and expand as you drive south. Pines, palms, and mangroves frame ocean views of every conceivable shade of blue. Great whipped-cream clouds are backdropped by an immense sky, and you are cruising, albeit by car, toward the end of the road.

The Keys

The Keys gleam like gems set in a sea that dazzles from transparent turquoise and milky emerald to deep sapphire. Strung on a ribbon of concrete and steel better known as the **Overseas Highway,** this archipelago curves 100 miles from Biscayne Bay to Key West. Nearly 70 miles west of the highway's end in Key West are a few leftover jewels, which Ponce de Leon christened the Tortugas (Spanish for turtles).

These frost-free islands, warmed by the Gulf Stream in winter and cooled by the trade winds in summer, appear to be an uncomplicated antidote for the winter weary. Nothing in their swaying palms or glistening sandy beaches offers the slightest hint of a tempestuous past.

Yet early history of the Keys is peppered with both drama and tragedy. Ponce de Leon, who claimed Florida for Spain in 1513, charted the Keys and named them Los Martires (The Martyrs), because from a distance they looked like men who were suffering. The name proved to be

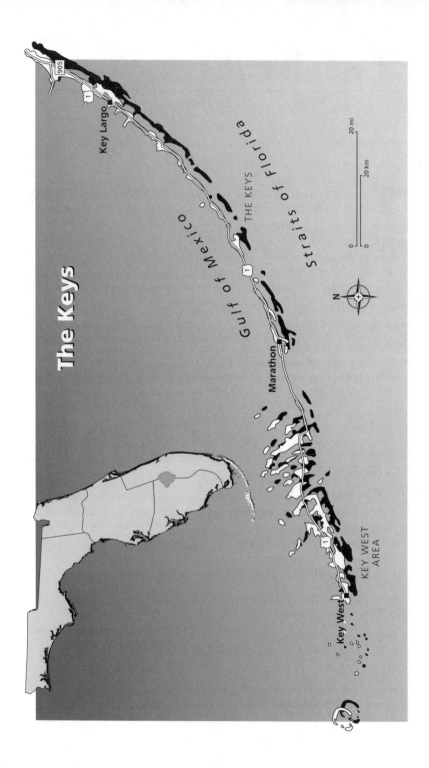

The Keys

Gulf of Mexico

Straits of Florida

THE KEYS

Key Largo

Marathon

Key West

KEY WEST AREA

N

20 mi

20 km

TOP EVENTS IN THE FLORIDA KEYS

Underwater Music Festival,
Big Pine Key, July,
(800) 872–3722

Fantasy Fest,
Key West, October,
(305) 296–1817

prophetic. Spanish ships, laden with gold and treasures from Central America, were routinely plundered as they passed the islands. Such famous pirates as Black Caesar, Blackbeard, and Lafitte found the Keys' many inlets and coves ideal for concealing their ships and stashing their booty.

By the turn of the century, the Keys were more than ready for tycoon Henry Flagler's incredible scheme to link them to the mainland by rail. His idea was to extend his famous Florida East Coast Railroad across 100 miles of water and twenty-nine islands. As one of the founders of Standard Oil, Flagler had plenty of wealth to devote to this grand project popularly known as Flagler's Folly. At age seventy-five, having spent a lifetime responding to improbable challenges, he could afford to ignore those who said it couldn't be done. Besides, it didn't seem like such a big deal. "All you have to do," he said, "is to build one concrete arch, and then another, and pretty soon you will find yourself in Key West."

Unfortunately, the railroad turned out to be an economic failure. To make matters worse, a horrendous hurricane tore through the Keys in 1935, destroying embankments and even sweeping a train into the sea.

Flagler's Folly

*H*enry Flagler's dream railroad was finally completed on January 21, 1912. The next day, when Flagler arrived aboard the first official train, Key West staged the largest celebration the island had ever seen. School children turned out to welcome the railroad's mastermind. Flagler walked on a thick carpet of roses gathered from local gardens to receive accolades from an excited citizenry. It was an emotional moment for the eighty-three-year-old visionary, whose last great dream had finally become reality. His life's work completed, Flagler was to die the following year.

Despite early rave reviews, the railroad proved to be an economic disaster. Cargoes fell well below optimistic projections, and too few wealthy visitors could be lured so far from the mainland. The Great Depression dealt a lethal blow to the staggering enterprise, but it was violent weather that finally finished it off.

The worst hurricane the area had ever known devastated the Keys on Labor Day in 1935. A 20-foot wall of water smashed the islands, and the barometer registered 26.35, the lowest reading ever recorded in the Western Hemisphere. The storm swept a train into the sea and washed away many miles of track along with most of the embankments. The death toll, estimated at about 500 people, also included one railroad, a magnificent achievement whose moment in the sun was over.

After nearly two and one-half years of relative isolation, the impoverished people of the Keys were delighted when the state of Florida built the 128-mile Overseas Highway. The highway, a continuation of U.S. 1, is an incredible engineering feat consisting of 113 miles of roadway and forty-three bridges.

Residents of the Keys, buoyed by their new accessibility, placed their hope for the future in tourism, a hope that has become reality. More than a million tourists each year seek out the Keys' subtropical climate and easygoing island lifestyle. They are usually in quest of an off-the-beaten-path experience, and they are rarely disappointed with what they find. You can traverse the highway in less than three hours; but then, you can also see the Mona Lisa in less than a minute. The point is to take your time and enjoy. There are lots of things to see and do, but you will need to slow down to fully absorb and appreciate the natural beauty that surrounds you.

The Upper Keys, those nearest the mainland, stretch from Key Largo through Long Key. Key Largo is the base for the nation's first underwater park. *John Pennekamp Coral Reef State Park,* 21 miles long and approximately 4 miles wide, protects forty species of coral and 650 species of fish on the only living reef along the Atlantic Coast. The reef, which was severely damaged by commercial souvenir hunters in the 1930s and 1940s, has recovered under the park's protection. These spectacular coral gardens were saved by a conservation movement spearheaded by John Pennekamp, an associate editor of the *Miami Herald,* whose stories fired up public interest in this national treasure.

Dive shops abound in Key Largo, as do scuba diving courses culminating in certification. Skin divers, snorkelers, and passengers on glass-bottom boats revel in the park's clearwater views to 60 feet, which include colorful coral formations, exotic fish, turtles, and old sailing wrecks. *Christ of*

The Conch Republic

*T*his friendly freewheeling community once seceded from the Union, established the Conch Republic, and demanded foreign aid from the U.S. government. Natives are called Conchs (pronounced "konks") after the mollusk that thrives in local waters, but transients abound. When we asked one waiter how long he'd been in the Keys, he checked his watch (for the time, not the date) before replying. All agree the attitude here is different. These mellow folks measure time by watching the sun rise over the Atlantic then strolling to the other side of the island to watch it slide into the Gulf of Mexico.

the Deep, a replica of Guido Galletti's *Christ of the Abyss* in the Mediterranean Sea, highlights one of the reef's natural underwater valleys.

A glass-bottom boat leaves three times daily (9:15 A.M., 12:15 P.M., and 3:00 P.M.) for a guided tour of **Molasses Reef.** You'll see high coral ridges, tunnels, and a variety of formations including elkhorn, staghorn, star, and brain coral without ever getting wet. Certified scuba divers may board a boat that leaves daily at 9:30 A.M. and 1:30 P.M. for trips to Molasses Reef, French Reef, or Benwood Wreck (depending on conditions). Snorkelers take advantage of a convenient dive platform on *El Capitan,* which leaves three times daily on two-and-a-half-hour reef

Where the Boys Are

Our son Stephen suggested he and his Dad celebrate Steve's spring break from college together. They returned home a week later wildly enthusiastic about their adventure in the Keys. What follows is Steve's version of the experience.

Air. We both needed air, but only Dad had it. Moving slowly to conserve oxygen, I gave the out-of-air signal. He took a big breath and passed the regulator to me. I remember his white knuckles and his eyes. Big eyes under water are the two-second warning signal. Dad's were huge.

I grabbed one quick breath instead of the standard two. We didn't need a problem with 25 feet of water overhead. On my next turn the regulator slipped from our hands and began blowing the precious air out in a great blast of bubbles.

Things were not going smoothly. With some difficulty we managed to get the regulator under control and were able to get a good breathing system going. Then the instructor appeared and turned my air back on. We had passed the buddy breathing test. I inhaled deeply.

For my spring break from my sophomore year in college, I suggested Dad and I chase adventure. I didn't want to look at things from a tour bus. I wanted something physical, something real.

We found it in a one-week scuba diving course in Key Largo. An impulse stop at a dive center turned out to be a good one. Our first thought had been to do some snorkeling, maybe spear a few fish later on. But the trip we wanted was canceled. That changed our free-flowing, let-it-happen vacation into an intense five-day SCUBA (Self-Contained Underwater Breathing Apparatus) Certification Course.

I learned a lot, and it wasn't only about diving. The day the class ended we all went out for dinner. The other participants said they envied us, not just because we could have a good time together, but because we cared about each other. They were right. Sharing air in the open ocean gave that caring a new dimension. I knew if things really went wrong, Dad came first.

I figure it's the least I could do. We do go way back.

trips. Usually the excursion heads for Grecian Rocks where you'll see colorful angelfish, parrotfish, and some harmless nurse sharks. For boat tour information call (305) 451–1621.

John Pennekamp Park also has canoe and kayak rentals as well as beaches and nature trails. The campsites are much in demand, so be sure to make reservations well ahead or get there early. John Pennekamp Coral Reef State Park, P.O. Box 487, Key Largo, FL 33037; snorkel reservations: (305) 451–1621; scuba reservations: (305) 451–6322; boating reservations: (305) 451–6325; camping reservations: (305) 451–1202; park number: (305) 451–1202.

At the *Key Largo Holiday Inn* you may see the *African Queen,* an old river freighter that Humphrey Bogart and Katharine Hepburn made famous in the 1951 film classic. The remodeled inn now has a Casa Blanca Lounge and Greenstreet's Restaurant. To take a tour on the freighter, call (305) 451–2121.

Theatre of the Sea in Islamorada (Spanish for Purple Isle) is the second-oldest marine-life park in the world. A fifty-minute tour includes a look at an extensive shark and ray collection and a dolphin show in a natural coral grotto. Who knows? This may be your only chance to be kissed by an affectionate sea lion or touch a shark (and come away with all your fingers intact). For information and reservations on the "Swim with a Dolphin" program, call (305) 664– 2431. Open 9:30 A.M.–4:00 P.M. daily. Theatre of the Sea is on U.S. 1, P.O. Box 407, Islamorada, FL 33036; (305) 664–2431.

From Indian Key Fill on U.S. 1, you can take boat tours of both Lignumvitae Key and Indian Key. Boat tours leave for *Indian Key* State Historic Site at 10:00 A.M. and 2:00 P.M. and for *Lignumvitae Key* State Botanical Site at 9:00 A.M. and 1:00 P.M. Closed Tuesday and Wednesday. Call (305) 664–4815 to arrange a tour and to get information. Lignumvitae was named for a type of hardwood tree with healing properties found growing here, and tours of the State Botanical Site reveal many other unusual plants. You'll be fascinated to learn how early Keys residents adapted the fruits, barks, and leaves of the forest to meet their needs. Rangers say this nature preserve "is the last place that truly represents the Keys as they were."

A once-thriving settlement at Indian Key (a state historic site) was completely destroyed during the Seminole Indian raid in 1840. The tropical foliage here is amazing. Only at the top of the observation tower are you eye level with the tops of towering century plants. A marvelous time to visit is May when tiny white butterflies are migrating from South America. **Long Key State Park** is noted for great fishing, swimming, snorkeling, boating, and camping. For information about the park contact Park Manager, P.O. Box 776, Long Key, FL 33001; (305) 664–4815.

The Middle and Lower Keys (from Long Key on to Key West) differ geologically from the Upper Keys, which are the boney skeletons of an ancient coral reef. While all the islands have as a base a thick blanket of limestone, those farther from the mainland are topped with a layer of Miami oolite, egg-shaped particles cemented into rock by the millennia.

Each island seems to have a distinct identity, but most activities still center on Key favorites—beachcombing, sunbasking, and fishing from bridge, beach, and boat. From Marathon to Key West, spearfishing is permitted 1 mile offshore. Marathon is the starting point for the famous **Seven-Mile Bridge,** the country's longest continuous bridge. Its 65-foot crest is the highest point in the Keys.

Once it was a strip joint; in fact, it was the only topless dancer bar on Marathon Key. Now Fanny's Bar is—ta da—the nation's only turtle hospital. Some would call this progress.

Unfortunately, **Hidden Harbor Turtle Hospital** came into being to solve a growing problem—turtles afflicted with multiple tumors. These tumors are symptoms of a debilitating disease known as Fibro-Papilloma that is now thought to have viral origins. This rapidly spreading epidemic may be affecting as much as 90 percent of the local turtle population and has shown up as far away as Barbados and Hawaii.

Back in 1986 Tina Brown, charter boat captain, and her partner, Richie Moretti, one-time auto mechanic, purchased the Hidden Harbor Motel and converted their saltwater pool for the display of marine life. Soon local anglers began bringing in turtles suffering from grotesque tumors, and it became clear that surgery was needed to save their lives.

Brown and Moretti bartered free fishing and diving trips for the services of a vet until they were able to get a vet on staff who would perform surgery in exchange for a room. They fund their hospital (which needs roughly $100,000 yearly) from proceeds of the Hidden Harbor Motel and give countless hours to the care of their reptilian friends.

They also give educational programs to local school children and presentations on turtles to the local museum. Currently Brown and Moretti are working with the University of Florida in hopes of finding a cure for a disease that is decimating an already endangered species.

The turtle hospital does not have regular visiting hours for the public, but they give a slide show to motel guests about three times a week as a thank you, since motel funds operate the hospital. You will be amazed at the modern medical offices—including an X-ray room, necropsy lab, and operating room—and saddened by the sight of so many sick turtles in the saltwater pool behind the hospital. The Hidden Harbor Motel, 2390 Overseas Highway, Marathon, FL 33050; (305) 743–5376 or you can reach the hospital at (305) 743–6509.

If it's late in the day and you need a place to sleep, why not consider a floating houseboat at dockside or a lighthouse apartment. *Faro Blanco Marine Resort* offers both as well as an assortment of cottages and condos, four restaurants, a full-service marina, Olympic-size swimming pool, charter fishing, tours, and dive lessons. The resort has facilities on both Atlantic and Gulf waters.

Faro Blanco is in Marathon, 110 miles southwest of the Florida mainland, two and one-half hours from Miami by car, an hour from Key Largo, or an hour from Key West. The resort is located at Mile Marker 48. Faro Blanco Marine Resort, 1996 Overseas Highway, Marathon, FL 33050; (800) 759–3276 or (305) 743–9018.

It's easy to whiz right by *Pigeon Key* as you drive across Seven-Mile Bridge. You might look down, see a cluster of old buildings on a tiny palm-sheltered island, and wonder what it's all about. Of course you'd like to take a closer look. Those with a yen to get off the fast track for a little while will be well rewarded by a brief sojourn to Pigeon Key.

This four-acre island, connected to the mainland by a bridge originally built by Henry Flagler for his famous Florida East Coast Railway, has a rich and colorful history. Today its future seems equally promising. Pigeon Key, virtually in the shadow of the Overseas Highway, is a certified Historic District listed on the National Register of Historic Places. From 1908 to 1935, this island served as a construction and maintenance camp for the railroad; the Pigeon Key Foundation has carefully restored seven buildings from this era.

Since the railroad days, Pigeon Key has been a center for the Road and Toll District, a site for the U.S. Navy, a fishing camp, and a research center for the University of Miami.

The potential for this idyllic island is limitless; it is on its way, gradually but certainly, to becoming a world-class center for environmental education, historical exhibits, and research.

Shuttle to Pigeon Key

Be sure to sign up for a tour and take the shuttle out to the island. You'll enjoy the ride. The shuttle is an attractive railroad car, modeled after the historic Florida East Coast Railway that leaves from the Pigeon Key Visitors Center on Knight's Key. This way you'll hear stories of the early railroad as you pass slowly over the Old Seven-Mile Bridge.

Once you reach the island, you'll learn about the heritage of the Florida Keys, the natural environment, and various disastrous hurricanes. Your guide will make memories of one-time residents come alive. And, yes, the island has a ghost—or at least a fairly juicy ghost story.

Be sure to see the museum showing the history of the island, the Overseas Highway, and the overseas railway as well as historical and cultural exhibits, including *Florinda,* a Cuban refugee vessel that carried twenty-four people to freedom. You'll see the Section Gang's Quarters (1909), a one-time dorm for railway workers (now the Education Center for the Pigeon Key Foundation); the Bridge Tender's House (1909); the Bridge Foreman's House (1916); Negro Quarters (1909); Honeymoon Cottage (1950); and others. Don't miss the 1930 *Home Movie* of a trip on the Florida East Coast Railway from Key West to Miami shown in the Education Center.

Pigeon Key is a delightful spot for a picnic (you're welcome to use the picnic tables), or you may want to just sit beside the sea and watch the colors shift from aquamarine to cobalt. Artists and photographers return time after time to capture the island's picturesque landscapes and seascapes.

The island's proximity to the Gulf Stream, Florida Bay, coral reefs, sea grass beds, and an abundant variety of marine life makes it an ideal setting for marine research. Mote Marine Laboratory plans to use the island's resources to study such vital concerns as water quality and the biological integrity of tropical marine ecosystems. Mote's Center for Shark Research will continue its study of sharks as an ecologically and economically valuable marine resource.

Approximately 45 miles from Key West, 100 miles southwest of Miami, and $2^2/_{10}$ miles due west of Marathon, Pigeon Key is connected to the mainland by the Old Seven-Mile Bridge.

Sounds interesting but how do you get to Pigeon Key? Walkers, joggers, cyclists, and skaters are welcome to go out to Pigeon Key via the Old Seven-Mile Bridge at any time during regular hours (9:00 A.M.–5:00 P.M. seven days a week) for a small admission fee. Access to the island is at Mile Marker 48 at the west end of Marathon.

One thing you can't do is drive your car to Pigeon Key, as regulations prohibit private cars on the old bridge. You may, however, leave your car in the parking lot at the east end of the Old Seven-Mile Bridge.

The best way to experience this historic island is to begin and end your trip at the Pigeon Key Visitors Center on the Atlantic side of Knight's Key. Even if you don't have time to meander about Pigeon Key, take a moment to browse the visitors center's intriguing selection of environmental and historical books and gifts.

The shuttle service to Pigeon Key leaves Knight's Key on the hour from 10:00 A.M. to 4:00 P.M. Visitors are welcome to stay as long as they wish and to return on any shuttle. The last shuttle returns to the visitors center at 5:00 P.M. Why not make a day of it? Pigeon Key Foundation, P.O. Box 500130, Marathon, FL 33050; (305) 289–0025; Web site: www. pigeonkey.org.

Prettiest beach in the Florida Keys? Consider **Bahia Honda State Park** just south of Marathon's Seven-Mile Bridge. The idyllic, palm-shaded beach at Bahia Honda (Spanish for deep bay) resembles a tropical island in the South Pacific. Pines, palms, and mangroves frame ocean views that shift from turquoise and violet to milky emerald and navy blue. The water temperature ranges from the low to mid-80s, and refreshing Caribbean trade winds keep this sunbaked subtropical island comfortable year-round.

This southernmost state park for camping is the perfect place to while away the hours beachcombing, swimming, snorkeling, fishing, exploring, and bird-watching. Be sure to stroll the nature trail to see some of the unusual botanical growth (satinwood trees, spiny catesbaeas, and dwarf morning glories) on this unique spit of land, as well as the many beautiful and rare birds (white-crowned pigeon, great white heron, roseate spoonbill, reddish egret, osprey, brown pelican, and least terns) that pass through here.

For a glorious view climb to the overlook, which includes the first two spans of the original Flagler train trestle and the abandoned narrow span where more than one RV lost an outside mirror in a highway squeeze play. Many of the old bridges in the Upper and Lower Keys, including this one, offer anglers spots to dangle their hooks for mackerel, bluefish, tarpon, snook, grouper, and jewfish. According to a park ranger, tarpon fishing in Bahia Honda rates among the best in the country.

Two campgrounds—one fairly open near the marina and west swimming area, the other shady and more secluded—tempt RVers and tent campers to linger. Typical of Florida state parks, this one is clean and well maintained. Reservations are suggested, especially around holidays. The campsites are reserved for those who call ahead (reservations taken up to eleven months in advance). There are six cabins, which also may be reserved in advance. Bahia Honda State Park, 35850 Overseas Highway, Big Pine Key, FL 33043; (305) 872–2353.

Dainty Key deer wander through the slash pines and mangrove swamps on Big Pine and a few surrounding keys. This fragile subspecies, thought to have been stranded when the Wisconsin Glacier melted, is the smallest of all whitetail deer. From 26 to 32 inches in height, the deer average 38 inches in length and weigh between 30 and 110 pounds. By 1954 hunting and destruction of habitat had reduced the population of deer to fifty. The establishment of a *National Key Deer Refuge* protected the herd, which has stabilized at about 300. These deer, the size of a large dog, are still threatened with extinction, primarily because of loss of habitat and ill-advised feeding by residents and visitors. Feeding can cause the deer to congregate and bring them in contact with such death traps as cars, canals, fences, and dogs. It is now against the law to feed the deer.

National Key Deer Refuge is north of U.S. 1 on Key Deer Boulevard (SR 940). The refuge headquarters is in the Winn Dixie shopping center on Key Deer Boulevard, Big Pine Key. Best times to see deer are early morning, late afternoon, and early evening on the north end of Key Deer Boulevard and No Name Key. *Blue Hole,* a rock quarry with an alligator guarding a sign that says PLEASE DON'T FEED THE ALLIGATORS, is nearby. For information contact the Refuge Manager at (305) 872–2239.

If you don't feel romantic on *Little Palm Island,* you'd better check your pulse. This is the place romantics dream about, a secluded South Seas kind of island abloom with lush tropical foliage including a dense grove of soaring Jamaican coconut palms. And get this—you don't have to jet the vast reaches of the South Pacific to find this idyllic retreat. It's just 3 miles offshore in the heart of the Florida Keys.

Once upon a time, this five-acre island served as a fishing camp and private getaway for Presidents Roosevelt, Truman, Kennedy, and Nixon plus a string of other dignitaries and celebrities. Since 1988 it's been a luxury resort for those seeking the ultimate escape from reality.

As you approach the island, you'll catch a glimpse of thatched roofs peaking from beneath luxuriant greenery. These roofs belong to fourteen stilted villas scattered throughout the island. Each private abode comes with a secluded, wraparound sundeck, an enticing rope hammock strung between gracefully curved palm trees, and an ocean view.

Inside you'll find a living room, an expansive bedroom with king-sized bed draped in gauzy, for-effect-only mosquito netting, and a sitting area. The dressing area and bathroom, complete with whirlpool bath, open directly to a bamboo-fenced, totally private outdoor shower. Go ahead and pinch yourself. Try to remember this is not Fiji; this is Florida.

Every modern comfort is at your disposal, from a minibar to a wet bar with plenty of coffee and tea. However, you will not find the spirit-jarring intrusions of television, telephones, and alarm clocks. They are banned from the island. After all, this is supposed to be a romantic hideaway.

Tropical islands usually unveil their flaws on closer inspection. What Little Palm Island reveals is a heated lagoonlike freshwater pool fringed by palms, a waterfall, flowering shrubs, birds, and a sugar-white sandy beach.

You now have a tough decision. Do you simply relax and enjoy the ambience, or do you take advantage of the resort's many activities? Kayaks, canoes, sailboats, fishing equipment, and snorkeling gear are complimentary. You may want to perk up your appetite with a workout in the exercise room near the Gift Boutique.

Perhaps you'd rather go scuba diving or snorkeling or try your hand at deep-sea fishing. Several offshore and mainland excursions are offered, and guided nature tours by canoe or sailboat are popular. Divers will definitely want to join an excursion to nearby Looe Key to explore the wonders of the last living coral reef in North America.

If your idea of a vacation is simply to relax and be pampered, you'll want to indulge yourself with a spa treatment including a relaxing massage, a facial, and a manicure or pedicure.

Little Palm Island is a delightful spot to enjoy wildlife. Great white herons, little green herons, night herons, frigate birds, white ibis, brown pelicans, osprey, skimmers, egrets, sandpipers, roseate spoonbills, manatees, dolphin, Key deer, and loggerhead turtles are common sights in

OTHER ATTRACTIONS WORTH SEEING IN THE FLORIDA KEYS

The Maritime Museum of the Florida Keys, Key Largo

Florida Keys Wild Bird Rehabilitation Center, Tavernier

Dolphin Research Center, Grassy Key

Museum of Natural History of the Florida Keys, Marathon

Key West Aquarium

The Curry Mansion, Key West

Bahama Village, Key West

the four separate nature preserves near the island and on the surrounding ocean flats.

The island is on the flyway for birds making their spring migratory trip north from the Caribbean basin and Central and South America. Bird migration peaks in early May and continues throughout the month. More than one hundred migratory species include blackpoll warblers, palm warblers, falcons, kestrels, orioles, tanagers, bobolinks, cuckoos, ovenbirds, and black-bellied plovers.

The resort dock is a favorite hangout for tarpon, bonefish, angelfish, snapper, lookdown fish, and snook. Sometimes in the evenings hundreds of great tarpon roll around in the deep water at the end of the dock.

You'll notice a sign by the outdoor dining room indicating it is off limits to Key Deer. These deer know a good menu when they catch wind of it. These diminutive mammals often swim over to Little Palm from a neighboring island to see what's going on. If they don't show up for dinner, you can commandeer a canoe the next day and paddle to nearby Big Munson Island, home to a herd of about thirty endangered deer.

One thing all resort guests seem to enjoy is eating. The island's gourmet cuisine combines regional cuisine with Caribbean and Oriental influences. It's hard to beat an entree of locally caught stone crab claws, but perhaps the rack of lamb, seared with mustard, and served with a Madeira sauce will do just that. If you're in the mood for a totally decadent dessert, select the bittersweet chocolate soufflé with Guanaja chocolate sauce or the passion fruit crème brûlée.

You may order breakfast served in your room or on your private deck. For lunch and dinner you may dine in the airy dining room, outdoors on a spacious terrace, or a few steps down on the resort's pristine sandy beach. The Tropical Sunday Brunch buffet is an island tradition, and the chef creates a different seven-course feast each Thursday. You don't need to be a resort guest to take advantage of the superb cuisine on any day, but you do need a reservation. The public may make dining reservations by calling (305) 872–2551.

Little Palm Resort is at the western end of the Newfound Harbor Keys, where the Gulf of Mexico meets the Straits of Florida. The island is a fifteen-minute launch ride from its Shore Station on Little Torch Key.

Little Torch Key is on Overseas Highway U.S. 1 at Mile Marker 28.5, approximately 28 miles east of Key West International Airport, 22 miles south of Marathon Airport, and 120 miles southwest of Miami International Airport.

Transfer and van service to the Little Torch Key Shore Station is available from both Key West and Marathon Airports. Limousine service can be arranged from Key West, Marathon, and Miami International Airports. Seaplane service is available from Miami. Advance notice is required for all these services. Little Palm Island, 28500 Overseas Highway, Little Torch Key, FL 33042; (305) 872–2524 or (800) 3– GET–LOST.

Now here's a batty idea—a high-rise for bats. This weather-beaten, 35-foot wooden tower was built to solve a problem. You see, Righter Clyde Perky wanted tourists to enjoy his guest cottages, restaurant, and marina, but they were turned off by hordes of dive-bombing mosquitoes. Perky knew bats had a ravenous appetite for mosquitoes, so he built them the most comfortable lodging he could think of and decorated it with sex-scented bat droppings imported from Texas. Unfortunately, the bats never got wind of the project (although the neighbors certainly did), and the tower remains uninhabited. Modern spraying techniques have largely done away with the mosquito problem, and who can say the tower isn't a success in its own right—after all, it has survived several hurricanes and is listed on the National Register of Historic Places. The **Perky Bat Tower** is near Mile Marker 17 on the Gulf side of U.S. 1 on Sugarloaf Key.

End of the Road

*K*ey West Cemetery, *bordered by Francis, Angela, and Olivia Streets, is a browsable tribute to a truly off-the-beaten-path community. Most of the tombs are above ground, many identified only by first names or nicknames. You'll want to read the epitaphs, including the infamous "I told you I was sick."*

There are separate sections for those of the Jewish and Catholic faiths, and many Cuban crypts are adorned with a statue of a chicken. The chicken usu-ally denotes Santeria, an odd mix of Catholicism and animist beliefs held by descendants of former slaves from Africa.

Find the statue of a tiny Key deer, and you will be in a special section of the cemetery devoted to pets. And don't miss the monument to the crewmen of the battleship USS Maine who died in Havanna harbor at the beginning of the Spanish-American War in 1898. The monument is marked by the statue of a single sailor.

Key West Area

At the end of the Overseas Highway where the Atlantic meets the Gulf of Mexico is Key West, the southernmost city in the continental United States. Here the Calusa Indians made a final stand against invading tribes from the north. The Spanish, who came upon the grisly remains of the battle, named it *Cayo Hueso,* which translates to the "island of bones." Eventually this was anglicized into Key West.

Unruffled by the crosscurrents of its cultural heritage, this exotic community has long been a mecca for writers, artists, and other well-knowns. The claim is that Key West is not really a place,

Perky Bat Tower

but an attitude. The community's freewheeling spirit once led it to secede from the Union, establish the Conch Republic, and demand foreign aid from the United States government! On this 5-by-3-mile island Tennessee Williams spent the final years of his life, Harry Truman had his **Little White House,** and John James Audubon painted tropical birds.

Stop in to visit the six-toed cats (direct descendants of those loved by "Papa" Hemingway) at the **Ernest Hemingway Home and Museum.** Hemingway bought this Spanish Colonial–style house in 1931 and wrote a number of novels here. You'll see memorabilia, original furnishings, and exotic trees and plants from around the world. Open daily 9:00 A.M.–5:00 P.M., 907 Whitehead Street, Key West, FL 33040; (305) 294–1575.

More Hemingway memorabilia is on tap at **Sloppy Joe's,** Papa's favorite bar at 201 Duval Street, Key West, FL 33040.

The **Audubon House** contains many of John J. Audubon's original engravings as well as a video about his life. Authentically restored with eighteenth- and nineteenth-century furnishings, this early-nineteenth-century house is now a public museum. Once you've seen the incredible bird life on the Keys, it's not hard to understand why this famed naturalist-artist spent so much time here. The Audubon House is at 205 Whitehead Street at Greene Street, Key West, FL 33040. Open daily 9:30 A.M.–5:00 P.M.; (305) 294–2116.

The *Mel Fisher Maritime Heritage Society Museum* has treasures recovered from Spanish galleons that have been slumbering on the ocean floor for centuries. Along with more than 150 pounds of gold are silver bullion, emeralds, diamonds, copper, brass cannons, rare antiques, and a wonderful collection of historic artifacts. All told, the treasure, worth more than $40 million, is one of the largest displays of its type anywhere.

Feast your eyes on gold doubloons and discs, more than fifty gold bars, and thirty-five gold chains—including one measuring 12 feet and weighing more than six pounds. The prize piece from the salvaged collection is a gold poison cup featuring a bezoar stone that changes color when it comes in contact with a toxic substance. You just can't be too careful! Mel Fisher's Gold Exhibit is at 200 Greene Street, Key West, FL 33040. Open 9:30 A.M.–5:00 P.M. daily; (305) 294–2633.

Once shipwrecks were the area's economic mainstay. Settlers from the mainland, the Bahamas, and Europe flocked to the Keys to partake in the rich harvest of the sea. In 1825 Congress legislated that all salvage taken from wrecks in United States waters must be taken to a United States port for arbitration. Key West, as the islands' first permanent settlement, became the center for the auction of cargoes and repair of ships. By the 1830s wrecking had made Key West the wealthiest city, per capita, in the entire United States of America. The long dreary years of economic draught that followed were not endured in vain. Had the town enjoyed a history of uninterrupted prosperity rather than prolonged recession, its architectural treasure trove might have been leveled to make way for more modern buildings.

The *Wrecker's Museum* in the Oldest House in Key West is actually two houses, typical of 1830s "conch" construction. Browse the displays on the wrecking industry that once made Key West such a wealthy community. Don't miss the elegantly furnished dollhouse, the old kitchen house, and large garden. Guided tours daily 10:00 A.M.–4:00 P.M.; Sunday noon–4:00 P.M. Maintained by the Old Island Restoration Foundation, 322 Duval Street, Key West, FL 33040; (305) 294–9502.

A massive restoration effort, centered on *Duval Street,* is currently saving classic buildings that infuse the city with its Old World air. The architecture is a melange of Bahamian, Spanish, New England, and Southern styles. The Oldest House (circa 1829) in Key West is typical of small residences of that time. Many old homes were built in the 1850s by master ship carpenters who insisted on the best materials and used wooden pegs instead of nails. These handsome homes with wide verandas and gingerbread trim suggest a slower, more gracious era. Some of the most attractive, known as "conch" houses, were built in sections in the Bahamas and shipped over on schooners.

If you can possibly schedule your visit to coincide with *Old Island Days,* which begin in January and end in March, do so. The residents of this small island community wear bright red and white to mark the festivities as the entire island celebrates its heritage with house and garden tours, food fests, plays, flower shows, sidewalk art festivals, and even a conch-shell blowing contest. For information contact Florida Keys and Key West Visitors Bureau, 402 Wall Street, Key West, FL 33040; or call (305) 294–1241 (arts and crafts show information) or (305) 294–9501 (house tours); (800)–LASTKEY.

Natives of Key West are called *Conchs* (pronounced "konks") for the mollusk that thrives in local waters. This favorite local delicacy appears in chowders, fritters, and conch salad and as conch steak. Don't leave the islands without sampling stone crab, Florida lobster, shrimp, and fresh-off-the-boat swordfish, yellowtail, and red snapper. This is the perfect place to indulge in traditional Cuban dishes. Be sure to try a bowl of black bean soup and some *bollos* (pronounced "bowyows"), hush puppies made with mashed, shelled black-eyed peas instead of cornmeal. For dessert, Key lime pie, made from the piquant Key limes that flourish here, wins hands down.

Tourists who take the *Conch Tour Train,* an open-air tram, get a good look at the restoration area as well as the island's major points of interest. This one-and-a-half-hour tour promises "sixty of the most unusual historical sites you've ever seen." Boarding locations are Mallory Square and Roosevelt Avenue. Tours leave approximately every half hour 9:00 A.M.–4:30 P.M. daily. Contact Conch Tour Train at No. 1 Key Lime Square, Key West, FL 33040; (305) 294–5161.

History buffs will want to visit the *East Martello Tower Museum,* part of the nineteenth-century effort to fortify the country's southern boundary. Ground was broken for East Martello Tower in 1861, but the fort was never involved in a battle. A large collection of artifacts from the Keys (including implements used in cigar making and sponge diving) is housed in the fort's long series of casements, and two permanent art collections are on display. East Martello Gallery and Museum is adjacent to the airport at 3501 South Roosevelt Boulevard, Key West, FL 33040. Open 9:30 A.M.–5:30 P.M. daily; (305) 296–3913.

You'll get a commanding view from the newly restored 110-foot tower of the lighthouse in the *Key West Lighthouse Museum.* Built in 1847, the museum pays tribute to the unique military history of the Florida Keys and contains many military artifacts. Open daily 9:30 A.M.–4:30 P.M. Key West Lighthouse Museum, 938 Whitehead Street, Key West, FL 33040; (305) 294–0012.

Key West's newest state park, dedicated on July 4, 1985, is *Fort Zachary Taylor.* This pre–Civil War fortress is a reminder of a time when Union troops occupied Key West during the Civil War. To uncover Fort Taylor's mysteries, Howard England worked alone for nine years with bucket and shovel to uncover the country's largest known collection of Civil War cannons. He assembled a small museum with artifacts, photographs, and a model of the original fort. The park, with one of the finest natural beaches on the island, is an ideal spot to swim and picnic. Open 8:00 A.M. to sunset every day. Fort Taylor, P.O. Box 289, Key West, FL 33041. For information call (305) 292–6713.

At Key West arrangements can be made to fly 68 miles west to *Fort Jefferson* and *Dry Tortugas National Park.* The low-flying seaplane passes over shifting sandbars, clearly identifiable sharks, and an old Spanish wreck that has coughed up millions of dollars' worth of treasure. Passengers look down on the Marquesas, a ring of islands considered by some to be the only atoll in the Atlantic Ocean.

The Tortugas were considered of great strategic importance to the United States. Because the U.S. War Department believed the nation that occupied these islands could protect navigation in the Gulf, it decided to fortify them. Construction began on Fort Jefferson in 1846. Complete with 50-foot-high walls and a water-filled moat, the hexagonal fort covered most of sixteen-acre Garden Key. It was to be the strongest link in the chain of coastal forts that reached from Maine to Texas during the first half of the 1800s.

Federal troops occupied Fort Jefferson throughout the Civil War but saw little action. Although work continued on the fort for thirty years, it was never completed, primarily because the new rifled cannon introduced during the war had already made it obsolete. Used as a military stronghold for captured deserters during the Civil War, Fort Jefferson continued as a prison for almost ten years after the fighting had ceased.

The fort's most famous prisoner was Dr. Samuel Mudd, the physician who set John Wilkes Booth's broken leg after Booth assassinated Abraham Lincoln. Brought here in 1865 and sentenced to a lifetime of hard labor, he earned an early pardon by tirelessly tending to the victims of a yellow fever epidemic that swept through the fort. Be sure to see the orientation slide program before taking the self-guiding tour.

Snorkeling is especially good off the moat walls of Fort Jefferson. Coral formations and brilliant tropical fish provide fine opportunities for underwater photography. Saltwater fishing is good most of the year, and no fishing license is required.

Fort Jefferson Visitors Center is open 8:00 A.M.–5:00 P.M. Public transportation to the fort is available from Key West by seaplane or boat. Those who want to go by private boat may purchase nautical charts at marinas and boating supply outlets in Key West. Boaters should be aware of the possibility of extremely rough seas. The Tortugas are isolated, and you must provide for yourself. No housing, water, meals, or supplies are available. Camping is permitted in the grassed picnic area. For more information write the Superintendent, Box 6208, Key West, FL 33041; (305) 292–6713. For information on charter boats and flights, contact the Greater Key West Chamber of Commerce, 402 Wall Street, Old Mallory Square, Key West, FL 33040; (305) 294–2587 or (800) LASTKEY. For information on a ferry trip (8:00 A.M.–7:00 P.M.) from Key West to Dry Tortugas National Park, call (305) 294–7009 or (800) 634–0939.

Ponce de Leon discovered the Dry Tortugas in 1513. The islands were named by the Spanish explorer for the abundance of sea turtles ("tortugas" in Spanish) he found there. Later "dry" was added to the name to indicate the lack of fresh water. For most of the next 400 years the islands were nominally part of the Spanish colonial empire. Spanish patrol vessels frequented the area, as did Spanish ships, especially those laden with treasure passing just offshore en route from Mexico to Havana. Many ships wrecked on these reefs and shoals due to fierce storms and navigation errors.

Frigate birds with 7-foot wingspans soar above the cerulean waters surrounding the *Dry Tortugas.* Sooty terns, which have turned Bush Key into a rookery, lay their eggs in shallow depressions on its warm sandy beaches. The Tortugas also host noddy terns, brown and blue-faced boobies, and a variety of passing songbirds en route from Cuba and South America. During the nesting season from March to October, Bush Key is reserved for birds only. All keys, other than Garden Key and Loggerhead Key, are closed during the turtle season from May through the end of September.

Visitors should not leave Key West without seeing the ***southernmost point*** in the continental United States. (The Big Island of Hawaii claims the honor for the nation.) Chinese immigrant Jim Kee began selling shells here in the late 1930s, and his descendants still cater to tourists' yen for souvenirs.

Some of Key West's appeal is its temperature, which varies only twelve degrees and averages a balmy 77°; and some is its luxuriant palms, hibiscus, oleander, bougainvillaea, and fragrant frangipani blooms. But the city's greatest charm is that it is a true original.

Few other communities have the good sense to celebrate such a daily marvel as the sunset. The crowd starts to gather at **Mallory Docks** about half an hour before the main event. The Cookie Lady arrives on her bicycle and does a bustling business selling warm brownies and cookies. Locals show off their parrots and pet iguanas. Some juggle, dance, sing, or swallow flaming swords. All the entertainment is free (although the entertainers do pass a hat). After the sun's final farewell, everyone heartily applauds the performance.

For those who have purposely strayed far from the beaten path, it is an entirely appropriate celebration—a fine way to end a day or, for that matter, a book.

STATE PARKS IN THE KEYS

Bahia Honda State Park
(305) 872–2353

Curry Hammock
State Park
(305) 664–4815

Fort Zachary Taylor
State Historic Site
(305) 292–6713

Indian Key State
Historic Site
(305) 664–4815

John Pennekamp Coral
Reef State Park
(305) 451–1202

Lignumvitae Key State
Botanical Site
(305) 664–4815

Long Key State
Recreation Area
(305) 664–4815

Windley Key Fossil Reef
State Geological Site
(305) 664–4815

PLACES TO STAY IN
THE FLORIDA KEYS

KEY LARGO
Ramada Limited Resort
& Marina,
99751 Overseas Highway at
Mile Marker 100;
(305) 451–3939

Marina Del Mar,
527 Caribbean Drive at
Mile Marker 100;
(305) 451–4107

Westin Beach Resort,
97000 Overseas Highway;
(305) 852–5553

Marriott's Key Largo Bay
Beach Resort,
103800 Overseas Highway;
(305) 453–0000

ISLAMORADA
Kon-Tiki Resort, Route 1,
Box 58, Overseas Highway
at Mile Marker 84.5;
(305) 664–4702

Pelican Cove,
84457 Old Overseas
Highway at Mile
Marker 84.5;
(305) 664–4435

Cheeca Lodge, P.O. Box 527,
Overseas Highway at Mile
Marker 82; (305) 664–4651

MARATHON
Marathon Hotel and
Marina,
13201 Overseas Highway at
Mile Marker 54;
(305) 289–0222

Hawk's Cay, Overseas
Highway at Mile Marker 61,
Duck Key; (305) 743–7000

KEY WEST

Holiday Inn Beachside,
3841 North Roosevelt
Boulevard; (305) 294–2571

Galleon Resort & Marina,
617 Front Street;
(305) 296–7711

Pier House, 1 Duval Street;
(305) 296–4600

Hilton Resort and Marina,
245 Front Street;
(305) 294–4000

Wyndam,
1435 Simonton Street;
(305) 296–5000

Little Palm Island,
28500 Overseas Highway,
Little Torch Key;
(305) 872–2524

PLACES TO EAT IN THE FLORIDA KEYS

KEY LARGO

Mrs. Mac's Kitchen,
Mile Marker 99.4, Overseas
Highway; (305) 451–3722

The Italian Fisherman,
Mile Marker 104, Overseas
Highway; (305) 451–4471

ISLAMORADA

Manny and Isa's Kitchen
(Cuban), Mile Marker 81.6,
Overseas Highway;
(305) 664–5019

Marker 88, Mile Marker 88,
Overseas Highway;
(305) 852–9315

MARATHON

Kelsey's (seafood),
1996 Overseas Highway;
(305) 743–9018

KEY WEST

Cafe Des Artistes (French),
1007 Simonton Street;
(305) 294–7100

Godfrey's Restaurant at the
La-Te-Da Hotel, 1125 Duval
Street; (305) 296–6706

Keybosh, corner of Duval
and Southard Streets; (305)
294–2005

Louie's Backyard,
700 Waddell Avenue;
(305) 294–1061

Pier House Restaurant,
Pier House Resort, 1 Duval
Street; (305) 296–4600

Appendix

Recommended Reading about Florida:

Gift from the Sea, Anne Morrow Lindbergh

Islands in the Stream, Ernest Hemingway

To Have and Have Not, Ernest Hemingway

Cross Creek, Marjorie Kinnan Rawlings

The Yearling, Marjorie Kinnan Rawlings

Key West, Burt Hirschfeld

Condominium, John D. MacDonald

Flamingo Road, Robert Wilder

Florida: The Long Frontier, Marjory Stoneman Douglas

The Search for the Atocha, Eugene Lyon

Treasure of the Atocha, R. Duncan Mathewson III

The Everglades, Archie Carr

The Everglades: River of Grass, Marjorie Stoneman Douglas

The Other Florida, Gloria Jahoda

Ninety-two in the Shade, Thomas McGuane

Mile Zero, Thomas Sanchez

Rabbit at Rest, John Updike

Breaking and Entering, Joy Williams

For Young Readers:

The Yearling, Marjorie Kinnan Rawlings

Save the Florida Key Deer, Margaret Goff Clark

APPENDIX

The Vanishing Manatee, Margaret Goff Clark

The Endangered Florida Panther, Margaret Goff Clark

The Threatened Florida Black Bear, Margaret Goff Clark

Florida's Vanishing Wildlife, Peter Bramley

Early People of Florida, Eva Costabel

Avast Ye Slobs! Florida Pirate Trivia, Carole Marsh

Gold Shines Forever! The Discovery & Recovery of the Spanish Treasure Ship Atocha, Carole Marsh

Kids Explore Florida, Susan Moffat

Henry Flagler, Builder of Florida, Sandra Sammons

Florida, Lynn Stone

Slave Ship: The Story of the Henrietta Marie, George Sullivan

Chessie, The Meandering Manatee, Carol Amato

The Pink Motel, Carol Brink

Freddy Goes to Florida, Walter Brooks

Panther Glade, Helen Cavanagh

Freedom River, Marjory S. Douglas

The Boy Who Loved Alligators, Barbara Kennedy

Shadows in the Water: A Starbuck Family Adventure, Kathryn Lasky

Index

A

B

C

INDEX

INDEX

About the Authors

Diana and Bill Gleasner, an award-winning writer/photographer team, have thirty published books to their credit as well as hundreds of articles for national and international magazines and newspapers. As professional travel photojournalists who have roamed the globe in search of fascinating travel experiences, they admit a continuing addiction to Florida. The Gleasners are members of the Society of American Travel Writers and the Travel Journalists Guild.

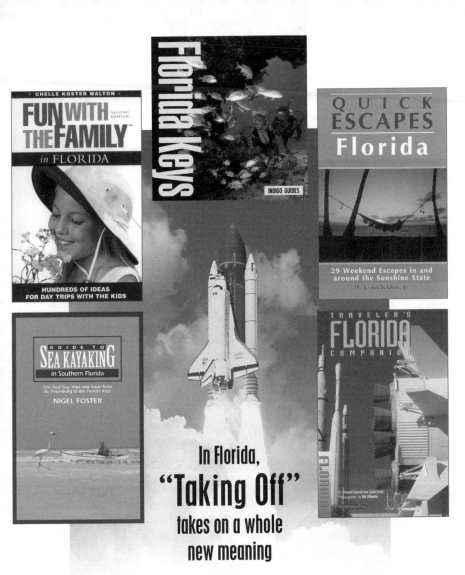

In Florida, "Taking Off" takes on a whole new meaning

And the variety of attractions are out of this world.

From the spectacular natural beauty of the Everglades and the Keys to the high-tech sophistication of Cape Canaveral and Miami, not to mention the fun and fantasy of Disneyworld, you'll find adventure, recreation, and points of interest to be shared and enjoyed by all. At The Globe Pequot Press, the sky's the limit when it comes to the wealth and variety of valuable information you'll need to reach new heights in your travel experience.

Take off with

The Globe Pequot Press

To order, contact your local bookstore   or call 800-243-0495 • www.globe-pequot.com